Another victory for bestselling author
Stephen E. Ambrose—

AMERICANS AT WAR

"The names of ordinary soldiers fill Ambrose's books; he does them honor, once again, in this collection, by reminding us of their heroism as well as that of their leaders."

—The New Orleans Times-Picayune

"Fascinating and provocative."　　　*—The Dallas Morning News*

"[Ambrose] demonstrates deep knowledge and common sense about mankind's most senseless activity."　　　*—Time magazine*

"Historical accounts sparkle . . . as readable as a novel."

—The Jackson Clarion-Ledger (MS)

"A fascinating, insightful collection . . . Ambrose convinces you that you are a participant in history."　　　*—The Houston Chronicle*

continued . . .

Praise for the New York Times *Bestseller*

UNDAUNTED COURAGE:

Meriwether Lewis, Thomas Jefferson, and the Opening of the American West

"Ambrose takes us into the interior of an adventure filled with high romance and personal tragedy involving the greatest expedition ever undertaken in the history of this country."

—Paul Theroux, *Chicago Tribune*

"*Undaunted Courage* is a work of love: rhapsodic and heroic."

—David M. Shribman, *The Wall Street Journal*

"A fine and important book, intelligently conceived and splendidly written."

—Blanine Harden, *The Washington Post Book World*

"A swiftly moving, full-dress treatment of the expedition . . . A lively retelling of the journey of the two captains conveyed with passionate enthusiasm by Mr. Ambrose."

—Alvin M. Josephy, Jr., *The New York Times Book Review*

" 'If I was ever in a desperate situation,' [Ambrose] declares, 'I would want Meriwether Lewis for my leader.' When it comes to assaying American history, one could say the same for Stephen Ambrose."

—Malcolm Jones, Jr., *Newsweek*

AMERICANS AT WAR

Stephen E. Ambrose

BERKLEY BOOKS
NEW YORK

AMERICANS AT WAR

A Berkley Book / published by arrangement with
University Press of Mississippi

PRINTING HISTORY
University Press of Mississippi edition published 1997
Berkley trade paperback edition / October 1998

The Penguin Putnam Inc. World Wide Web site address is
http://www.penguinputnam.com

ISBN: 0-425-16510-8

BERKLEY®
Berkley Books are published by The Berkley Publishing Group,
a member of Penguin Putnam Inc.,
375 Hudson Street, New York, New York 10014.
BERKLEY and the "B" design
are trademarks belonging to Berkley Publishing Corporation.

146122990

CONTENTS

INTRODUCTION

My experiences with the military have been as an observer. The only time I wore a uniform was in naval ROTC as a freshman at the University of Wisconsin, and in army ROTC as a sophomore. I was in second grade when the United States entered World War II, in sixth grade when the war ended. When I graduated from high school in 1953 I expected to go into the army, but within a month the Korean War ended and I went to college instead. Upon graduation in 1957 I went straight to graduate school. By the time America was again at war, in 1964, I was twenty-eight years old and the father of five children. So I never served.

But I have admired and respected the men who did fight since my childhood. When I was in grade school, World War II dominated my life. My father was a navy doctor in the Pacific. My mother worked in a pea cannery, beside German POWs (Africa Corps troops captured in Tunisia in May 1943). Along with my brothers—Harry, two years older, and Bill, two years younger—I went to the movies three times a week (ten cents six nights a week, twenty-five cents on Saturday night), not to see the films, which were generally real clinkers, but to see the newsreels, which were almost exclusively about the fighting in North Africa, Europe and the Pacific. We played at war constantly: "Japs" vs. marines, GIs vs. "Krauts."

In high school, I got hooked on Napoleon. I read various biographies and studied his campaigns. As a seventeen-year-old freshman, in naval ROTC, I took a course on naval history, starting with the Greeks and ending with World War II (in one semester!). My instructor had been a submarine skipper in the Pacific and we all worshiped him. More important, he was a gifted teacher who loved the navy and history. Although I was a premed student with plans to take up my father's practice in Whitewater, Wisconsin, I found the history course to be far more interesting than chemistry or physics. But in the second semester of naval ROTC, the required course was gunnery. Although I was an avid hunter and thoroughly familiar with shotguns and rifles, the workings of the five-inch cannon baffled me, so in my sophomore year I switched to army ROTC.

Also that year, I took a course entitled "Representative Americans" taught by Professor William B. Hesseltine. In his first lecture, he announced that in this course we would not be writing term papers that summarized the conclusions of three or four books; instead we would be doing original research on nineteenth-century Wisconsin politicians, professional and business leaders, for the purpose of putting together a dictionary of Wisconsin biography that would be deposited in the state historical society. We would, Hesseltine told us, be contributing to the world's knowledge.

The words caught me up. I had never imagined I could do such a thing as contribute to the world's knowledge. Forty-five years later, the phrase continues to resonate with me. It changed my life. At the conclusion of the lecture—on General Washington—I went up to him and asked how I could do what he did for a living. He laughed and said to stick around, he would show me. I went straight to the registrar's office and changed my major from premed to history.

Over the next week, Mr. Hesseltine's teaching assistants showed us students around the historical society library. Here were the old newspapers, there the manuscript room with letters, diaries and the rest, here the old magazines, there the scholarly journals. Then we picked a name from a list. I chose Charles Billinghurst, a one-term congressman from Milwaukee. He was interesting for two reasons: he was one of the first

Republican congressmen, and he was heavily involved in railroad building (I knew by then from his lectures that Mr. Hesseltine put great stress on the importance of understanding railroad developments if you were going to understand politics).

Never can I forget the magic of that passage of discovery. Opening those musty old newspapers, I was thrilled. I devoured them, reading the advertisements, the notices, the news stories (oh, the joy when I found a speech by Billinghurst). I read his letters in the manuscript room, and found diary entries about him from contemporaries. I felt in touch with the past.

That past fascinated me because of two overwhelming questions: how could the Civil War have happened? And, how could the men of the Union and Confederacy be brought to such a passion that they would hurl themselves at each other as they were to do at Gettysburg? I have long since extended my research to before and after the Civil War, but those two questions—how do wars happen? and how do men do it?—have been the lodestar of my career. By immersing myself in the documentary remains of the time, I felt I was getting along in finding answers.

I remember the moment when I completed the paper. The flush of pride I felt when I thought, I know more about Charles Billinghurst than any other living person, has not been equaled. Only later did I realize that no one else wanted to know anything about Billinghurst; only much later did I realize that if I told the story right, I could make them want to know. (When I started talking about writing a book on Meriwether Lewis, one prominent historian told me to forget about the Lewis and Clark Expedition because "nothing happened." Another advised dropping the idea because no one was interested in a dead white male who violated sacred Indian territory. And my publisher said the same.)

I took as many history courses as the degree requirements would allow. The University of Wisconsin History Department in the mid-1950s had a superb faculty. Howard Beale, Merle Curti, William A. Williams, Merrill Jensen, Vernon Carstenson, Fred Harvey Harrington and many others were at the top of their fields. Those of us who were privileged to be history majors at that time knew then and know now that this was the best history department in the country. And the star, for me, was Mr. Hesseltine. In the spring semester of my sophomore year, his lecture course was on the Civil War. It was rich in content, richer in drama, and richest of all when he fought the battles on the blackboard. He was highly opinionated about the generals—and usually wrong, I felt. He encouraged argument. I embraced it. The exchange taught me to read. I devoured books on the generals, then went forth to do battle with him.

I lusted for more. I wanted to see, touch, feel these battlefields. In July 1955, I rode a bike from Wisconsin down to Shiloh, where I slept on the battlefield. Then deeper into Mississippi I rode, down to Vicksburg. There I met Ed Bearss, the park historian. We spent the next day wandering over the battlefield. Ed knows more about this battle—and many others—than any living person, and is justly famous for his abilities as a raconteur. We would stop at this or that spot and Ed would describe for me the way A Company of the 51st Illinois advanced over here or fell back over there, getting the story down to the level of the individual soldier. I learned a lot that day, most of all that if I wanted to tell stories like Ed did, I needed to know more.

Back in Madison, I talked my way into Mr. Hesseltine's graduate seminar, and began working on a biography of General Henry Halleck. It was my mentor's idea. I think he wanted me to broaden my perspective, which was narrowly on the military side of the Civil War. Halleck, as Lincoln's chief of staff, let me study a military man yet forced me to study the politics of the war as well. Even better, Halleck provided insights into how a citizen army is created in a democracy, almost overnight, and how a democracy fights a war.

In 1957, upon graduation, I went to Louisiana State University to earn my M.A. degree under the famous T. Harry Williams, himself a Hesseltine student. Williams was the star, by far, but it was a solid department with excellent teachers and I learned a great deal from them.

Williams was much like Hesseltine, argumentative and opinionated. I loved arguing with him. He liked to pour scorn on me. I'd read another half-dozen books or so and return to refute him. Meanwhile I was his teaching assistant and attending his lectures. There has never been a better platform performer. He strutted, he waved his arms, he spun a web, he told stories. He was unconscionable in the way he milked the drama of the Civil War. It was a privilege to be present.

In 1958, I returned to Madison for my Ph.D. work under Mr. Hesseltine. For my dissertation I did a biography of Emory Upton. In 1960 it was off to the University of New Orleans for my first teaching job. My courses on the second half of American history forced me to begin studying World War I, World War II, and Korea. I realized how much more I needed to know.

Almost four decades later, I still do and I'm still researching. Americans at war continue to fascinate me. My search for the answers to the questions of why we go to war and how we fight the war has taken me into diplomatic and political history. But whether I'm researching and writing about Nixon, Eisenhower, or an airborne company in World War II, those questions remain my lodestar.

All nations make war in their own way. The American way is the theme of these essays. "Hitler should beware the fury of an aroused democracy," Dwight Eisenhower wrote his brother Milton on the day World War II started. That is the theme of the American way. After four decades of study, what impresses me most is how far superior democracy is to all other forms of government in making war. Hitler was sure that the opposite was true. He believed that a totalitarian government was inherently and overwhelmingly more efficient than democracy, with its squabbling parliamentarians representing this or that interest group. That is true enough during peace time, but when war comes and everyone in the democracy becomes a member of the team, eager to do his or her duty, ready to accept and exercise individual initiative, the result is an explosion of power, as indicated in "The War on the Home Front" in this collection.

Teamwork is the word that best describes the way democracies make war, whether in intelligence collection and deception measures, or on the home front. It takes time for a democracy to make up its mind, however, as the essay on American entry into World War II in this volume describes; sometimes it doesn't happen, as the pieces on Vietnam indicate.

But while it is heartening to study an aroused democracy at war, it is depressing to have to deal with the death and destruction inherent in war. To study and write about My Lai, or Hiroshima and Nagasaki, or atrocities in general, is to be reminded painfully of how awful war always is, and of the way in which, while it brings out the best in some men, it brings out the worst in others. It makes me wince whenever I hear in an interview or read in a letter or memoir of some of the atrocities committed by Billy Yank, or Johnny Reb, or the GIs, or the grunts. Worse are accounts of how this buddy died, or that buddy lost his leg.

I've spent a lot of my career studying small units in action. For me, the appalling losses are compounded by the knowledge that it was the natural leaders, the junior officers, who went down in the greatest numbers. Always in my subconscious is the thought, What life was cut off here? A genius? It is impossible to imagine what he might have invented; we do know that his loss was our loss. A budding politician? Where might he have led us? A builder? A teacher? A scholar? A novelist? A musician? I sometimes think that the biggest price we pay for war is what might have been. The loss of these young men is the unmeasurable part of the cost of war—which is one reason why democracies are so hesitant to get into them. The immediate cost, in lives and destruction, is terrible enough to make democracies hesitate.

Mr. Hesseltine was a "great man" historian. People made history, he told us. Nothing is inevitable. Leaders set policy and order action. There is opposition. If it goes to the limit, the issue will be decided on the battlefield. Throughout the process, leaders make choices. So leave aside social forces or economic determinism, Mr. Hesseltine said, and let's talk about Mr. Lincoln and General Grant, Mr. Davis and General Lee. He was right. In four decades of teaching, I've always found that what the students want to know about American history, first of all, is: Who were our heroes? What did they do?

So my approach to war and politics has been biographical, as is reflected in this collection. I've done biographies of a variety of leaders, starting with Billinghurst and continuing to James Newton, Emory Upton, Henry Halleck, Crazy Horse, Custer, Dwight Eisenhower, Richard Nixon and Meriwether Lewis. A disparate list. The only thing they have in common is that they were leaders. Ike and Dick were as different as a bright sunny day and a dark thunderstorm. A basic principle with Eisenhower was to tell the truth; with Nixon, it was to lie. MacArthur, as can be seen in the piece reprinted here, almost always lied his way out of difficulties. Yet each of these men was an effective, even great, leader.

When you get down to a small unit level, however, there are elements of leadership that are tried and true. For all his showmanship, George Armstrong Custer knew what they were. Never tell your men to do something you won't do yourself. Always see to their needs first—food, shelter, clothing, equipment. Make certain they have dry socks. Push them to but never beyond the breaking point. Convince them that they have more in them to give than they ever thought possible. "Follow me" are the operative words, not "go take that hill."

But these easily stated yet hard-to-follow maxims do not apply at the level of general officer or president. I've been writing biographies of leaders for forty years and I have yet to discover any basic principles of leadership that I can pass on. Each national leader has his or her own style, a reflection both of the individual's personality and of the times in which he or she lived. That is what makes history so fascinating.

People are the leaders and the led. I once attended a session at the American Historical Association convention that was essentially a debate over these propositions: Lincoln emancipated the slaves; the slaves emancipated themselves and Lincoln had to follow. The debate was vigorous, one side arguing that only Lincoln could have led a democracy in which a majority of voters were opposed to emancipation to accept it, the other side maintaining that by running away from their plantations whenever Federal lines got close enough to make it feasible, slaves freed themselves and forced Lincoln to act, helped considerably by northern pressure to put some ex-slaves into uniform. My own conclusion was that you can't have a leader without followers, and you can't have followers without leaders. Without Lincoln's sense of timing and persuasive power, and without his moral sense and courage, it is impossible to imagine how emancipation might have come about. But without the pressure on him from self-freed blacks and from a demand that they do their share of the fighting, Lincoln would have been unable to bring it off.

I once talked to a seminar of local historians in New Orleans. I told them about Operation Fortitude. They loved the details of how it was done, highly intellectual matters of breaking codes and deceiving the Germans. At the conclusion, in a throwaway line, I said, "Of course, none of this would have mattered if the infantry had failed to do its duty, because in the end it came down to the poor sons-of-bitches making the attack." I thought it was so obvious a truth that I was almost embarrassed to make it, but the professors were indignant. One of them said, "Here you've spent an hour showing us how we won, and then assert that it was infantry that won the battle, when you have just proved the opposite."

Different perceptions. For my part, I'll stick with Mr. Hesseltine's maxim that history is about people, leaders and led.

It is the essential theme of this collection of essays. Their subjects range from the Civil War to some guesses about war in the twenty-first century, but throughout they are about people.

Bay St. Louis, Mississippi
February 24, 1997

AMERICANS AT WAR

STRUGGLE FOR VICKSBURG

The Battles and Siege That Decided the Civil War

At a time when the Civil War went badly for the Union, President Abraham Lincoln looked at a map and commented to a visitor, "See what a lot of land these fellows hold, of which Vicksburg is the key. . . . Let us get Vicksburg and all that country is ours. The war can never be brought to a close until that key is in our pocket."

By October 1862, the Federals had gained control of the Mississippi River from its mouth upstream to Port Hudson, in Louisiana, and from the river's sources down to Vicksburg, Mississippi. As long as the Confederates held the 130-mile stretch between those two towns, they could maintain communications with the western third of their nation and draw reinforcements and supplies. By denying the use of the great waterway to the Union, they prevented the reopening of normal traffic between the Northwest and New Orleans.

Lincoln was right. Vicksburg was the key and until that key was in the Federal pocket the war would continue. But wresting it from the Confederates seemed an impossibility.

With a population of nearly 5,000, the town stood on a 200-foot bluff on the eastern bank of the Mississippi, just down from where the river made a hairpin curve. Between there and Memphis the line of bluffs ran far inland, and the area adjacent to the river was low and swampy.

Across the river the ground was often inundated, and always nearly impassable for an army. From the north, the Yazoo River blocked the landward approach. To the east and south, staunchly Confederate Mississippians inhabited the countryside.

Soon after a Federal fleet seized New Orleans in April 1862, the Confederates began fortifying Vicksburg, first with batteries below the town to command the river approach from the south. Later, they mounted guns above the town and along the river, making Vicksburg impregnable to an attack from the water and creating a long gantlet past which boats found it dangerous to run. With good reason Vicksburg became known as the Gibraltar of America.

Long before Lincoln made his comment about Vicksburg, Ulysses S. Grant recognized its importance and began pondering how to secure this key that would both lock off the trans-Mississippi territory of the Confederacy and unlock the southern hold on the "Father of Waters."

No one knows for sure just when Grant conceived his strategy for penetrating the heartland of the Confederacy by stabbing south along the great waterways leading into it. A visitor to the small Union headquarters at Ironton, Missouri, in the summer of 1861 found the shabby, insignificant-looking new brigadier sitting under a tree in front of a cabin, drawing lines with a red pencil on a map. Grant explained that these were the invasion routes that high command should adopt and pointed out that one ran down the Mississippi past Vicksburg.

Two years were to elapse before Sam Grant was in a position to put his ideas into effect, but he never abandoned them.

The little spring beside which Grant dreamed his dreams now bubbles from a swale in the lawn of a Catholic school, and there is a simple shaft erected by his comrades of the 21st Illinois to mark the nearby site of his headquarters. But the greatest monument to this quiet little man is the fruition of those early plans which he converted into one of the most decisive campaigns of all time.

It is a classic campaign, one that professional soldiers still study. With the single exception of air power, it contained the major elements of warfare later exemplified in World War II. There were mobile forces and even partisans striking far behind the lines of the main forces, and joint (Army-Navy) operations on a scale not seen again until the landings in North Africa in 1942. There were amphibious assaults, forced marches, pitched battles, field engineering of great resourcefulness, logistical triumphs, and intelligence and counterintelligence activity of a sophisticated nature. Finally, there was a siege in which courage and endurance were commonplace, and imaginative approaches to diverse problems were everyday occurrences.

STRATEGY OF THE CAMPAIGN

The scope of the campaign, the size and type of problems encountered and overcome, and its strategic importance are together enough to make it unique. But above all else, Vicksburg stands out because of the way in which one man dominated the entire campaign. Seldom in history has an individual so totally imposed his will upon his own forces, those of the enemy, and an operation. Ulysses S. Grant and Vicksburg are names that history will link together forever.

The campaign gave Grant an opportunity to show his skill in nearly every aspect of the soldier's trade. For each test he proved he was prepared and capable. His outstanding characteristic was flexibility of mind; he was always able to change his plans when confronted with a change in the situation. His relations with all but one of his chief subordinates were excellent. He was superb in handling troops. If throughout the long winter of 1862–63 he was not able to keep his superiors—a crabby General in Chief and an impatient President—completely satisfied, he did convince them that a change in commanders would be a mistake. He solved a potentially explosive political problem with tact, delicacy, and understanding. He was keenly aware of the vital importance of logistics and saw to it that his men were never critically short of food or without ammunition. Though not an inspirational leader, he was ever steady and generated confidence and trust. In this campaign he managed his frontal assaults capably and broke them off before they became blood baths. His ability to maneuver large bodies of troops over great distances was truly outstanding.

Fittingly, Grant himself began the strategic campaign that culminated in the fall of Vicksburg when, in February of 1862, he captured Forts Henry and Donelson in northwestern Tennessee. Thus began the operations to open the Mississippi River, a task that would be the major objective of the Union forces in the West for the next year and a half.

Grant took command of the Department of the Tennessee on October 25, 1862. General in Chief Henry W. Halleck informed him that substantial reinforcements would soon come to the theater. It was characteristic of Grant that he started his campaign within a few days, and that he never turned back. His plans were flexible and he tried various routes of approach, but he kept his face ever toward his objective.

On November 4 Grant started from Bolivar, in south-central Tennessee, with the idea of advancing along the axis of the Mississippi Central Railroad to Jackson, the capital of Mississippi. The Confederate forces facing him, commanded by Lieutenant General John C. Pemberton, fell back behind the Tallahatchie River. When this line, which Pemberton fortified, was outflanked by Federal cavalry and an infantry force from Arkansas that crossed the Mississippi at Helena, the Confederates retreated to Grenada and began digging in south of the Yalobusha River. Pemberton's retreat was almost a rout. Grant remarked after the war that had he known this he would not have been so meticulous in maintaining his supply lines and staying so close to the railroad, but would have moved right on to Jackson. But, being unaware of the enemy situation, Grant advanced cautiously, stopping to rebuild bridges, repair the railroad, and bring up supplies to advance depots. Although his cavalry made a dash into Holly Springs on November 13, his infantry did not arrive there until the 29th. By December 5 he still had not reached Grenada.

Perhaps Grant's reluctance to display the kind of boldness that had won him Forts Henry and Donelson was the result of a confused command system, one that made it difficult for him to advance with confidence. He was not sure at this time that he was being supported by the authorities in Washington. Essentially the high command there consisted of three men—President Lincoln, Secretary of War Edwin Stanton, and General in Chief Henry Halleck. Lincoln and Stanton were politicians who, with no prewar military experience, had handled well the administrative details of the largest war in which the United States had ever been engaged. Inevitably they were irritated when their generals were unable to use the large numbers of men they had raised and armed to conquer the South. Thus they were receptive when, in August 1862, John A. McClernand, an Illinois Democrat wearing a major general's uniform, had come to them, cursed the West Pointers for being too cautious, and said he could give them Vicksburg by Christmas. Lincoln and Stanton arranged for McClernand to raise a private "army" in the Northwest, with which he would launch an attack down the Mississippi River against Vicksburg. Even though he would be in Grant's theater, he would operate independently.

Evidently Lincoln and Stanton were embarrassed by what they had done, or else they feared the West Pointers would sabotage the operation, for they hesitated to tell Halleck about it and when they did they ordered him to keep it secret.

Everything was at cross-purposes. Halleck approved of neither the plan nor McClernand, whom he considered a pompous, foolish person and a poor general. Grant and his most esteemed subordinate, Major General William T. Sherman, distrusted McClernand as a soldier and disliked him as a man. McClernand in turn was outspoken in his contempt of all West Pointers.

Eventually Halleck spoiled McClernand's grandiose plans through a complex series of machinations that had a simple goal: to deprive McClernand of the force he was enlisting. As fast as McClernand raised troops in the Northwest, Halleck sent them to Memphis, where they were in Grant's Department and thus quite properly under the latter's control.

By early December Halleck had managed to tell Grant obliquely most of the "secret" (which had been discussed in the newspapers anyway), and Grant sent Sherman to Memphis to organize the new levies into units. The object was then to get them on their way to Vicksburg before McClernand became aware that he was being euchred. The latter, full of suspicion and indignation, finally hastened to Memphis, but he was too late.

INITIAL THRUSTS SOUTHWARD

Grant's plan had called for a single, overland thrust on Jackson and Vicksburg. He now changed it, possibly (at least in part) to thwart McClernand. Thus Union forces would make a two-pronged attack, one Grant's original overland drive and the other Sherman's amphibious effort down the river.

Three divisions of Sherman's force left Memphis on December 20, just a few days before McClernand arrived. All of Halleck's, Grant's, and Sherman's moves had been carried out more or less surreptitiously. For Grant this was risky; he did not yet have the press and public opinion solidly behind him, and the Government attitude was unknown. One aspect of the situation did give him reassurance: it had become obvious that Halleck was going to support him all the way. Halleck and Grant had had their differences early in the year, when Grant served under the other in the West, but now when it was a choice between McClernand and Grant, Halleck made his preference clear.

Grant might also have drawn comfort from the Confederate command structure had he known it. Pemberton, a native of Philadelphia and a graduate of West Point, had in mid-October assumed command of the Confederate forces in Mississippi and East Louisiana. A nervous man, Pemberton was unsure of himself and incapable of furnishing bold, aggressive leadership. When Grant started south Pemberton reported to Richmond that his situation was desperate. His statements caused such keen concern in the higher Southern echelons that President Jefferson Davis himself went west by rail to confer with Pemberton and inspect the defenses of Vicksburg. He was accompanied by General Joseph E. Johnston, whom Davis had appointed to command all forces between the Appalachians and the Mississippi. Considering the communications system available to Johnston, this was an impossibly large theater to control. An additional complication was that Johnston and Davis, both Military Academy graduates, hated each other.

Johnston vainly tried to avoid the assignment, protesting that no one could effectively control such a theater. He then asked Davis for more troops. Davis told him to transfer them from the other major army in his command, Braxton Bragg's, which was in Tennessee. Johnston argued that it would be easier and wiser to pull reinforcements from Arkansas, where Lieutenant General Theophilus T. Holmes had 20,000 men. Davis agreed; then to Johnston's disgust he wrote a friendly note to Holmes "suggesting" that he send some men. No troops came.

Before Davis returned to Richmond, Johnston had one more conversation with him. A pessimist by nature, Johnston must have sounded like a veritable Cassandra. He said the theater was too large, each of the two armies too small, and they were too far apart to support each other. All was lost. Davis told Johnston to do the best he could, and left.

Grant and Sherman, meanwhile, had paused to regroup. Major General Earl Van Dorn, commanding Pemberton's cavalry, and at the front facing Grant, decided to avoid a head-on collision. He slipped past Grant's left flank, got into his rear, and wrecked his supply base at Holly Springs. The Confederates destroyed or carried away a million dollars' worth of rations, forage, and ammunition.

Grant decided he had better pull back to Memphis and Grand Junction, where he could get fresh supplies by water from the big Union supply base at Columbus, Kentucky. Then he would rebuild the railroad from Memphis to Grand Junction which, because of its damaged condition, he had not used before, and repair any fresh damages caused by Van Dorn on the line. After a new supply reserve had been accumulated he would resume his overland advance. During the retrograde movement Grant restricted his men to short rations and sent out wagons fifteen miles on both sides of the road to scour the country for food and forage. To his amazement he found that even this narrow zone would support his force for two months.

Grant tried to inform Sherman of this withdrawal, but his wire communications to the rear had been torn down by Rebel raiders commanded by Brigadier General Nathan B. Forrest. Pemberton, unknown to Sherman, reinforced the garrison at Vicksburg. Still, on December 21, Sherman learned that Van Dorn had captured Holly Springs. He might have guessed that this would cause Grant to turn back; but Sherman was determined to push on. He was so intent on reaching Vicksburg before McClernand that in his hurry to get away he had left behind part of a pontoon train. In the fighting that followed, this error of Sherman's cost the Union dearly.

Sherman arrived on the Yazoo eight miles north of Vicksburg on December 26. For three days he debarked his four divisions and worked them through the difficult swamps and bayous to a position from which he could assault across Chickasaw Bayou against the ridge just north of Vicksburg. He made this attack on the 29th. The Confederates, thanks to reinforcements which the suspension of Grant's overland drive had released, easily repulsed the Union troops with severe losses. Sherman fell back to Milliken's Bend.

There, on January 2, McClernand finally caught up with the expedition. In a towering rage he showed Sherman his orders from the President placing him in command. Sherman at once relinquished the command and, in his own words, "subsided into the more agreeable office of corps commander."

McClernand named his force "The Army of the Mississippi." He eagerly agreed to Sherman's suggestion that he move the army back up the Mississippi to the mouth of the Arkansas River, then steam up that stream to take the main Confederate position on it, the Post of Arkansas. McClernand had independently planned a similar campaign before he caught up with Sherman. Both generals felt this move necessary to relieve a growing threat to their right flank and rear, for the Confederates were preparing to descend the Arkansas with gunboats capable of raiding Union shipping. Indeed, one supply boat had already been captured.

McClernand got under way quickly, before Grant could interfere (Halleck had finally obtained from Lincoln orders that placed McClernand under Grant's general direction). On January 11 McClernand captured the Post of Arkansas. He then wrote Grant proposing that he penetrate deeper into Arkansas.

Grant was furious. He told McClernand to get back to the Mississippi immediately. He also wired Halleck that McClernand had gone off on a wild goose chase. Halleck telegraphed Grant: "You are hereby authorized to relieve General McClernand from command of the expedition against Vicksburg, giving it to the next in rank or taking it yourself." McClernand returned to Milliken's Bend. Grant arrived there on January 29. The next day he took personal command of all forces operating against Vicksburg.

When Grant took command, McClernand protested bitterly. He had already told Lincoln, "I believe my success here [at the Post of Arkansas] is gall and wormwood to the clique of West Pointers who have been persecuting me for months. How can you expect success when men controlling the military destinies of the country are more chagrined at the success of your volunteer officers than the very enemy beaten by the latter in battle?" Lincoln, who was learning to rely more upon his professional advisers, especially Halleck, ignored the communication.

Grant's first act was to divide his forces into four army corps. He split McClernand's Army of the Mississippi into the XIII Corps under McClernand and the XV Corps under Sherman. His own forces were distributed into the XVI Corps (Hurlbut) and the XVII Corps (McPherson). Grant assigned to the XIII Corps the duty of garrisoning the Arkansas bank of the Mississippi. McClernand thought this was an attempt to relegate him to a subsidiary role in the campaign. He sent to Lincoln through Grant a formal complaint, citing Lincoln's original intention that he should command the expedition. Meanwhile in his personal contacts with Grant, McClernand was clearly insubordinate—and insufferable.

Grant wisely chose to ignore him and go on with his business, disregarding McClernand's insubordination. Grant realized that McClernand was an important politician in Illinois, that Lincoln desperately needed the support of War Democrats, that McClernand was among the first members of Congress from the Democratic Party to pledge himself to a vigorous prosecution of the effort to save the Union, and that he had given up his seat in Congress to take the field. Such men are rare enough in any war, and Grant felt that he should make every effort to overlook McClernand's faults.

CAMPAIGN OF THE BAYOUS

By the time Grant assumed command, winter rains had made the land around the river's bank impossible for any but the most limited operations. Still, Grant felt he could not stand idle for three months. Grant had good reasons for conducting a vigorous bayou campaign, although he was sure none of his efforts would be fruitful. The North had become discouraged. It was common talk, even among strong Union men, that the war would prove a failure. The elections of 1862 had gone against the Republicans. Voluntary enlistments had practically ceased. Had the North's second largest army stood idle over the winter or fallen back it would have fed the already rampant defeatism.

As Grant explained later, "It was my judgment at the time that to make a backward movement . . . would be interpreted by many of those yet full of hope . . . as a defeat, and that the draft would be resisted, desertions ensue, and the power to capture and punish deserters lost. There was nothing left to be done but to *go forward to a decisive victory*. This was in my mind from the moment I took command."

Through the winter Grant kept the troops busy, as he made four attempts to reach the high ground east and south of Vicksburg. The engineers tried to dig a canal that would divert the Mississippi and thus leave Vicksburg high and dry. The men labored for weeks in an effort to provide a water route from Lake Providence south to the Ouachita and then to Red River, which would allow the gunboats and transports to get below Vicksburg without having to run the Confederate batteries. Two attempts were also made to get into and along the Yazoo River above Vicksburg.

All these efforts involved an enormous amount of material and tremendous exertion by the troops. If they did no practical good in terms of the campaign itself, they nevertheless were of great benefit. The activity kept the generals from conspiring among themselves while the men, being constantly busy, had little time to grumble. The work gave newspaper reporters something to write about and stimulated the North's interest and morale. Perhaps most important, when spring came and Grant finally set out, the troops he commanded were in good physical condition. Their muscles were hard, they were used to life in the field instead of the soft life of a permanent camp, and they had learned to get along on short rations.

GRANT BYPASSES VICKSBURG

At last, in late March, the river began to recede, the roads to dry out, and Grant concentrated his troops at Milliken's Bend, Young's Point, and Lake Providence "preparatory to a final move which was to crown the long, tedious, and discouraging labors" with success. By March 29 Grant had evolved his plan. He told Halleck he would move his army south of Vicksburg in barges and small steamers, through the series of bayous west of the Mississippi. Some overland marching would be necessary, but it should not be difficult in the drier weather. At the same time Rear Admiral David D. Porter's gunboats and large transports would run past the Vicksburg batteries. They would meet the troops south of Vicksburg and ferry them across the river. Grant had discussed the plan with Porter, who then approved it. This was fortunate for the army, since Porter's command was independent, and Grant could not give him orders. McClernand also agreed with the plan, but Sherman and McPherson strongly urged Grant to return to the overland approach east of the river.

Two months later, when Grant was besieging Vicksburg, he overheard Sherman telling the visiting governor of Illinois, "Grant is entitled to every bit of the credit for the campaign; I opposed it. I wrote him a letter about it." In his letter Sherman had said that by crossing the river south of Vicksburg, Grant would be putting himself voluntarily in a position that an enemy would be willing to maneuver for a year to get him into. Grant chose to regard the letter as unofficial and did not keep a copy. Years later Sherman himself gave a copy to Grant's biographer, General Adam Badeau, who printed it.

When Halleck received Grant's plan he approved it, with the proviso that Grant should help Major General Nathaniel P. Banks before moving on Vicksburg. Banks, operating out of New Orleans, was attacking Port Hudson. Grant replied that once across the river he would send a corps to aid Banks, and Halleck was satisfied. As a diversion, Grant sent a small cavalry force, under Colonel Benjamin Grierson, on a raid through central Mississippi. Grierson's justly famous raid, which began on April 17 and ended on May 2, was a huge success. He broke railroad lines at a number of crucial places, frightened the citizenry, and caused Pemberton to send the Confederate cavalry and a division of infantry after him in a hopeless chase.

Another, almost as important a diversion, was the dispatch, early in April, of Major General Frederick Steele's division to Greenville. Going ashore, the Federals drove inland to Deer Creek and then turned south, inflicting much damage in an area from which Pemberton's commissary drew much of its hogs and hominy. To counter this thrust, Pemberton's subordinate at Vicksburg, Major General Carter L. Stevenson, ordered out a strong column. Steele then retired and reported back to Grant at Milliken's Bend. Because of this expedition, Stevenson gave scant notice to intelligence reports telling of a Union advance southward from Milliken's Bend.

As a secondary diversion Grant left Sherman at Young's Point; late in April Sherman made a feint on the Yazoo that held some of Pemberton's force in place.

Throughout April, Grant's main force, led by McClernand's XIII Corps, worked its way down the west bank of the river. The area was flat bottom-land cut by numerous bayous. Road construction was a hard, muddy, disagreeable task that required much corduroying. The troops had to improvise a number of bridges, using whatever material was at hand and their own ingenuity. By April 29 McClernand's and Major General James B. McPherson's corps had joined at Hard Times, where they met Porter's fleet, which in a spectacular movement had passed the batteries at Vicksburg.

Although the Federals had been moving south since the last day of March, Pemberton had done little to meet the threat. He did not even know about Grant's movements until April 17 and not until the 28th did he foresee a Union attack on Grand Gulf. Even then he sent the local commander, Brigadier General John S. Bowen, only some 5,000 reinforcements, raising Bowen's total force to 9,000—far inferior to Grant's more than 24,000 men. Pemberton had been begging Johnston for reinforcements, but disagreements at higher levels—Johnston wanted to take men from Arkansas, while Davis said he should make transfers from Bragg—prevented action.

Pemberton, however, could have done much more with what he had. But he was besieged with reports of the great damage being done by Grierson, had an exaggerated idea of Grierson's strength, and had consequently sent all his cavalry and thousands of infantry after the Yankee raider. He kept a large force north of Vicksburg to meet the threat Sherman posed, and hesitated to weaken the garrison at Port Hudson for fear Banks would pounce on the fort (this last was partly Davis' fault as he had repeatedly stressed the importance of Port Hudson).

The result of the poor intelligence work was that just when Pemberton should have been concentrating to meet and oppose Grant's crossing of the river, he had his force dispersed all over the state. Pemberton's subsequent discomfort was primarily due to his own indecision.

On April 29 Porter, at Grant's request, bombarded the Grand Gulf batteries. Grant hoped to cross his troops in the transports and assault craft, but the batteries proved too strong and, after consultation with Porter, Grant decided to land farther downriver. He planned to go to Rodney, but when a Negro informed him that a good solid road led inland from Bruinsburg he decided to cross there. On April 30 Grant got McClernand's corps and part of McPherson's corps across.

It would be impossible to improve on Grant's own description of his feelings at this point: "When this was effected I felt a degree of relief scarcely ever equalled since. Vicksburg was not yet taken, it is true, nor were its defenders demoralized by any of our previous moves. I was now in enemy territory, with a vast river and the stronghold of Vicksburg between me and my base of supplies. But I was on dry ground on the same side of the river with the enemy. All the campaigns, labors, hardships, and exposures from the month of December previous to this time that had been made and endured, were for the accomplishment of this one object."

GRANT MOVES TO ISOLATE VICKSBURG

From this point on, until the siege began, Grant moved with amazing speed. Brushing the Confederates aside with short, hard blows wherever he met them, he moved his force inland to Jackson, then westward to

Vicksburg. He hardly ever took the obvious route, always left himself with alternatives, and kept Pemberton thoroughly confused. No other campaign of the Civil War, and few others in all military history, were so successful at such small cost. In view of this operation, it is difficult to explain the prevalence of the widely held view that Grant was slow and deliberate—a bludgeon general rather than the wielder of a rapier.

As soon as Grant was across the river he ordered Sherman to bring the bulk of his force south. Leaving Major General Frank Blair's division to guard his depots and supply line west of the river, Grant then set out inland with McClernand's corps and part of McPherson's. The troops marched along the Rodney road south of Bayou Pierre toward Port Gibson, a small village where there was a network of roads leading to Grand Gulf, Vicksburg, and Jackson. McClernand, in the lead, hoped to beat Bowen to the bridge over Bayou Pierre on the route that led to Grand Gulf, but he had wasted valuable time because of poor staff work. His men had not received their three days rations prior to crossing the river and he had to wait while they were issued. By the time he reached Thompson's plantation, five miles west of Port Gibson, it was after midnight.

In any case the Confederates were already there. Brigadier General Martin E. Green and an advanced detachment of Bowen's force had arrived late in the afternoon and taken up positions to contest the Yankee advance. Because the cavalry was off chasing Grierson, Bowen had no firm idea where the Federals were, but he guessed that they would try to cross the bayou and invest Grand Gulf. Therefore he sent one brigade to hold the bridge and cover Port Gibson, while he prepared to move with the other as necessary.

For General Green the night of April 30–May 1 passed slowly. All was silence about him. No scouts had reported in; he began to fear that Grant had taken a wholly unexpected route, or perhaps even reembarked his troops for another try at Grand Gulf. At 12:30 A.M. the tension became more than he could bear, and he rode forward to make sure that Lieutenant Tisdale and his outpost were alert.

Coming up to the Shaifer house he found a small area of chaos. Mrs. A. K. Shaifer and the other women of the house had panicked at the news the Yankees were coming. They were frantically trying to load their most valuable household effects into a wagon in which they proposed to flee to Port Gibson. The panic of the ladies allowed the overwrought Green to get control of himself. He calmly told them that the Yankees could not possibly arrive before daylight, and that they therefore had plenty of time to load their wagon.

He had hardly spoken the comforting words when a crash of musketry shattered the stillness. One ball smashed through the west wall of the house and several more buried themselves in the wagon-load of furniture. A brief horrified silence gave way to shrieks of dismay. Abandoning both household goods and dignity, the ladies scrambled into the wagon and whipped the team frantically toward Port Gibson and fancied safety. Green, both chagrined and amused, ordered Tisdale to contest the Yankee advance, then galloped back to make sure that the gunfire had alerted his command. The land campaign for Vicksburg was under way.

During the remainder of the night the troops exchanged sporadic fire with little result. The night was so dark and the country so broken that Brigadier General Eugene A. Carr, senior Union commander on the spot, decided to wait until dawn before deploying his division further.

BATTLE OF PORT GIBSON, MAY 1, 1863

Dawn revealed to General Carr a terrain of incredible complexity. It was an utter maze of ridges, each more or less flat-topped and of equal height, but running in all directions. Each ridge was separated from its neighbor by a steep-sided ravine filled with a jumble of trees, vines, and immense and almost impenetrable cane brakes. The ridge tops were chiefly cultivated fields except where there were groves of trees around plantation buildings. Visibility was excellent from the ridge tops but the ravines were jungles that closed tightly about men moving through them, so that each man's world was a tiny green-walled room only a few yards across.

McClernand, nervous, eager, and excited, rode up at daybreak. He had just passed a fork in the road and had no idea which of the routes before him led to Port Gibson. The inevitable Negro "contraband" appeared to explain that both did, and that at no point did the two roads, which followed ridges, diverge more than a mile or two. They were separated, however, by a deep vine- and cane-choked ravine, so that one flank could not reinforce the other except by marching back to the junction of the roads. Bowen's men were in position on both roads, hoping to hold off McClernand until reinforcements under Major General William W. Loring could arrive from Big Black Bridge.

McClernand immediately decided to attack along both ridges and simply push the Confederates out of the way. He put the divisions of Hovey, Carr, and A. J. Smith on the right flank and that of Osterhaus on the left. With an entire corps passing through one road junction there was not much room for maneuver, and it took a few hours to get everyone into position. Neither attack got off until after 8 A.M. By then Bowen himself had arrived. Instantly recognizing that he had the whole of Grant's army in front of him, he sent couriers to the rear to bring up all possible reinforcements.

In retrospect this was the critical moment of the Vicksburg campaign. Grant was still involved in an amphibious operation. His force was inevitably divided, with one of his three corps still on the west bank of the river and over half of another still engaged in disembarking and in unloading the transports. If Pemberton could have struck while Grant was thus off balance, with one foot in the water and the other on land, he certainly would have spoiled Grant's plans and he might have even destroyed his army.

But Pemberton utterly failed to take advantage of the opportunity. Because he had voluntarily given up his cavalry he was operating in the dark. Not until the battle had been joined did he learn that contact had been made. Then he sent elements of two divisions toward Port Gibson and telegraphed Johnston, demanding reinforcements. Johnston at once wired back: "If Grant's army lands on this side of the river, the safety of Mississippi depends on beating it. For that object you should unite your whole force."

As always, Johnston's strategic insight was impeccable. His advice, however, was worthless. Pemberton had five divisions scattered through the triangle formed by Port Gibson, Jackson, and Vicksburg. He had only one division and two brigades of another at the scene of the opening battle. He was simply in no position to prevent Grant from establishing himself on the east bank. Pemberton must have winced the next day when Johnston again wired him: "If Grant's army crosses, unite all your forces to beat it. Success will give you back what was abandoned to win it."

Johnston had been ill, and in any case never had his heart in the campaign. He approached it with the attitude that the result was a foregone conclusion, never showed any enthusiasm for his assignment, made no real effort to control or direct Pemberton, and was so weighted down with pessimism that he evidently felt that sending more troops to Pemberton was simply to waste them. There is no evidence that he ever made a determined attempt to get reinforcements to the hard-pressed Pemberton. In a typical "my hands are tied: there is nothing I can do" message to the Confederate War Department the day after the Battle of Port Gibson, he transmitted Pemberton's call for reinforcements and commented "They cannot be sent from here without giving up Tennessee."

The upshot was that Bowen was left by his superiors to fight his battle alone. Grant, meanwhile, reached the field just as the battle was getting into full swing and inspected both flanks in person. McClernand's progress was slow but steady. He could not begin to deploy all his troops on one road, and in any case Confederate fire made a direct advance along the ridge unprofitable. He therefore sent men into the ravines on both sides to attempt to outflank Bowen. Once in the ravine, however, the smoke of battle, coupled with the vines and underbrush, made it virtually impossible to maintain any sense of direction, and regiments found themselves moving at odd angles to the direction their officers supposed. Great gaps opened at some points, while at others regiments jammed up. Still the weight of the advance was enough to force the enemy to give ground.

On the left Brigadier General Peter J. Osterhaus, a Prussian who was the most distinguished of the foreign-born generals who served the Union, was having great difficulty. At 8:15 he had tried to rush the

Rebel position. He had gained about 400 yards, then had come to a sudden stop when he hit the main enemy lines. When he found time to check his position, Osterhaus discovered that his attack had carried his men into the middle of a concave system of ridges, and that the diverging movements caused by peculiar arrangement of the ravines had opened huge gaps in his lines. The 42d Ohio faced the middle of the Rebel line with the 49th Indiana on an odd eccentric to the left. Between the Hoosiers and the 118th Illinois on their left there was a gap of more than 200 yards. A well-led Confederate counterattack might roll up his entire line.

But the Rebels had no fresh troops. Grant meanwhile, as soon as McClernand's men had passed the road junction, rushed elements of McPherson's corps forward. Throughout the day McClernand begged Grant for more men. Grant consistently insisted that McClernand, who had sent Brigadier General Alvin P. Hovey to help Carr, on the right, already had more men on his very limited front than he could use effectively. A brigade of Major General John A. Logan's division (which had crossed the river that morning) reached the Shaifer house about noon and Grant ordered it to support McClernand's right. Logan's next brigade to reach the field was sent to assist Osterhaus.

While Union reinforcements reached the field in division strength, Bowen received his only reinforcements—about one and a half brigades coming up from Grand Gulf and Vicksburg. Osterhaus, with a superiority of over three to one, moved some troops into the ravine on his left, and sent a series of skirmish lines forward. There was a great deal of noise, tremendous confusion, and clouds of smoke before the Confederates fell back.

On the right McClernand, never a subtle general but a firm believer in applying the greatest strength in the smallest space, prepared a direct frontal smash. He concentrated so many men on his narrow front that the regiments were stacked up two, three, and four deep. The two leading regiments got within eighty yards of the Confederate artillery before the men had to seek shelter. Two more regiments followed, the men shouting and forming a single irresistible mass. The Confederates had two batteries double-shotted with canister for a last telling volley, but before the gunners could fire their pieces the Yankees swept over them, capturing two guns of the Botetourt Virginia Artillery. Gleefully the Union men manhandled these guns around and fired them at the backs of the fleeing Rebel troops.

McClernand's column moved forward along the Rodney road. About a mile beyond Magnolia Church the vanguard encountered a strong force of Confederates posted in a deep hollow. Here Bowen had deployed the brigade (William E. Baldwin's) that had just arrived from Vicksburg, after marching forty-four miles in twenty-seven hours. The half brigade (Francis M. Cockrell's) that had come from Grand Gulf that morning would constitute Bowen's reserve.

In this difficult country it took several hours for McClernand and his three division commanders to form their troops in line of battle. The Federals then advanced into the cane-choked hollow, but within minutes the enemy checked their forward progress. Bowen in the meantime had taken a desperate gamble. He sent Cockrell with his two regiments far to the left. Taking advantage of the terrain, Cockrell was able to assail McClernand's right, which was not refused, and roll up one Union brigade. To counter this thrust McClernand was compelled to rush artillery and infantry to his right. Superior numbers soon told, and the Confederate success was nullified. But by this time dusk was at hand, and the day's fighting was over.

It had taken all day but the Confederate position was finally gone. Bowen had fought magnificently; no other Confederate leader would do as well in the campaign to follow. A West Point classmate of McPherson and the ablest general in Pemberton's army, Bowen was a severe disciplinarian. His jet-black hair, bushy eyebrows, and luxuriant chin beard tended to draw attention away from his sleepy eyes and rather frail constitution. He was unable to withstand the rigors of the siege, contracted severe dysentery, and survived the campaign by only a few days. But he had made his contribution; it could have been decisive. For eighteen hours he had held up Grant's entire army, inflicting over 800 casualties. Had he received any help at all, Bowen might have driven Grant into the river. But Pemberton had let his best chance go by.

Grant rode up to McClernand's headquarters just after the successful assault at Magnolia Church. Governor Richard Yates of Illinois was there; together the three men rode forward to inspect the captured position. The men cheered lustily as they passed along the line. Grant was impassive as always, but the cheers were heady to McClernand and Yates. The two politicians were so overwhelmed by the sight of all those voters that they simply had to stop and make brief congratulatory addresses to the troops. Yates said a few words, then McClernand shouldered him aside and exulted, "A great day for the Northwest!"

Grant watched quietly, then suggested that perhaps the advance should be resumed. McClernand, beaming, agreed, and got the pursuit started. Bowen had led part of his force over Bayou Pierre to cover Grand Gulf (which he evacuated the next night), while the remainder slipped northeastward over the Little Bayou Pierre (South Fork of the Bayou Pierre) and then took a more northerly route toward Vicksburg, crossing Big Bayou Pierre (the Bayou's north fork) at Grindstone Ford. He fired the three bridges behind him. When darkness fell Grant let his weary men make camp.

The next morning Grant moved through Port Gibson to Little Bayou Pierre; he at once set his men to work bridge-building. Lieutenant Colonel James H. Wilson, two years out of West Point and soon to achieve fame as a cavalry leader, supervised the construction. Using material obtained from wooden buildings, stables, fences, and the like, and going into the water himself to work as hard as the men, Wilson quickly had the bridge finished. Grant crossed, and by evening that day (May 2) had reached Bayou Pierre.

A BOLD DECISION

Grant had planned to solidify his position around Grand Gulf and south of the Big Black, then send McClernand's corps to assist Banks at Port Hudson. Once that operation was completed, Grant would move north with his entire army reinforced by that of Banks. But on May 3 Grant learned that Banks was on a chase up Red River and would not be ready to invest Port Hudson for several weeks.

The news was extremely frightening. Grant had bet everything he had on this campaign only because he was convinced he could move faster than the Confederates. Outwardly taciturn, he was filled with an inner tension, a compulsion to get moving. The trouble was that he had no assured line of supplies. The road from Milliken's Bend down to Hard Times was so bad and so exposed to attack that Grant hesitated to supply his army that way. Material could not be brought up from New Orleans as long as the guns at Port Hudson were still firing. Transports and barges could run the batteries at Vicksburg, but only at what would be an increasing cost as the Confederate gunners improved with practice.

Grant made the boldest decision of the war. He declared that he would move inland without occupying the countryside. He would have the men carry enough hardtack, coffee, and salt to get by on, load his wagons to the bulging point with ammunition, and depend on the countryside for whatever else he needed. He did arrange to have heavily guarded supply trains come out of Grand Gulf each day.

Grant's next problem was where to attack. McPherson, on May 5, had conducted a reconnaissance north of the Big Black River which revealed that Pemberton had finally concentrated his troops and was having them dig in to oppose an attack from the south. Grant may have known that Johnston was attempting to build up a force at Jackson, that President Davis had dispatched troops from the East, and that any reinforcements to Vicksburg had to come through Jackson. He therefore adopted a favorite Napoleonic maneuver and advanced so as to get between the two forces, hopefully to destroy the weaker one first, then turn on the stronger.

By May 7 Grant had McClernand up to Big Sand Creek with McPherson at Rocky Springs. Sherman had reached Hard Times, crossed the river to occupy Grand Gulf, and caught up with the other two corps in a couple of days. On May 11 Grant pushed Sherman's corps out in front of McClernand's, which had halted near Cayuga, while McPherson prepared to advance on Raymond from Utica. Sherman and McClernand marched together to Auburn, where McClernand branched out almost straight north on the Telegraph Road toward Edwards' Station while Sherman moved on eastward to Dillon's plantation. If it proved necessary, Grant had lateral roads available so that any one corps could support another at any time.

Still, Grant was taking a risk. If Pemberton had organized the countryside so that spies and scouts could be reporting, or if he had retained his cavalry for reconnaissance, he might have descended quickly on the nearest Union corps and isolated and destroyed it. But he had neglected to make either of these elementary preparations and as a result was completely in the dark about Grant's movements. He was, in addition, under orders from Davis to hold Vicksburg and from Johnston to concentrate and attack Grant. Under the circumstances he decided to take an indecisive course, which suited his temperament in any case, collect his forces along the Big Black River, and await developments. He did send Bowen forward to occupy Edwards' Station and a brigade, Brigadier General John Gregg's, from Jackson to Raymond.

BATTLE OF RAYMOND

When Gregg marched into Raymond on the afternoon of May 11 the populace hailed his men as saviors. The village seethed with rumors of the approach of a Yankee column from Utica. Gregg asked where he could find the headquarters of Colonel Wirt Adams, expecting to find the cavalry commander busy receiving reports on the enemy's movements. Gregg's request was met with blank stares—Adams had exactly five men in the village.

Adams' absence was due to a masterpiece of ambiguity by Pemberton. The latter, after ordering Gregg to Raymond, had sent a message to Adams: "General Gregg is ordered to Raymond. Direct your cavalry there to scout thoroughly, and keep him informed." What Pemberton meant was that Adams should take all his cavalry to Raymond and carry out this mission. Adams, however, read the message to say that the cavalry he already had in Raymond (five men) should scout thoroughly and keep Gregg informed. Adams therefore proceeded with his original plans and, while Gregg marched into Raymond, rode into Edwards' Station.

The result was that a Union corps was bearing down on an unsuspecting Rebel brigade, and again the Yankee forces, though outnumbered in the area, had overwhelming superiority at the point of contact. In the engagement that followed, the Southerners again showed that given equal numbers they were more than equal to their enemy. In part this was due to a misreading of the situation by McPherson, who overestimated his opponent's strength, a natural mistake—he just could not believe that a brigade would challenge a corps to pitched battle. He therefore advanced cautiously, enabling Gregg to engage the Union regiments piecemeal.

The battle itself, on May 12, was even more confused than that at Port Gibson. The Confederates kept attacking, wildly hitting advancing Union regiments and forcing them to retreat. On two occasions John A. Logan personally rallied his men. Once the 20th Ohio, seeing a Texas regiment sweep down upon its flank, began to waver and prepared to run. Logan dashed up and with "the shriek of an eagle turned them back to their place." One Ohioan gave Logan his just due: "Had it not been for Logan's timely intervention, who was continually riding up and down the line, firing his men with his own enthusiasm, our lines would undoubtedly have been broken at some point."

The whole battlefield was a bowl of dust and smoke; no one could see what was really going on. The Confederates would probably not have fought had they known what they were up against. Considering some of the things they did, however, it is possible that a knowledge of the odds would have simply spurred them to greater efforts. For example, late in the day Colonel R. W. MacGavock found himself on a bare spur just as a pause occurred in the battle. As the smoke and dust lifted, he and his men were exposed to McPherson's entire corps artillery. Joyfully switching fire to the only visible target, the Union gunners began to rake MacGavock's ranks with shell fire. Meanwhile a blue line of infantry, sharpshooters thrown out in advance, began to come up the hill. MacGavock realized that if he fell back the entire Southern position would go with him. If he stayed, he would be cut to pieces by the Yankee artillery and the charging infantry.

He could think of only one thing to do. A tall, commanding man who habitually wore a long gray cloak with a brilliant scarlet lining, Mac-

Gavock dramatically threw his cloak back. There he stood, a compelling crimson figure, at the head of his troops. Every eye on the battlefield turned toward him. He waved his arm forward and shouted for a charge. At that instant a Union sharpshooter cut him down, but his men rushed forward with irresistible force, screaming for vengeance. They broke the Yankee line and sent it running.

Somehow this was not the way a battle between a brigade and a corps was supposed to go; in the end inevitably the weight of the Union attack made itself felt. The Confederates slowly fell back, even though Gregg continued to find the best defense was a good offense. Whenever a Yankee regiment appeared, the Rebels facing it would move forward threateningly, making as much noise as possible. Soon, however, the Confederates found themselves nearly surrounded, with the enemy well around both flanks. Gregg retired.

One Confederate brigade had held up a Union corps for a half a day, at a cost of 515 casualties. McPherson suffered almost an equal loss in killed and wounded, but because his missing total was only 37 his casualty list ran to only 442.

The bone-weary, hot, dusty, thirsty 20th Ohio led the Union advance into Raymond. Coming into the shaded village from the brazen sun, they were astonished to find a tremendous picnic spread beneath the stately live oaks along the streets. The ladies of Raymond had prepared the feast for Gregg's soldiers, to be eaten upon their "return from victory." Gregg had moved through the village so fast, however, that the men had not touched the food. The boys from Ohio gratefully took their places and by the time the following regiment reached town the food was gone.

Grant received McPherson's report of the battle while at Sherman's headquarters. He knew from his scouts that Pemberton was concentrating at Edwards' Station, partly to block the Federal movement to Vicksburg, partly to pose a threat to the Grand Gulf-Raymond road over which Grant was bringing up reinforcements and the heavily guarded trains. During the day, Sherman in the center and McClernand on the left had forced their way across Fourteen Mile Creek, as they turned their columns toward the Vicksburg-to-Jackson railroad. Grant also knew that a couple of the Confederate regiments coming all the way from the eastern seaboard had reported to Gregg after he had retreated through Raymond. More would be coming and their route would be via Jackson. If Pemberton were finally going to concentrate all his units, Grant wanted his pulled together too. He also wanted to cut Pemberton off from any possibility of receiving outside aid, and at the same time destroy the communications and manufacturing center of Mississippi, which was Jackson. Grant therefore "decided at once to turn the whole column toward Jackson and capture that place without delay."

Grant issued his orders on the night of May 12. He directed McPherson to Clinton, almost directly west of Jackson and astride the Vicksburg-to-Jackson railroad; once McPherson had occupied Clinton he would sever Pemberton's direct communications with Johnston, who was building up a force in the capital. Grant told Sherman to start at 4 A.M., marching through Raymond toward Jackson. McClernand would follow and occupy Raymond.

Grant was now deep in hostile territory, with large enemy forces on either side of him. The Union troops were in the position Sherman had said the enemy would be willing to maneuver for a year or more in order to get them into. Meanwhile General Banks, on Red River, was pleading for reinforcements.

Grant had been in a similar position in February 1862, at Fort Donelson. Then as now he did not panic. (The modern slang expression is an excellent description of Grant in such a situation: "He kept his cool.") Neither did he take foolish chances. He kept his troops in supporting distance of each other, making constant reconnaissances to enable each corps to know at all times where the most practicable routes were in case it became necessary for them to concentrate. More important, he moved so rapidly, as well as audaciously, that he had the Confederates constantly and thoroughly confused.

McPherson reached Clinton early on May 13. The men immediately cut the telegraph line and began destroying the railroad. Sherman got into Raymond before the last of McPherson's command had left. McClernand had the most difficult mission; his spearhead, which had forced its way across Fourteen Mile Creek, was in contact with the formidable force Pemberton was concentrating at Edwards' Station. To keep the Confederates off balance while he broke contact, McClernand bluffed an attack, and the Confederates began digging in. McClernand, covered by this feint, sent three of his divisions eastward across Bakers Creek, and by the time Pemberton and his generals realized what had happened, McClernand's corps had stolen a day's march on them.

McClernand reached his encampment in good order. The next morning, May 14, McPherson marched at dawn for Jackson; so did Sherman. When the two corps reached the Confederate entrenchments around the city they would be about two miles apart. McClernand sent one division to Clinton, another behind Sherman, and a third to Raymond.

JOHNSTON GIVES UP JACKSON

By the afternoon of the 13th Grant's position was as nearly perfect as the human mind and hard marching could make it. He had two corps threatening Jackson; a division, Hovey's, at Clinton that could either hold off Pemberton or reinforce McPherson; another division behind Sherman for support; a division at Raymond that could take either road and reinforce Hovey or Sherman; and two more divisions (one of which, Blair's, had recently crossed the river) farther back within one and one-half day's march of Jackson. These last divisions, under McClernand's command, were threatening Pemberton and, if not needed at Jackson, were one day's march from there on their way to Vicksburg and on two different roads leading to that city.

The Confederate position, by contrast, approached the ludicrous. Johnston, who had arrived in Jackson on the evening of the 13th, had nothing like enough men to hold off two corps. Although the total Confederate strength in the whole area of operation was still greater than Grant's, the third battle of the campaign was about to be fought with the Union forces—who were invading and were in the heart of enemy territory—again in great superiority. Grant stood squarely between the two Rebel armies. Johnston ordered Pemberton to move on Clinton, where the two separated forces could unite. Pemberton, however, had other ideas. He was considering moving southeast to attack and destroy Grant's trains and the two divisions guarding them.

Within Jackson, Johnston had only some 6,000 men to defend the capital. "I am too late," he wired the Secretary of War. At 3 A.M. on May 14 he issued an evacuation order, even though he then was facing two corps, which had not yet begun their final advance on Jackson. In short, Johnston's pessimism was so great that he decided to retreat before any pressure was exerted and before he could possibly be certain that the Union concentration was aimed at Jackson.

At 5 A.M. McPherson and Sherman started out for Jackson. It had rained most of the night; with daybreak the rain began to fall in torrents, turning the roads into sheets of mud. At places along McPherson's route the road was covered by a foot of water. The wheels of the ambulances, guns, and limbers quickly converted the road into a bottomless quagmire, through which the artillery horses strained in vain to pull the heavy caissons. The sodden infantrymen put their shoulders to the wheels. Curses quickly lost in the sound of falling water rang out whenever an officer or courier dashed past on his horse and splashed sheets of mud and water on the straining infantrymen.

Despite everything the men moved forward. By midmorning they had reached the outer Confederate lines. McPherson's leading division, Brigadier General Marcellus M. Crocker's, deployed. McPherson sent word back to the following division, Logan's, to hurry forward. Just then the rain abated slightly and McPherson organized an immediate assault. As he prepared to give the order to charge, another terrific downpour commenced, with the water coming down in buckets. McPherson, afraid to allow his men to open their cartridge boxes lest the water ruin the ammunition, called off the attack to wait for the rain to subside.

Sherman's vanguard, meanwhile, had worked its way forward and had reached Lynch Creek, which was nearly overflowing. A small Confederate force covered the bridge. As soon as he heard the enemy artillery contesting his advance Sherman rode forward, made a hasty reconnaissance, and ordered an immediate attack. Just then the rain ceased. It was 11 A.M. The men dashed forward, crossed the bridge, and drove the Rebels back. By early afternoon Sherman had forced the enemy into the main Jackson entrenchments (dug earlier by slave labor and citizen volunteers), where his assault came to a halt.

Grant was with Sherman, and the two officers conferred on the next move. Sherman pointed out that the enemy trenches extended as far to his left as he could see. To the right his vision was obstructed, and he decided to send a scouting party to reconnoiter in that direction. Sherman, Grant, and some staff officers, standing in front of a cottage as they talked, presented an obvious target to the Rebels. Just as the scouting party rode away several shells whistled over the infantry line and exploded nearby. Neither Grant nor Sherman turned a hair.

The scouts, led by Sherman's chief engineer, Captain Julius Pitzman, found that the trenches to the right were unmanned. Pitzman returned to the main force and gathered up the 95th Ohio for a flanking operation. As the regiment was placing its flag as a symbol of victory on the earthworks, an old Negro ran up to the men waving his hat and yelling at the top of his voice, "I'se come to tell you-all that the Rebels is left the city, clear done gone. You jes' go on and you will take the city."

With considerable difficulty the Ohio soldiers got the old man calmed down enough to ask him, "Why are the Rebs still firing their battery if they have left the place?"

"Ho!" he laughed, "there is only a few cannoneers there to work the guns to keep you back."

The Negro offered to guide them and the men agreed to follow. Sure enough, he led them right into the unsupported and unguarded rear of the Southern artillerymen. Shouting joyfully, the Yankees surged forward, through the backyards and over fences, pounced on the Confederates, and bagged themselves six guns and fifty-two prisoners. Sherman could now walk into Jackson.

The northern jaw of the Union pincer was prepared to close. When the rains let up, Crocker decided not to waste time on such an inferior force, especially one that was challenging him two miles outside its earthworks. He sent his whole line charging forward on the double with banners unfurled, bayonets fixed, and the men cheering wildly.

The Rebels resisted for a few minutes, then retreated to their main trench system. Shortly after they arrived they pulled out of the city.

Johnston had already left; Gregg was in command. Gregg, learning that Sherman had closed up against the Jackson fortifications, and of the repulse of the men facing McPherson, and receiving a message that the army's supply train had left Jackson en route to Canton, decided he had done enough. He ordered his remaining men, except for a number of artillerymen manning the guns, to retreat along the Canton road and protect the rear of the wagon train. It was these artillerymen whom Sherman's troops captured.

At 3 P.M. McPherson learned that the enemy had vanished from his front. He sent Crocker's division on into the city while directing a brigade of Logan's division to march cross-country and attempt to cut off Gregg's retreat. Either the brigade did not march fast enough (the men had been marching or fighting in deep mud since 5 A.M.) or the order did not reach them soon enough. In any case Gregg escaped.

At 4 P.M. Grant, McPherson, and Sherman met in the Bowman House to exchange congratulations, count the cost of victory, and plan new blows against the enemy. The Union forces had 299 casualties, the Rebels 845. In addition, the victors had captured seventeen cannon.

If Grant had been thinking of savoring his victory and letting his men rest for a day or two, McPherson gave him news that dispelled this notion. General Johnston had the previous day sent an order to Pemberton, dispatching it via three messengers. One of the couriers was widely known as a fire-eating Rebel civilian whom the Union authorities had expelled from Memphis some months earlier for making public statements threatening and disloyal to the Union. His expulsion and subsequent flight into Confederate-held territory had received considerable publicity. Actually the man was an undercover Federal agent, and the whole affair had been stage-managed. He became a trusted Confederate messenger, and when Johnston sent him with orders to Pemberton, he took them first to McPherson. Thus the latter had the order before Pemberton, and showed it to Grant.

Grant eagerly grabbed the message. It directed Pemberton to proceed to Clinton and strike at Grant's rear. Johnston would try to unite with him there. Grant knew that Johnston's force was retreating to the northeast, but Pemberton did not. Presumably Pemberton would obey orders and should soon be setting out for Clinton.

Grant decided to concentrate at Bolton, the nearest point where Johnston could swing around and effect a junction with Pemberton. He told McPherson to march at earliest dawn and sent a courier to McClernand. After giving the tidings of the fall of Jackson, Grant ordered McClernand to "turn all your forces toward Bolton Station, and make all dispatch in getting there. Move troops by the most direct road from wherever they may be on receipt of this order."

One can only stand amazed at Grant's ability. The Confederates did not concentrate at Bolton or Clinton, which would have been their best move, so no battle was fought there. Had they done so, however, Grant would have fought them on at least equal terms—with his fresh troops in the forefront.

Grant told Sherman to occupy the rifle-pits around Jackson, and to destroy the railroad tracks in and about Jackson, and all the property belonging to the enemy. The conference then adjourned, and Grant retired for the night to sleep in the bed Johnston had occupied the night before.

By 10 A.M. on May 15 all of McPherson's corps had gone and Sherman was ready to begin the destruction. The chief purpose was to eliminate Jackson as a communication center, since Grant did not have enough troops to leave an occupying force. Sherman therefore started with the railroads. He would line a regiment up in single file parallel to the tracks. At a given signal everybody would bend over, grab a tie, and heave, this turning up on edge a section of track equal in length to the regiment. The men then piled up the ties, placed the rails on top of the pile, and started a fire. When the iron was cherry red in the middle, teams of brawny soldiers would grab the ends and twist the rails around a convenient tree. The results were called "Sherman's neckties."

Sherman burned all the factories in the town, many of the public buildings, and some private ones. His men found a supply of rum; the inevitable result was indiscriminate burning, against which Sherman protested bitterly.

During the morning Grant and Sherman visited a large textile factory. The plant manager and the employees, most of them women, simply ignored the presence of the two generals and went on working. The looms were producing tent cloth with C.S.A. woven into each bolt. Grant meditated on this industrious scene for a few minutes, then turned to Sherman and suggested that the women had done work enough. Sherman told the women they could leave, taking with them all the cloth they could carry. He then burned the factory.

BATTLE OF CHAMPION HILL

Sherman spent the night of May 15–16 in Jackson, marching for Bolton on the 16th. The Confederates re-occupied Jackson but the Union mission had been accomplished. Jackson was now worthless as a transportation center, her war industries were crushed, and the Confederate concentration that had aimed at saving Fortress Vicksburg was scattered to the winds. And Grant, now well concentrated, was marching due west toward Vicksburg.

Pemberton, meanwhile, had finally started to move. He had so far committed the inexcusable blunder of doing nothing. When he received Johnston's order to strike Grant's rear at Clinton, Pemberton held a council of war. There, incredibly, he raised with his commanders the question, "Should we obey the theater commander's order?" A heated discussion followed. A majority voiced a desire to march to the southeast and destroy Grant's trains and the two divisions guarding them. Pemberton himself wished to hold the line of the Big Black, repulse the Federals, and then counterattack. Sensing the mood of his generals and soldiers, Pemberton announced he would ignore Johnston and strike out for Auburn and cut Grant's supply line.

The next morning, May 15, Pemberton set out. The rains, however, had swollen Bakers Creek, and at the Raymond crossing the stream was unfordable. The Confederates spent most of the afternoon in waiting for the water to subside. Pemberton finally turned northeast and marched his troops into the main Vicksburg-Jackson road, where a bridge crossed the creek. They then marched eastward, turned into a plantation road, and after a seven-mile detour, the head of the column was back on the Raymond road. It was midnight before the rear brigades had crossed

Bakers Creek. When the army camped, the troops lay down where they halted. Six miles separated the vanguard from the rear guard.

Early the next morning, May 16, Pemberton received a later order from Johnston, one written after the fall of Jackson. Again Johnston wished to attempt to unite the forces at Clinton. This time Pemberton decided he would do as ordered; he sent a message to that effect to Johnston.

Grant, meanwhile, had McPherson and McClernand converging on Champion Hill. The two contending armies were unaware on the night of May 15–16 that they were camped within four miles of each other. At 5 A.M. two railroaders reported to Grant that Pemberton was at Edwards' Station preparing to move east. His force was estimated at 25,000 men.

Grant's first thoughts were to get up reinforcements. He had planned to leave Sherman in Jackson for two days, in order to complete the destruction of the city. Now he sent orders to Sherman to move as soon as possible westward, and to put one division with an ammunition train on the road immediately. Sherman was to tell the division commander to march with all possible speed until he reached the rear of McPherson's corps.

In sharp contrast to the way in which orders were acted upon in the Confederate army, Sherman had a division on the road within an hour, and his other division was soon out of Jackson. A. J. Smith's and Blair's divisions on the 15th had marched from Auburn to Raymond. Passing out of Raymond, they had advanced a short distance up the Edwards road and had camped. Hovey's division of McPherson's corps had marched westward from Clinton. A clean-shaven politician from Indiana who had received a promotion for his good work at Shiloh, Hovey had spent the night at Bolton. McClernand sent Hovey forward, while Grant, who was preparing to ride forward from Clinton, sent a message to McPherson to clear his wagons from the road and follow Hovey as closely as possible. McClernand had two roads available for his four remaining divisions; Grant told him to move on the enemy by both, but cautiously and with skirmishers to the front to feel for the enemy.

A. J. Smith, leading McClernand's advance on the southernmost road, was the first to encounter the enemy's pickets. Shortly thereafter, Osterhaus, spearheading McClernand's column on the Middle road, and later yet, on the Vicksburg-Jackson road, bumped into the Rebels. McPherson, hearing the scattered fire, tried to hurry his men forward, but Hovey's wagons were occupying the road and delayed the advance. McPherson sent word back to Grant at Clinton, describing the situation. Grant immediately mounted his horse and rode forward. In a short time he had got the wagons off the road and cleared the way for McPherson. By then, too, Hovey's skirmishing had increased in intensity, and now amounted almost to a battle.

Champion Hill, Pemberton's accidental choice of a battlefield, was well suited to the defense. One of the highest points in the region, it commanded all the ground to the north and southwest. The position would be especially formidable against attack by columns advancing via the Raymond and Middle roads. As contact was made early with General McClernand's columns advancing via these roads, Pemberton concentrated his troops along the ridge extending to the southwest and commanding Jackson Creek. To reach the Confederates' main line of resistance, McClernand's troops would have to deploy and advance across fields commanded by Pemberton's artillery.

It was not until midmorning that Pemberton and his generals learned of Hovey's approach. To meet this threat to their left, the Confederates rushed several brigades to hold the ridge extending northwestward from the crest of Champion Hill. Fronting this ridge were several ravines which ran north, then westerly, terminating at Bakers Creek. These ravines were overgrown with trees and underbrush. The weakness of this position was its length. So long as Pemberton was compelled by the presence of McClernand's troops on the Raymond and Middle roads to keep one half of his army posted on the ridges west of Jackson Creek, he would be unable to commit sufficient troops to hold the entire ridge overlooking Bakers Creek. Thus Pemberton's left flank rested in the air.

As the two armies confronted each other the stage was seemingly set for the climax of the campaign. After months (indeed, almost a year) of maneuvering in the west, the two major forces stood directly opposite each other. Pemberton had his troops on the field well in hand, but before the day was over he undoubtedly would wish that he had with him the two divisions he had left to hold the Vicksburg area, when he marched out to battle Grant. Pemberton's total strength on the field was about 23,000, opposed to Grant's 32,000.

To the winner of the battle that followed would go the final victory in the campaign for the Mississippi River. Champion Hill is thus, at first blush, one of the decisive battles of the Civil War.

Such a view of Champion Hill is superficial.

While Grant, through superior strategy and maneuvering ability, had gained a distinct advantage by splitting Pemberton and Johnston, all could be lost if he were defeated at Champion Hill. At this time Grant was deep in hostile country with a formidable force under Pemberton to his front and Johnston's rapidly growing army in his rear. By the 15th Johnston's scattered brigades outnumbered Sherman's two divisions at Jackson. In addition, there were two fresh Rebel divisions in Vicksburg, which on the morning of the 16th were as close to Champion Hill as Sherman. Grant, like Lee at Gettysburg, had to carry his ammunition with him. A two days' battle would have exhausted his supply of artillery ammunition.

If Grant were checked at Champion Hill, he would have to pause to regroup, and this would have allowed the Confederates to bring up fresh troops. The next battle would have found many of his batteries with nearly empty caissons. If Grant should decide to turn aside following a repulse at Champion Hill, he would either have to head for Grand Gulf or the Yazoo. Such a march would expose his flanks to Confederate attack.

As for the approach of Sherman's corps, it would have had little effect if Grant had been routed. Sherman's troops did not reach the Bolton area until long after dark on the 16th. The officers had pushed the men hard, and thousands had straggled. Some regiments in Tuttle's division melted to company strength. A thorough examination of diaries and journals offers convincing evidence that it would have been late on the 17th before Sherman's two divisions could have effectively interfered at Champion Hill.

When the battle opened, Pemberton's men, who had been marching and constructing earthworks for the past two weeks, were tired but eager to come to grips with the Yankees. McPherson's, on the other hand, had been marching and fighting for more than eight straight days. McClernand's were not quite so hard-pressed, but they too had done their share of tramping over the countryside. Sherman's, coming up in reserve, had done more marching than either of the others. In addition, the Union troops had been living on hardtack, fresh meat, and coffee for over a week. When the day ended, however, it was the Confederates who were exhausted, the Yankees who were ready for more. Grant's winter campaign to make the men work, in order to get into peak physical condition, had paid off.

As soon as Grant had cleared the road for McPherson he sent word to McClernand to push forward and attack. "These orders were repeated several times," Grant later recalled, "without apparently expediting McClernand's advance." The main weight of the battle therefore fell on Hovey and Logan.

Grant's criticism of McClernand may have been colored by personal feelings. It was about 2:30 before McClernand received the orders. He then issued instructions for his division commanders "to attack the enemy vigorously and press for victory." It was the division commanders who really failed to push the attack. Grant gives full credit to Hovey, whose division was, after all, a part of McClernand's corps. If McClernand is to be blamed for the failure of his other division commanders, he should in all justice receive part of the praise heaped on Hovey.

By 10:30 Hovey's and Logan's divisions advanced to attack the Confederate left. Hovey on the left at 11:30 charged up out of a hollow and wrested from the Confederates a battery posted on the crest of the salient angle. (Brigadier General Alfred Cumming's Georgia brigade opposed Hovey's advance.) Pushing on, Hovey's men captured a second battery at the crossroads. Logan's division in the meantime was locked in a savage contest with S. D. Lee's Alabamians. On the extreme Union right, a brigade led by John Stevenson turned Pemberton's left, held by Seth Barton's Georgians, and captured two batteries. By 1:30 Pemberton's left had been mauled and hurled back almost a half mile with the loss of sixteen guns and several thousand prisoners.

The Rebels of Bowen's division counterattacked with great dash and elan. Most of Pemberton's troops had stood helplessly by the past couple of weeks while Grant marched all through Mississippi, or so it seemed; now, unleashed, they fought as only men in a desperate situation can fight. At one point in the battle Colonel Francis Cockrell, commanding a Confederate brigade, led a charge holding his reins and a large magnolia flower in one hand while he brandished his sword with the other. The men followed, shouting gleefully.

The result of these attacks was to drive Hovey back, and he had to relinquish his captured guns. For the rest of the day the battle on Champion Hill raged, increasing in intensity. Hovey sent out innumerable pleas for reinforcements; he lost nearly one-third of his division. Hovey later called Champion Hill "a hill of death," and added that "I never saw fighting like this."

Grant did what he could to help. Crocker's division of McPherson's corps arrived just as it seemed that Bowen's Missourians and Arkansans would destroy Hovey's division and capture Grant's ordinance trains parked near the Champion house. Grant rushed one brigade into the breach torn in the Union line by the onrushing Rebels and bolstered Logan with a second. Hovey meanwhile got three batteries in action where they enfiladed Bowen's advancing lines.

The advance by John Stevenson's brigade of Logan's division had carried it to a position from which, if he made a direct forward movement over open fields, he could get directly in Pemberton's rear and eliminate all possibility of escape. He did slide forward a little and got near the road leading down to Bakers Creek. Grant, who had been with Hovey, rode up, but neither he nor Logan realized the significance of Stevenson's position. Just at that moment a messenger arrived from Hovey with another plea for reinforcements—Pemberton had reinforced Carter Stevenson on Champion Hill after noting McClernand's disinclination to attack. Grant told Logan to rush John Stevenson to Hovey's aid, which uncovered Pemberton's line of retreat. Years later Grant admitted, "Had I known the ground as I did afterwards, I cannot see how Pemberton could have escaped with any organized force."

With Crocker moving into the breach the Confederate position on Champion Hill began to crumble. McClernand, meanwhile, had started to increase the pressure on the Confederate right. At the same time another brigade (Ransom's, of McPherson's corps), which had crossed the river at Grand Gulf a few days before, came up on the Rebels' right.

By 4 P.M. Pemberton decided to withdraw. He had lost nearly 4,300 men, while inflicting on Grant losses of 2,400. As in all previous engagements the Confederate enlisted men had fought well, and the regimental and brigade commanders, along with one division commander, Bowen, had done good work. At the higher level dissension and incompetence had spoiled the effort. Early in the battle one division commander, Loring, said he would "be willing for Pemberton to lose a battle provided that he would be displaced," and Loring and other generals openly laughed at Pemberton's orders. Another Confederate officer said Pemberton was "to all appearances—so far as my judgment could determine—as helpless and undecided as a child."

Pemberton left Loring to cover the retreat. The withdrawal began smoothly enough, but soon took on the aspects of a rout. Organization was lost, men fled for Vicksburg's fortifications as individuals, officers galloped about frantically trying to find their units, while artillerists looked for their guns. One Confederate officer confessed that what he saw on Champion Hill "made it look like what I have read of Bull Run," and the dispirited soldiers chattered wildly that the Yankee-born Pemberton "has sold Vicksburg."

Carr drove across Bakers Creek, swung to the southwest, and was able to shell the Raymond road, along which Loring's division would have to pass if it were to rejoin Pemberton. Finding the Federals on his flank and rear, Loring drifted off to the southeast, made a forced march to Crystal Springs, during which his men abandoned their cannon and supply wagons, and finally moved north to join Johnston at Jackson.

ACTION AT BIG BLACK

Pemberton rode through the already prepared breastworks guarding the Big Black and sent a fresh brigade in to man the works. He left instructions to move all the wagons to the left bank and to clear the roads for the passage of the defeated army. Then, thoroughly exhausted, he crossed the river with his staff, established his headquarters at Bovina, and settled down for a night's rest.

The men of Carter Stevenson's division were the first to reach the river; after their day with Hovey and Logan they were much too weary to do more fighting and they crossed the river. When they reached Bovina, Stevenson let the men flop down beside the road. They were instantly asleep.

Bowen's division came next. One of Pemberton's aides told him to defend the bridgehead until the whole force, including Loring's division (whose position was unknown to the Confederate main force) was across the river. Bowen's men, bone-tired and almost out of ammunition, were still—like their commander—of sound spirit. They filed into the trenches to extend the line.

At the same time, Sherman was on the road from Jackson to Bolton. He reached the Bolton area at 2 A.M. on the 17th; after four hours' rest he had the men on the road again, taking a route north of that followed by Grant's other two corps. Grant's idea was to send Sherman around to the left of the Confederate line, then have him swoop in behind Pemberton and keep him from getting back to Vicksburg. McPherson and McClernand would pursue the Confederates by the direct road to Vicksburg.

Grant's advance division, Eugene Carr's of McClernand's corps, began the pursuit at 3:30 A.M. (staff work in the Yankee divisions was outstanding, as was discipline; almost every day of the campaign the men were in full march when the sun rose). Shortly after daybreak they bumped into the main Confederate position. The east bank, where the Confederates were drawn up, was low bottomland, with a bayou running irregularly across its front. The bayou was grown up with timber, which the Rebels had felled into the ditch, and there was a foot or two of water in it. The position was naturally strong; it had been strengthened by using cotton bales and throwing dirt over them to make breastworks. Carr came up almost on the exact center of Bowen's line; his left brigade (Benton's) anchored its left near the railroad, while his right brigade, under Michael Lawler, occupied the woods between Benton's right and the river, which at this point flows from east to west.

If May 16 and Champion Hill belonged to Hovey and Logan, May 17 and the Battle of the Big Black was Lawler's. A mountainous man, weighing over 250 pounds, he fought in his shirt sleeves and sweated profusely. So huge was Lawler that he could not make a swordbelt go properly about his waist and wore his sword suspended by a strap from one shoulder. Grant once said of him, "When it comes to just plain hard fighting I would rather trust old Mike Lawler than any of them." A native of County Kildare, Ireland, Lawler was a veteran of Winfield Scott's advance from Veracruz to Mexico City. Lawler and his regiment had been mustered into service by U. S. Grant, then a captain serving on the staff of the Adjutant General of Illinois. He enforced discipline in his young heroes by knocking down recalcitrants with his fists, feeding emetic to drunks in the guardhouse, and by threats of violence to officers and men alike.

This morning Lawler moved his brigade through the woods to within 400 yards of the enemy line. There, next to the river, was a meander scar, a scar deep enough to hide his brigade. From it he could launch a short, quick assault on the Confederate left center. To get to it, however, he would have to cross an open field exposed to fire from some detached rifle pits. Lawler did not hesitate. Leaving one regiment behind to protect his artillery, he dashed across at the head of the other three. Losing only two men, he was now safe and snug almost within a stone's throw of the Southern works. Lawler, after calling up the regiment left to protect the artillery, massed his four regiments in columns of battalions, with the brigades on a two-regiment front so that his attack would be a narrow battering ram rather than spread out in the usual manner. He told the men not to bother to fire, but to keep moving forward until they reached the enemy parapet. When his preparations were complete, he had the regimental commanders order "Fix bayonets." Pouring sweat, he heaved his great bulk up on his horse, jammed the animal in the flank with his heels, leaned forward to help his horse clear the scar, and bellowed "Forward!"

The regiments roared out of their shelter and ran toward the Confederate line. The dumbfounded Rebels barely had time to get off one vol-

ley before the assault column hit them. The charge was one of the short-
est of the Civil War—it lasted just three minutes.

Completely outmanned, with bayonets and the stocks of muskets
raining down on their heads, the Rebels fled. Lawler had broken the entire Confederate line south as far as the railroad. All along that line
Rebels were scampering to the rear, desperate to get across the river before they were cut off.

The Indiana regiments and the Illinois units came over the barricade
north of the railroad and captured a gun. Private James S. Adkins of the
33d Illinois, exhilarated by the bloodless victory, leaped astride the gun
tube, waved his elbows up and down at his sides, and crowed like a
rooster. Then, curious, he tugged at the lanyard. The gun went off, hurling a shell close over the heads of the units coming up in support, and
bucking Adkins head over heels into the dirt. Miraculously, no one was
hurt.

Grant was near the middle of the Union line. Shortly before the
charge began, a staff officer rode up and gave him a letter of May 11
from Halleck. In it the General in Chief ordered Grant to return to
Grand Gulf and to cooperate from there with Banks against Port Hudson, then return with the combined force to besiege Vicksburg. Grant
quietly told the officer that the order came too late. Grant had served
under Halleck before, and he realized that the General in Chief would
not have given him the order if he had known Grant's position. The officer insisted that Grant had to obey, and was increasing the intensity of
his argument when the sounds of an attack broke forth. Grant later described what happened: "Looking in that direction, I saw Lawler in his
shirtsleeves leading a charge upon the enemy. I immediately mounted
my horse and rode in the direction of the charge, and saw no more of
the officer who had delivered the dispatch."

The Confederates on the west bank, before all the retreating men got
across, fired the turpentine-soaked railroad bridge and the steamer *Dot*.
Pemberton had ridden up from Bovina; he took one look and immediately decided against making a further stand along the Big Black. He
just had too few men to prevent the Union troops from crossing. Sadly
he ordered his division to withdraw the twelve miles to Vicksburg. Rid-

ing back to Bovina with a staff officer, he morosely muttered, "Just thirty years ago I began my cadetship at the U.S. Military Academy. Today, the same date, that career is ended in disaster and disgrace."

Grant's men spent the rest of the day (Lawler's charge ended at 11 A.M.) cleaning up the battlefield and building bridges over the Big Black. They had captured 1,752 prisoners, 18 cannons, 1,421 stand of small arms, and 5 battle flags, at a cost of 39 killed and 237 wounded. The bridge building, as always in Grant's army, was superb. McPherson himself directed the construction of one of the four. He used bales of cotton to make a pontoon bridge. General Ransom supervised the building of another. He had trees felled on opposite banks of the river, dropped them into the water so that their tops interlaced. Taking lumber from nearby buildings, he then laid a roadway across the trees. Working through the night, the army had four serviceable bridges ready on the morning of May 18.

GRANT'S PINCERS CLOSE ON VICKSBURG

That morning Grant sent his three corps forward, McClernand's on the road paralleling the railroad, and McPherson's and Sherman's along the Bridgeport road. About three miles northeast of Vicksburg, Grant, who had pushed ahead, overtook Sherman's vanguard and turned it into the Graveyard road while a staff officer was left to point out the route McPherson was to take—the Jackson road. As the three corps approached the city, McClernand's would be on the left, McPherson's in the center, and Sherman's on the right.

By late afternoon on the 18th, Sherman's advance was in contact with Confederates posted on the ridge fronting Vicksburg defenses. Before darkness put a stop to the fighting, Sherman had discovered a road branching off from the Graveyard road and leading toward the Yazoo. Steele's division was turned into this road. Under the cover of darkness, Pemberton recalled the troops that had been contesting Sherman's approach, and they took position alongside their comrades on the earthworks extending from Fort Hill to Stockade Redan.

Steele's division early on May 19 resumed its advance. Grant and

Sherman soon joined Steele. Grant was anxious to secure a base of supplies on the Yazoo above Vicksburg and Steele was headed straight toward Walnut Hills—the Confederate defensive position which Sherman had tried unsuccessfully to carry the previous December. So impatient were Grant and Sherman that they moved past the advance column and were riding well up with the advanced skirmishers. The enemy still occupied some detached works along the crest of the hill, although Pemberton had already decided to shorten his lines, and made no serious attempt to hold Walnut Hills. Shots rang out, and minie balls whistled past the generals' ears. Ignoring them, Grant and Sherman rode to the crest of the ridge.

Sitting there on their horses, they took possession of the most important single piece of real estate in the Confederate States of America. As long as Pemberton held that chain of hills no Union force could approach Vicksburg from the upper Mississippi. For a year and a half the western armies of the United States had concentrated their effort on gaining control of these few square miles. As Sherman and Grant watched the men spread out over the heights, they felt the most intense satisfaction. Grant could now reopen his communications with the north, receive supplies and reinforcements, and conclude the campaign.

Sherman turned to Grant and said, quietly, that up to this moment he had felt no positive assurance of success. Now he realized that this was the end of one of the greatest campaigns in history. Vicksburg was not yet captured, and much might still happen, but whether captured or not, the campaign was a complete success.

Johnston agreed. He telegraphed Pemberton to cut his losses and get out. "If Haynes' Bluff be untenable Vicksburg is of no value and cannot be held," Johnston wrote. "If therefore you are invested in Vicksburg you must ultimately surrender. Under such circumstances, instead of losing both troops and place you must if possible save the troops. If it is not too late, evacuate Vicksburg and its dependencies and march to the northeast."

Pemberton held a council of war, which concluded that it was impossible to withdraw—a strange conclusion, considering that McClernand's force, on Grant's left, extended only a little south of the Southern

Railroad of Mississippi. Pemberton decided to ignore not only Johnston's good advice but, once again, a positive order. When informed of Pemberton's decision, Johnston exhibited remarkable self-restraint—he advised Pemberton to hold out while he attempted to gather a relief force. His labors, however, were in vain.

By June 4 Johnston had gathered a force of 31,000, and between them he and Pemberton outnumbered Grant. At this time he was notified by the authorities in Richmond that no more reinforcements could be diverted to Mississippi. Instead of boldly seizing the initiative, while the Confederates had numerical advantage, Johnston allowed one of his division commanders to go on leave. Not until June 22, when this officer returned from leave, did Johnston organize his army to take the offensive. At this time, thousands of reinforcements, rushed from points as far away as Central Kentucky and Rolla, Missouri, had reported to Grant. The Federals now held a decisive numerical advantage. As time for the Vicksburg defenders ran out, Johnston continued to drag his feet. It was July 1 before he put his troops in motion.

The threat of a move by Johnston against his rear forced Grant to keep forces on the Big Black guarding the crossing. On June 22 when reports, which were later proved untrue, reached Grant that Johnston had forced his way across the Big Black, he rushed additional troops eastward and placed Sherman in charge of a seven-division army. Sherman's task was to smash Johnston should he cross the Big Black.

ASSAULT OF MAY 19

On the morning of May 19 Grant, figuring that the Confederates were so demoralized by the events of the past two weeks that they would crumble at the first sign of pressure, ordered a general assault. On the left and in the center the Union troops managed to gain some important positions for gun emplacements, but did not even come close to driving the Confederates out of their trenches. Obviously the Rebels could still fight. Sherman, on the right, learned this lesson best.

The key position in the enemy works opposite Sherman was the Stockade Redan complex. He gave Frank Blair's division the job of taking it. The ground in front of the redan was exceedingly rugged, consisting of a ravine covered with timber that Confederate working parties had cut six months earlier. Attempting to charge through this area, the men found it impossible to maintain a line of battle. As the Rebels poured small arms and artillery fire upon them, they instinctively searched out a place of concealment and stopped there, pinned down.

On Blair's right the 1st Battalion, 13th U.S. Infantry, tried a charge. When the commander called out "Forward!" the Regulars sprang across the hill behind which they had formed. Charging on the double, they passed through a deadly beaten-zone that was being swept by canister and shell. Men began to fall, some killed instantly, others with an arm or leg torn off. Crossing the ravine, the Regulars were caught in a crossfire between the enemy in the Stockade Redan and those in the 27th Louisiana Lunette on the left of the stockade.

Color Sergeant James E. Brown was shot through the head and killed. Another soldier instantly picked up the colors, and was immediately shot. In all, five different men were killed or wounded as they sought to carry the colors forward. The Regulars closed to within 25 yards of the Stockade Redan, began to falter, and finally scrambled back for cover behind fallen timber and stumps.

After the battle a count revealed that the flag of the 13th U.S. Infantry had 55 bullet holes in it. The battalion had lost 13 percent of its personnel in the attack. Sherman called its performance "unequaled in the Army" and authorized the regiment to insert "First at Vicksburg" on its colors.

There were other acts of heroism that day. Sherman decided he could not withdraw his corps until it was dark; meanwhile the men fired by volley at any Confederate who stuck his head above the parapet. The Rebels replied by cutting short the fuses of their shells, then rolling them down the hill into the Yankee masses. Occasionally the Union men could catch the shell and throw it back; more often it ripped apart legs and arms.

Late in the afternoon the Yankees discovered they had almost exhausted their ammunition. Volunteers raced through the felled timber to fill boxes and hats with the cartridges rifled from dead and wounded men. Orion P. Howe, a 14-year-old musician in the 55th Illinois, volunteered to go to the rear and order up fresh supplies. While dashing through the timber he caught a minie ball in his leg. Undaunted, he staggered on. At the point of exhaustion he reached General Sherman himself and reported on the critical ammunition shortage. Sherman called for volunteers to lug the heavy boxes of cartridges forward, and every man of the nearby Company C, 12th Iowa, stepped forward. Musician Howe was subsequently awarded the Medal of Honor for his services on that bloody day.

At dark, the Union troops withdrew. Grant's attempt to storm his way into Vicksburg had failed. He had gained some advance artillery emplacements and some good staging areas for use in future attacks, but at a fearful price. He had lost 157 killed, 777 wounded, and 8 missing, as against a total Confederate loss of about 250.

GRANT TRIES AGAIN

Following the failure on the 19th, Grant could either accept the situation and settle down for a siege operation or he could try another assault. He decided upon the latter course. Both he and his army were rather cocky at this point; five times they had met the Confederates in battle and routed them. The repulse of the 19th was an obvious fluke. The lesson of the campaign seemed to be that when Yankees attacked, Rebels ran. There were other more substantial reasons for another try. Johnston, in Grant's rear, was busily raising a relief force, and Grant wanted to destroy Pemberton's army before Johnston could come to his aid. If Grant could take Vicksburg immediately, he would not have to call upon Halleck for reinforcements and could, in fact, send men to the other theaters of war. Finally, in Grant's own words, "the first consideration of all was—the troops believed they could carry the works in their front, and would not have worked so patiently in the trenches afterwards if they had not been allowed to try."

The attempt was to cost them dearly. Pemberton's men, given a decent chance, could fight as well as any men on earth. And, in their entrenchments, they were powerfully placed. One of McPherson's staff officers described the position: "A long line of high-rugged, irregular bluffs, clearly cut against the sky, crowned with cannon which peered ominously from embrasures to the right and left as far as the eye could see. Lines of heavy rifle pits, surmounted with head logs, ran along the bluffs, connecting fort with fort, and filled with veteran infantry." On the slopes in front of the works were felled trees, with their tops interlaced, forming an almost impenetrable abatis. "The approaches to this position were frightful—enough to appall the stoutest heart."

Still Grant—and his men—wanted to try, and on the morning of May 22 they did. Grant had his corps commanders set their watches by his, then called for a simultaneous assault at 10 A.M. The attack would be preceded by a heavy preliminary artillery bombardment. Sherman would aim at the Stockade Redan, McPherson at the stronghold on either side of the Jackson road, McClernand at the defenses flanking the railroad and Baldwin's Ferry road.

Sherman, who had failed in his direct attack across the ravine in front of Stockade Redan on May 19, decided to attack directly down the Graveyard road. He would spearhead his attack with a "forlorn hope," consisting of 150 volunteers. These men, carrying timbers in their hands, would move at the double down the road and fill in the ditch fronting the stockade.

The attack moved off promptly at 10 A.M. The "forlorn hope" came through a curve in the road at full speed. The road at that point cut through a hill, then turned directly toward the redan. When the "forlorn hope" emerged from the extremely narrow cut they were 150 yards from the enemy and presented a perfect target. The Rebels cut loose, and most of the men were either killed or wounded. The remainder took cover in the ditch in front of the stockade. The 30th Ohio followed, to suffer the same fate. On their heels came the 37th Ohio. When that regiment started to emerge from the cut most of the men took one look and "bugged out," throwing themselves on the ground and refusing to advance farther. This choked the narrow cut, and Sherman's assault ground to an abrupt stop. Sherman made no further attacks that morning, even though only slightly more than 1,000 of his nearly 15,000 men had been engaged. After his experiences of the previous December and of May 19, he had had about enough of assaulting Fortress Vicksburg.

In the center McPherson never got any organized attack going. He put only 7 of his 30 regiments into action, and they all except those of John Stevenson's brigade stopped at the first sign of opposition.

Things went better on the left. McClernand sent Carr, who had the advantage of having Lawler's brigade in his division, storming the 2d Texas Lunette and the Railroad Redoubt. The 99th Illinois carried its flag across the Confederate works at a point 50 yards south of the lunette. Lawler, charging the Railroad Redoubt, drove the 30th Alabama out of its rifle pits and planted several Union colors there. Elsewhere McClernand's men pushed up to, although not through, the Rebel lines.

The enemy was soon able to contain the penetration McClernand's corps had achieved, and the Yankees were unable to do much about it. If Sherman and McPherson were guilty of not making strong enough commitments that morning, McClernand made the mistake of throwing everything he had into the first rush. With no strategic reserve he was unable to exploit his opportunities, and in fact could barely hold what he had gained.

With his entire corps engaged, McClernand appealed to Grant to have Sherman and McPherson resume the attack, arguing that he could achieve a breakthrough with more help. Grant thought McClernand was exaggerating his success (or so at least he claimed later), but felt he could not ignore the request and ordered Sherman and McPherson to renew their assaults as a division in favor of McClernand. At 3 P.M. Sherman sent Mower's brigade spearheaded by the 11th Missouri charging down the Graveyard road four abreast. As the regiment emerged from the fatal cut in the road, it was riddled by Confederate fire. Those Missourians who were not killed dashed forward and took cover in the ditch alongside the survivors of the "forlorn hope" and the 30th Ohio. Sherman suspended the attack.

McPherson launched a half-hearted assault on the 3d Louisiana Redan, which got nowhere.

McClernand, meanwhile, was stuck. He could neither go forward nor disengage. At 5:30 counterattacking Confederates recovered the Railroad Redoubt. Finally, at nightfall, McClernand pulled his troops back. He was the only corps commander who really made an effort that day; if Sherman and McPherson had attacked with the same energy, the assault would probably have worked. But they did not, and later they—and Grant—were unduly skeptical about McClernand's penetration, which they claimed was a figment of his imagination. But in fact McClernand did get into the Rebel works and his report to Grant was accurate.

Grant's position in this affair is a strange one. If he really intended to try a full-scale assault, he should have been angry with Sherman and McPherson.

In any case Grant, in his report written on May 24, was quite unfair to McClernand. He showed a pettiness most uncharacteristic of the Commanding General. "General McClernand's dispatches misled me as to the real state of the facts," Grant said of the events of May 22, "and caused much of the loss. He is entirely unfit for the position of corps commander, both on the march and on the battlefield. Looking after his corps gives me more labor and infinitely more uneasiness than all the remainder of my department." Assuming that Grant really felt that strongly, that he did not immediately relieve McClernand can only be regarded as amazing. If McClernand was that bad, Grant was extremely derelict in his duty (not to mention his responsibilities to the troops in McClernand's corps) when he kept McClernand in command.

FALL OF McCLERNAND

McClernand smoldered. He was sure that if McPherson and Sherman—and of course Grant—had properly supported him his corps would be in Vicksburg. He was not, therefore, in a receptive mood when Colonel James Harrison Wilson visited him with an order from Grant directing him to send some troops to watch the crossing of the Big Black.

McClernand read the order, then snapped, "I'll be God-damned if I'll do it. I'm tired of being dictated to—I won't stand it any longer, and you can go back and tell General Grant." He added some more remarks of a similar character, then began to curse West Point generally. Wilson heatedly pointed out that McClernand was not only insulting the commanding general but Wilson himself, as Wilson was an Academy man, and offered to get off his horse and use his fists to get McClernand to apologize. The middle-aged general sized up the colonel in his mid-twenties and muttered, "I was simply expressing my intense vehemence on the subject matter, sir, and I beg your pardon."

Wilson, of course, reported the whole affair at Grant's headquarters, to everyone's great delight. Thereafter whenever anyone was heard using profanity—and it was a hard-cursing headquarters—Grant would laugh and explain, "He's not swearing—he's just expressing his intense vehemence on the subject matter."

McClernand's end came a couple of weeks later. He wrote an order of congratulations to the XIII Corps which, with some help from his headquarters, got into the papers. This violated a standing War Department regulation to submit such papers to army headquarters before publication; worse, McClernand had implied in the order that the XIII Corps alone had been responsible for the success of the campaign. Sherman bitterly remarked that the order was really addressed "to a constituency in Illinois," and McPherson said it was designed "to impress the public mind with the magnificent strategy, superior tactics, and brilliant deeds" of McClernand.

Grant asked McClernand if the order as published was genuine. McClernand said it was and he was prepared to stand by it. Grant finally decided to act and on June 18 relieved McClernand, putting E. O. C. Ord in his place.

Following the May 19 assault Grant held a conference with Porter and arranged for some good landing places along the Yazoo for transports and supply ships. He wired Halleck to say he was ready to receive reinforcements and supplies, which the General in Chief immediately began to send.

One afternoon a day or so later Grant took a ride along the rear of his fighting lines. Men began to glance at him as his horse moved slowly past. The soldiers generally did not love Ulysses Grant, nor were they awed by him—he was much too matter-of-fact a man to inspire such emotions. Besides, nothing about his personal appearance suggested greatness. The soldiers did respect him as a soldier, and as a man. He was the kind of person who invited honesty and was obviously approachable.

When Grant rode by, a soldier who had looked up stared at his commanding general for a moment, then said in a conversational tone, "Hardtack." Other soldiers glanced at Grant and took up the call; soon everyone in the vicinity was yelling "Hardtack! Hardtack!" at the top of his lungs. They were not expressing a deep-rooted hatred of Grant, or anything like that, nor were they blaming him for the bland diet they had been on for the past month. They were saying that they were terribly proud of what they had done, especially considering the conditions under which they had marched and fought, but now the time had come to create a more regular existence. In short, it was time that Grant, who had done so well so far, get them something better to eat than a straight hardtack and meat diet.

Grant reined in and told the soldiers he had made all the arrangements and they would soon have fresh bread and coffee. The men laughed and cheered. The bond between Grant and the Army of the Tennessee had been strengthened.

Grant was very good at this sort of thing. Men in an Illinois regiment remembered that one evening Grant strolled out, sat down by their campfire, and "talked with the boys with less reserve than many a little puppy of a lieutenant." Grant assured the boys that he had everything under control, said that Pemberton was a "northern man who had got into bad company," and insisted that the Union position could be held even if Johnston raised 50,000 men.

THE SIEGE

The siege went forward. Grant's basic plan was to hold on until starvation forced Pemberton to surrender—the classic strategy of siege warfare—but he also wanted to end it as soon as possible, in order to release his troops for other theaters. In addition, the sooner Pemberton surrendered the sooner Grant could turn Sherman loose on Johnston, who had raised a relief expedition.

June, therefore, was an active month. Most of the work was designed to get the Union lines closer to those of the Confederates, so that the next time there was a general assault the troops would not have to cross a quarter-mile or so of rough terrain before reaching the enemy works. Grant had his engineers plan approach trenches and mines (which could be used to blow gaps in the Confederate position), which the men then dug. The whole thing anticipated the more sophisticated trench warfare of the Western Front in World War I.

The only trained engineers in the Army of the Tennessee were the West Point graduates, and most of them were high-ranking officers with other duties. The few full-time engineers discovered, however, that the Western soldiers were handy jacks-of-all-trades who could do almost anything. One professional engineer declared that in the enormous task of constructing trenches, saps, batteries, and covered ways he could safely rely on the "native good sense and ingenuity" of the common soldier. "Whether a battery was to be constructed by men who had never built one before," he declared, "a saproller made by those who had never heard the name, or a ship's gun carriage to be built, it was done, and after a few trials well done. . . . Officers and men had to learn to be engineers while the siege was going on."

As soon as Grant established his base on the Yazoo, the General in Chief began to feed him reinforcements. By June 18 Grant's army was up to 77,000. Pemberton had no more than 30,000, all plagued by illness and malnutrition, and his supply of food and ammunition was strictly limited. Grant's lines ran from the Yazoo to the lowlands along the Mississippi above the city to the banks along the river to the south—twelve miles of camps, trenches, and gun emplacements on the hills and ridges. So tightly did Grant hold the ground that a Confederate defender wrote despairingly, "When the real investments began a cat could not have crept out of Vicksburg without being discovered." Among other things, this meant nothing—especially no artillery ammunition—got in to Pemberton, so that on top of all their other difficulties his men were forced to endure the constant Yankee artillery bombardment without being allowed to reply in kind. They did, however, have a good supply of powder and minie balls. One Yankee wrote home to say that although the Rebels had not fired a cannon for seven days, at least fifty rifle bullets had whizzed over his head in the last ten minutes.

Taking potshots at the Union lines was about all the Confederates could do. For the rest of their defense, according to one Yankee officer, was "far from being vigorous." The defenders seemed content to "wait for another assault, losing in the meantime as few men as possible."

The waiting was hard, both because the Confederates were short of nearly everything and because of the Union bombardment. Food was so short that the citizens of Vicksburg and the soldiers defending it were soon reduced to eating mule meat and pea bread. Medical supplies were almost nonexistent. Water was so scarce that officers posted guards at wells to make sure none was wasted "for purposes of cleanliness." On top of these privations, the citizens were forced to burrow underground or live in caves to avoid the well-nigh constant shell fire, which came both from Grant's artillery and Porter's fleet.

The ground was well suited to the building of caves, for it consisted of a deep yellow loess of great tenacity. Perpendicular banks cut through the ridges stood as well as if made of stone, and the citizens cut rooms for themselves in the embankments. In some cases two or more rooms were cut out, carpeted, and furnished with tables, chairs, and kitchen equipment.

In terms of some of the sieges of the 20th century, most especially that of Leningrad, conditions inside Vicksburg were not so terrible. They were, however, bad enough—certainly the worst any large group of Americans have ever been asked to undergo. The citizens compiled a proud record. There was some complaining, but no pressure on Pemberton from the city to surrender and end the suffering. The people got by, as people under siege have done since war began, by joking about their condition. They even had a newspaper, which by the end was being printed on the blank side of wallpaper. The citizens of Vicksburg, in short, endured.

The troops on both sides did the same. On the picket line Johnny Reb and Billy Yank discussed politics, the siege, and philosophy, traded coffee and hardtack for tobacco, and got to know each other. Occasionally they sent personal messages back and forth. Each army contained regiments from Missouri; one day the picket at Stockade Redan agreed to informal short truces. This area, when soldiers in blue and in gray might visit briefly a relative or friend on the other side, came to be called "Trysting place."

While the pickets got to know each other, under their very feet Grant's army dug tunnels. The Confederate counter-mined, but without success. Grant exploded the first mine, near the Jackson road, on June 25. The explosion of the mine was a signal for a heavy bombardment all along the line, accompanied by small arms fire. The mine blew off the top of a hill and created a crater into which an assaulting column charged, only to be checked by Confederates posted behind a parapet previously constructed to the rear of the work. A desperate battle ensued for possession of the crater. After twenty hours, Grant had McPherson recall his men, and another mine was commenced. On July 1 this mine was exploded. When this occurred, one of the Negroes who was countermining was thrown all the way into the Union lines. When asked how high he had gone, he replied, "Dunno, massa, but t'ink about t'ree miles." General Logan confiscated the Negro, who thereafter worked in his headquarters.

Grant exploded another mine on July 1, again without significant results. His engineers, meanwhile, had pushed forward everywhere, so much so that at some points only ten yards separated the two forces. Within a week or so Grant would be able to simply overwhelm the defenders, sending his men over the top and into the Confederate lines so fast that the Rebels probably would not even get off a volley. Grant set July 6 as the date for the final rush.

Johnston had plans of his own. On July 1 he finally put his 32,000 men and 78 cannon in motion toward Big Black. He had no illusions about any great victories; he did hope to so distract the Army of the Tennessee that Pemberton could break out.

Pemberton circularized his generals to see if that was possible, asking specifically if their men could stand a battle and a long hard march. Most of the generals thought not. Their men could hold the lines a while longer, but a campaign in the field was impossible. Brigadier General Louis Hébert summed it all up: "Forty-eight days and nights passed in trenches, exposed to the burning sun during the day, the chilly air at night; subject to a murderous storm of balls, shells, and war missiles of all kinds; cramped up in pits and holes not large enough to allow them to extend their limbs; laboring day and night; fed on reduced rations of the poorest kinds of food, yet always cheerful. . . ." All but one of Pemberton's generals told him it was time to surrender.

SURRENDER

At 10:30 A.M. on July 3, under a flag of truce, two horsemen approached the Union lines. One was a colonel on Pemberton's staff, the other General Bowen, who had fought so ably at Port Gibson and Champion Hill. Bowen was an old friend of Grant's, which may have influenced Pemberton's decision to send him on this mission. The Confederates carried a letter from Pemberton to Grant proposing an armistice and the appointment of commissioners to write a surrender formula. Pemberton knew that Grant wanted to get the whole business over in a hurry, and this knowledge gave him, he felt, bargaining power.

Bowen gave the note to A. J. Smith, who took it to Grant. The Union commander hoped to repeat his triumph at Fort Donelson and at the same time simplify matters, so his reply was short and to the point: "The useless effusion of blood you propose stopping . . . can be ended at any time you may choose, by the unconditional surrender of the city and garrison."

Bowen took the message to Pemberton at 3 P.M. Pemberton, Bowen, and a staff officer rode out. Grant, Ord, McPherson, Logan, and A. J. Smith, accompanied by several of Grant's staff, went forward to meet them. Grant and Pemberton walked away from the main group and had a conference near a stunted oak tree. Pemberton, excited and impatient, asked what terms Grant offered; Grant replied that he had said everything he had to say in his letter. Pemberton replied "rather snappishly" that in that case the conference might as well end immediately. Grant thought so too, and they walked back to mount up. Grant suggested that if he and Pemberton withdrew, perhaps four of their subordinates (Bowen and Montgomery for the Confederates, McPherson and A. J.

Smith for the Union) might be able to work out a satisfactory arrangement. Bowen patched things up, and before parting the two commanders agreed that at ten that night Grant would send another letter through the lines, one containing his final terms.

At dusk Grant called a meeting of all the corps and division commanders in the area—the nearest thing he ever had to a council of war. There was much to discuss. Vicksburg was unquestionably doomed—that was not at issue. The attack scheduled for July 6 would certainly be successful. But why pay the price? All Pemberton really wanted was to make sure his men were paroled instead of being sent north to a prison camp. Grant's officers urged him to make a deal, especially since shipping thirty thousand prisoners up the Mississippi would be an intolerable strain on Porter's fleet (something Pemberton already knew, as his intelligence service had intercepted and decoded messages wigwagged back and forth between Porter and Grant). Grant reluctantly agreed to abandon his unconditional surrender formula, and wrote to Pemberton proposing that the Southerners stack their weapons, give their paroles, and then go off to such camps for exchange prisoners as the Confederate authorities might suggest. Pemberton, who hoped that Grant would give generous terms in order to consummate the surrender on the nation's birthday, asked for some other minor concessions. Grant refused, and the deal was finally made.

Grant was later much criticized for allowing the Rebels to make their paroles. The critics contended that all or most of Pemberton's 30,000 men would soon be fighting again. Grant's reply was that "I knew many of them were tired of war and would get home just as soon as they could." Grant was mistaken, because many of the Confederates were back in ranks by November. A number of Carter L. Stevenson's soldiers were captured at Missionary Ridge, for instance.

On the morning of July 4 white flags began to flutter over the Confederate works. Logan's division and Sanborn's brigade were the first units to march into the city. Logan and Sanborn posted guards to keep unauthorized persons from entering or leaving and took charge of the captured people and property.

Sherman immediately moved his corps to the east in order to drive

Johnston off. He took time to scribble a note to Grant before departing. "I can hardly contain myself," he exclaimed. "This is a day of Jubilee, a day of rejoicing to the faithful, and I would like to hear the shout of my old and patient troops." But duty called. "Already my orders are out to give one big huzza and sling the knapsack for new fields."

Grant, typically, was more subdued. Greatness can take many forms, assuming one shape with a Douglas MacArthur, another with an Andrew Jackson. It is most appealing, perhaps, when couched in directness and simplicity. At the conclusion of the most momentous and successful campaign on the North American continent, the architect of victory sent the following report to the War Department: "The enemy surrendered this morning. The only terms allowed is their parole as prisoners of war. This I regard as a great advantage to us at this moment. It saves, probably, several days in the capture, and leave troops and transports ready for immediate service. Sherman, with a large force, moves immediately on Johnston, to drive him from the state."

In his operations during May 1863, Grant used the classic ingredients of military success—surprise, speed, and power: *Surprise* of Pemberton, who could not believe that Grant would move independently of a protected supply line; dazzling *speed* in which his divisions marched upward of 200 miles in two weeks, fighting five battles; and the application of superior *power* at each successive, critical point. As historian Francis V. Green wrote: "We must go back to the campaigns of Napoleon to find equally brilliant results accomplished in the same space of time with such small loss."

It is true that Pemberton was outclassed. Yet his soldiers, when given the benefit of good leaders such as Bowen and Gregg, fought with their customary skill and elan. As Grant said of them, when negotiating surrender terms with Pemberton, "Men who have shown so much endurance and courage will always challenge the respect of an adversary." Again, he offered a line of thought that does not often occur to our people: Americans do not fight wars to make permanent enemies, but ever strive to convert their ex-foes into allies. Grant suggests this in his statement: "The men had behaved so well that I did not want to humiliate them. I believed that consideration for their feelings would make them less dangerous foes during the continuance of hostilities, and better citizens after the war was over. . . . [Therefore] when they passed out of their works they had so long and so gallantly defended, between the lines of their late antagonists, not a cheer went up, not a remark was made that would give pain."

Instead, individual Yanks shared the food in their haversacks with Johnnies, and Grant ordered his commissary to issue ample rations to Pemberton's troops and to the citizens, both in the city and throughout the countryside recently passed over by the armies.

Tactically and strategically the results of the campaign were among the most decisive of the war. Abraham Lincoln, his cabinet, and the people in the North were enheartened after the previous long months of defeat and discouragement. The Confederacy, after Gettysburg and Vicksburg, never regained the military initiative. From hindsight, perhaps, the final outcome of the war was now inevitable. The commander at Port Hudson, on learning of the fall of Vicksburg, surrendered to General Banks. President Lincoln could now say, "The father of waters rolls unvexed to the sea."

CUSTER'S CIVIL WAR

George Armstrong Custer's most recent biographer, Robert M. Utley, concludes that, as a Civil War general, he "combined audacity, courage, leadership, judgment, composure, and an uncanny instinct for the critical moment and the action it demanded. He pressed the enemy closely and doggedly, charged at the right moment, held fast at the right moment, fell back at the right moment, deployed his units with skill, and applied personal leadership where and when most needed." These are the characteristics of a god.

Utley, former chief historian of the National Park Service, is *the* authority on the frontier army. His conclusions demand respect. In this case, however, he has allowed his romanticism about Custer (his title is *Cavalier in Buckskin*) to overcome his good judgment, as badly as did the *New York Times* reporter in 1864 who compared Custer to Napoleon.

Utley ranks Custer as a "great cavalry general . . . second in the Union army only to [Phil] Sheridan." Admirers of James Harrison Wilson will hotly dispute that call, but none will disagree with Utley's further point, that had Custer been killed in 1865, or retired from the army to go into business or politics, he would be known today as a solid Civil

War hero, rather than "as a folk hero of worldwide renown." His immortality comes from the Little Big Horn.

The contrast between the "boy general" of the Civil War and the Custer of the Little Big Horn has always fascinated Americans. The former never made a mistake; the latter made them by the score. The former was famous for his good luck, the latter for the breaks that went against him. The former was all but universally admired, while the latter is the object of continuous controversy, damned by many, still praised by a few.

But the contrast is more apparent than real. The Civil War Custer and the Custer of the Little Big Horn were the same man, using the same techniques and tactics, against enemies who were not all that dissimilar. Custer's follies at the Little Big Horn had their roots in Custer's Civil War. Custer lost his life and his command at the hands of the Sioux in 1876 because of characteristics he had displayed time and again in the Civil War. His undoubted audacity and courage were offset by a criminal lack of good judgment, a refusal to take the time to gather intelligence about the enemy, an insistence on attacking at the earliest possible opportunity, a petty jealousy toward his fellow officers, a monumental ambition, and a total disregard for the lives of his men.

War entails the taking of risks, to be sure, and every victory exacts its price. But there has to be some relationship between the risk and price, on the one hand, and the gain and reward on the other. Every war sees good men lost to no purpose, but that does not justify Custer's spendthrift attitude toward the lives of his men, much less give him a claim to being a great general. It does require that we look for the source of the disaster at the Little Big Horn in Custer's triumphs in the Civil War.

George Armstrong Custer was a war lover. He loved the smells, sights, and sounds of the battlefield. For him, no thrill compared to the saber charge. He was most thoroughly himself when he stood in his stirrups, bullets whizzing all around him, drew his saber, turned his head, and called out to the hundreds or thousands of young soldiers behind him, "Charge!"

Like George S. Patton, Jr., in 1945 when "his" war ended, Custer was disappointed in 1865 when his war came to a halt. He hardly knew what to do with himself. Only twenty-five years old, he had done it all, seen it all. Everything that followed, until the last day of his life, was anti-climactic.

The appeal of war for Custer had nothing to do with politics. He was not engaged in a crusade. Again like Patton, who liked and admired the Germans (and was contemptuous of his British and Russian allies), Custer admired and liked Southerners. Few men were as effective in making war on the Confederate States of America as Custer, but no other Union officer exceeded him in approval of the Southern way of life or in friendship with individual Confederate officers.

The war had some of the aspects of a game about it for Custer; it was as if he were a modern college football player, congratulating his opponents at the end of a hard-fought game. "I rejoice, dear Pelham, in your success," he wrote in 1862 to his West Point classmate John Pelham, who was making a name for himself in the Confederate artillery. At the end of the Peninsula campaign, in 1862, Custer took two weeks off from the war to attend the wedding in Tidewater, Virginia, of his West Point friend Gimlet Lea, currently an officer in the Confederate army. There were parties, and balls, and dancing, and the singing of such Southern songs around the piano as "For Southern Rights, Hurrah!" and "Dixie."

The innocence and romanticism of the scene are certainly appealing and offer an excuse for Custer—he was but twenty-two years old, and the girls were pretty, and the parties were fun. Still, by this time the war was more than a year old, tens of thousands had died, Custer was an officer on the staff of General McClellan, and his hobnobbing with the enemy was at best questionable conduct.

But Custer made up for it with the joy, the zest, and the aplomb with which he made war on his friends. Just a week or so earlier, he had led his first charge. McClellan was crossing the Chickahominy River, and he gave Captain Custer the honor of leading a company in the van.

"Why, that's Armstrong Custer!" the men of Company A, 4th Michigan Volunteer Infantry shouted when Custer took his place at the head of the column. Custer, born and raised in New Rumley, Ohio, had gone to Monroe, Michigan, to live with his sister as he attended high school.

Custer greeted the soldiers, some of them classmates, others old friends, cheerfully. There was handshaking all around. Then Custer straightened up in his saddle and shouted, "Come on, Monroe!"

When he got Company A in place, he called out, "Go in, Wolverines! Give 'em hell!" He was the first into the fray, and the last man to leave the field. As in every battle of his life, his bravery was breathtaking. No wonder McClellan, and later his other superiors, decided that if he wanted to hobnob with rebel officers, they would let him.

It is easier to describe Custer's courage than to account for it. For four years, he was at the head of every charge, never faltering, never turning back. But he was not suicidal. His life was precious to him, but only if he lived up to his own image of himself. He would rather die than ignore his duty or shirk danger. This attitude gave him the strength to overwhelm or at least overcome fear.

But there was more to his courage than just overcoming fear. He positively enjoyed combat. It had, for him, all the challenge and excitement of a football game, infinitely magnified. To switch to a different analogy, battle had for Custer some of the fascination of the hunt. In writing home about his experiences he used words like "the chase" or "the sport" and referred to his enemies as "the game." In one of his early actions he was leading ten men in pursuit of a small body of Confederate cavalry. It was, Custer wrote his sister, "the most exciting sport I ever engaged in." His target was a rebel officer mounted on a magnificent blooded bay horse. "I selected him as my game, and gave my horse the spur and rein. . . . The chase was now exciting in the extreme."

The horsemen cleared a fence. Custer gained on his quarry and called on him to surrender. When he refused, Custer fired his pistol. He missed. Again Custer called out, "Surrender." The man rode on. Taking careful aim, or as careful as he could from the back of a galloping horse, Custer fired again. A hit, right in the head. Custer kept the man's horse, saddle, fancy sword, and double-barreled shotgun as trophies. "It was his own fault," Custer wrote home. "I told him twice to surrender."

It was important to Custer that these acts of reckless bravery be witnessed by others because, as was the case with most of his classmates (West Point, 1861), his ambition burned bright, and, in the Civil War, rewards went to the brave far more than to the brainy. How badly the young heroes wanted the rewards can be seen in the standard toast they made at the beginning, middle, and end of a drinking bout: "To promotion—or death!"

In May 1863, Captain Custer went to his commander, General Alfred Pleasonton, to ask two favors. First, he wanted Pleasonton to appoint Lieutenant George Yates, a friend from Monroe, to the staff (throughout his life Custer liked to surround himself with friends and relatives; at the Little Big Horn, two brothers, a brother-in-law, and a cousin fought beside him). Pleasonton agreed. Then Custer asked to be recommended to Governor Austin Blair for command of a Michigan cavalry regiment, newly organized. Pleasonton made the recommendation; Custer backed it up with others from four additional generals and a prominent Republican judge in Monroe. Alas, it was to no avail; Custer was an outspoken war Democrat and a known admirer of McClellan (who would be Lincoln's Democratic opponent in the 1864 election), so Republican Blair was not about to give him command of a regiment.

Adding to Custer's dismay, Judson Kilpatrick, who had been a year ahead of Custer at West Point, was now a brigadier general commanding a brigade of three regiments. Custer had never liked Kilpatrick; he was in fact intensely jealous of the man. Toward the end of June 1863, when Custer was still a mere lieutenant serving on Pleasonton's staff, things got worse, as Kilpatrick took command of a full division of cavalry.

Kilpatrick got ahead, in Custer's view, because he was a Republican, but also because of his reputation, which can be summed up as "damn the losses, full speed ahead." Kilpatrick's nickname in the Army of the Potomac was "Kill Cavalry," and it referred to the Union as well as Confederate cavalry. He was a daredevil, reckless leader; when General William T. Sherman requested Kilpatrick's services, he commented, "I know Kilpatrick is a hell of a damned fool, but I want just that sort of man to command my cavalry."

Kilpatrick's meteoric rise was so much gall and wormwood for Custer. Still, he was not blinded by his jealousy, but rather learned from it. And what he learned was that the way to get ahead in the Union cavalry was to charge the enemy at every opportunity, and hang the losses.

He got his opportunity on June 27, 1863, in the midst of Lee's invasion of Pennsylvania. Lincoln replaced General Hooker with General George Meade as commander of the Army of the Potomac, and Meade undertook a general reorganization, even as his army marched to meet Lee. As part of that process, Pleasonton jumped Custer from lieutenant in the regular army to brigadier general of volunteers, and gave him command of a brigade of cavalry, the 2nd Brigade in Kilpatrick's 3rd Division of the Cavalry Corps, Army of the Potomac. The 2nd Brigade consisted of the 1st, 5th, 6th, and 7th Michigan Cavalry regiments. As the 5th was the regiment Custer had asked to command, one month earlier, only to be turned down by Governor Blair, Custer enjoyed some sweet revenge—tempered a bit by having to serve under Kilpatrick.

At twenty-three years of age, Custer was a brigadier general, responsible for the lives and success of a brigade of cavalry almost two thousand men strong. It was astonishing, in a way—how on earth could the army entrust so many men to one so young? Yet it was almost commonplace. Of the 120 cadets who graduated from West Point in 1860 and 1861, 14 became general officers in the Union army, 3 in the Confederate service. Custer was by no means the only "boy general" of the war, although at age twenty-three he was the youngest man in the history of the United States Armed Forces to wear stars on his shoulders.

He—and the other boy generals (who were almost all in the cavalry)—got the appointment because of his recklessness. The Union cavalry had done poorly in the first two years of the war, and it was generally felt that the cause was excessive caution. To beat the Confederates into submission, the high command wanted field officers who would fight the rebels, any time, any place, under any circumstances, no questions asked, and accept heavy casualties in order to inflict heavy casualties. Young, devil-may-care, ambitious youngsters like Custer were ideal for the job.

The best of these boy generals, in this author's opinion, was James Harrison Wilson (USMA 1860), while the most famous, by far, was Custer. More than any of the others, Custer took advantage of his opportunity, to the point that at the end of the war, at Appomattox, General Phil Sheridan, by then commander of the cavalry in the Army of the Potomac, purchased the small table which Grant and Lee had used and gave it to Custer's wife, with a note: "My dear Madam—I respectfully present to you the small writing-table on which the conditions of the surrender of the Confederate Army of Northern Virginia were written by Lt. General Grant—and permit me to say, Madam, that there is scarcely an individual in our service who had contributed more to bring this about than your very gallant husband."

In less than two years, Custer, who had been an obscure young lieutenant, had risen to the pinnacle. How did he do it?

He rose to the top over the backs of his fallen soldiers. As a general, Custer displayed one basic instinct, to charge the enemy wherever he might be, no matter how strong his position or numbers. Throughout his military career Custer indulged that instinct whenever he faced opposition. Neither a thinker nor a planner, Custer scorned reconnaissance, maneuvering, and all other subtleties of warfare. He was a good, if often reckless, small-unit commander, no more and no less.

Gleefully accepting every risk himself, Custer personally earned his reputation as the most daring, gallant, and courageous Union cavalry general of the war. The press loved Custer's methods, and the reporters made him into a genuine superstar.

Americans made heroes out of their generals, and the higher a general's losses, it seemed, the greater a hero he became. Losses that would have appalled George Washington, or Dwight Eisenhower, or even John Pershing (whose war was even bloodier than the Civil War), were accepted as routine in the Union army. Indeed, they were almost desirable, if the Confederate losses were anywhere near as large.

Consider. At Gettysburg, in his first battle as a general, in just three days Custer lost 481 men out of a brigade of approximately 1,700, or more than 25 percent. (The American army's bloodiest battle in World War II was at the Bulge, December–January 1944–45. In that month-long engagement, total losses were about 13 percent.)

At Gettysburg, Custer personally led the 1st Michigan Cavalry regiment, about four hundred men strong, in a saber charge against an entire enemy division. The charge did halt a Confederate advance, although that probably could have been done with less bloodshed by placing his men in a defensive position and throwing up breastworks. As Custer did the job, however, he lost eighty-six men in a few brief moments. But he also drew attention to himself and received high praise from his superiors for his boldness and willingness to seize the initiative.

In the Wilderness campaign of May 1864, Custer lost 45 percent of his brigade (98 killed, 330 wounded, 348 missing in a force of 1,700). It is necessary to point out that he was only doing what all the other generals were also doing; he was just doing it better. The sole idea the Union army had was to kill as many rebels as possible, no matter what the cost to the North. It was a strategy of annihilation, if annihilation can be called a strategy.

One reads Custer's battle reports today (and those of other generals) with a sense of wonderment. Heavy casualties were almost a point of pride with the Union generals, something to brag about, as they proved that the general had not shirked his duty, that he was willing, nay anxious, to get out there and fight. One hundred killed, three hundred wounded, two hundred missing, for no conceivable military advantage, but what did it matter, so long as a superior officer saw the charge or the newspapers reported on it?

The reality behind the casualty figures escapes us today, but it was there—farm boys without an arm or a leg, dragging out their existence, unable to work or support themselves or their families, men whose minds as well as their bodies were permanently crippled, young wives who never saw their husbands again, teen-age boys whose lives were cut short. The Union cause was about as just as men are ever likely to find in any war, certainly more noble and inspiring than most, but the price the North paid for victory was far higher than it should have been. And, clearly, Custer was one of the leading causes.

Of course, he never saw it that way. To lead men in combat as Custer did, he had to be able to ignore the horrors of war, and he did. Custer's eyes were blind to the field hospitals after a battle, with their stacks of amputated arms and legs. All he saw were the backs of his retreating enemies, never the dead cavalrymen lying around him.

In the fall of 1863, after a cavalry skirmish on the Rappahannock River (which Custer with his usual hyperbole pronounced "the greatest cavalry battle ever witnessed on this continent"), Custer wrote home: "Oh, could you but have seen some of the charges that were made! While thinking of them I cannot but exclaim 'Glorious War!'"

It was glorious for Custer, but what of his men? How did he get ordinary midwestern farm boys to follow him into the teeth of Confederate artillery or on a charge against rebel infantry lined up behind a stone wall?

First, he was active in looking after his troopers' interests. He worked hard at getting top-quality horses and arms for his men. He saw to it that they were well fed and quartered whenever possible. He strove to create an atmosphere of closeness, even uniqueness, in his outfits, in a conscious and successful attempt to make them into one big happy family.

His own flamboyance helped his men identify with him. He dressed and acted in such a way as to make certain that he stood out from the crowd, that he would always be the center of attention. Most enlisted men respond positively to the eccentric commander, if he is professionally competent and fair with them, and Custer's troopers were no exception. His outlandish uniforms, his flowing golden locks of hair, with curls down to his shoulders, and his bright red tie made him stand out. His men paid him the ultimate compliment of imitation; they wore red neckerchiefs around their necks.

In combat Custer was an inspiring sight. Usually out front, deliberately exposing himself to the enemy fire, and always at the head of the column when engaged in a saber charge, waving his hat, pointing with his sword toward the enemy, shouting encouragement to the men, he was awesome in appearance.

Custer backed that appearance with performance. He embraced the time-honored advice to all combat leaders: never send your men to do something you wouldn't do yourself. To begin with, Custer always rode with his men. He ate what they ate, slept less than they did, and pushed himself harder. His endurance was legendary. One observer wrote, "On the eve of the surrender . . . in one of those last strenuous days I came upon General Custer, sitting on a log, upright, a cup of coffee in his hand, sound asleep."

Custer's bravery was equally legendary and a source of pride and inspiration for his men. He once attacked a division with a squadron, without reconnaissance. "I'll lead you, boys," Custer called out as soon as he spied the enemy blocking his path. "Come on!"

The charge utterly failed, but he was cited for gallantry. The third day at Gettysburg, Custer rose to the head of his brigade. "Come on, you Wolverines!" he shouted, his voice clear and defiant as a bugle. Those who fought behind Custer testified to the magic of that call. In leading the charge, Custer was disobeying a direct order (a practice that would soon become a habit). "I challenge the annals of warfare to produce a more brilliant or successful charge of cavalry," he wrote in his report on the engagement.

At Brandy Station in the fall of 1863, Custer was surrounded (he was also surprised on three occasions and surrounded on two others). Riding ahead of the 5th Michigan, deployed in columns of squadrons, Custer stood up in his stirrups and shouted, "Boys of Michigan. There are some people between *us* and home: I'm going home, who else goes?" He ordered the band to strike up "Yankee Doodle" (Custer had the band with him always, playing stirring marches for his charges). Tossing his hat aside with a dramatic gesture, he drew his sword and rode back and forth at the head of the regiment, mad with battle ecstasy.

"You should have heard the cheers they sent up," Custer wrote. "I gave the command 'Forward!' And I never expect to see a prettier sight. I frequently turned in my saddle to see the glittering sabers advance in the sunlight. After advancing a short distance I gave the word 'Charge!'—and away we went, whooping and yelling like so many demons."

Sad to relate, the charge was not a success. An unseen ditch caused horses and men to pile up in an impossible melee. Custer lost his horse, then another (he had a dozen horses shot from under him in the course of the war); finally he got the men re-formed and managed to cut his way through to safety.

Most of Custer's charges were successful, however, at least in the sense of driving back the enemy, inflicting casualties, capturing booty. This was especially true after he became a division commander, in the fall of 1864.

One factor in his success, seldom mentioned by his admirers, was the quality of the enemy. Custer was lucky to become a division commander when he did. By 1864 the Confederate cavalry was worn out, run-down, badly outnumbered, and absolutely incapable of meeting the Union cavalry on even terms. Custer's opponents in his most successful battles, in Sheridan's Shenandoah Valley campaign and in the operations in the spring of 1865 leading up to Appomattox, were poorly equipped in weapons, riding inferior, half-starved horses, exhausted, suffering the agonies of dysentery and other enervating diseases. Custer's men, meanwhile, were newly conscripted, in good health, with fresh, strong, well-fed horses, armed with repeating rifles, and backed by plenty of artillery, with infantry support.

Still, the Rebel units he defeated were veteran outfits, fighting desperately under proven leaders. Custer's victories were hard-won. And the principle ingredient in them was his own example. A private who rode with Custer later summed it all up for his wife: "Custer commanded in person and I saw him plunge his saber into the belly of a rebel who was trying to kill him. You can guess how bravely soldiers fight for such a general."

The private failed only to add what a price they paid. Custer's Michigan cavalry brigade, while he commanded it, sustained the highest casualties of any cavalry unit of the Union army during the war, a total of 525 killed. Adding in wounded and missing, as a brigade commander, Custer suffered 100 percent losses.

Custer also lost every man at the Little Big Horn. In that battle, too, he was recklessly brave, wonderfully courageous, and criminally impetuous. Jealousy of fellow officers, unbridled ambition, an intense desire to be noticed and written about, and a disregard for the ultimate welfare of his men characterized Custer's generalship in Montana in 1876 as much as in Virginia in 1864–65. Rather than the child being father to the man, in Custer's case it was more that the child never became a man.

As a soldier, he reached his limits as commander of small units with specific tasks under the control of older, wiser officers. As an independent commander, he was a failure. To put it into a World War II context, Custer would have been outstanding as a regimental commander in one of the armored divisions, a disaster as division commander, and a catastrophe as an army commander. He was a long way short of being the great general Utley says he was.

"JUST DUMB LUCK"

American Entry into World War II

The fiftieth anniversary of American entry into World War II began a period of rethinking how and why it happened, using the fresh eyes of a new generation born since the war and growing up with its results. In Russia, for example, young scholars are asking what kind of a victory it was when the Soviet Union had 20 million killed and most of its European area devastated, only to end up with a tighter-than-ever Stalinist dictatorship. To that question older Russian scholars reply, ask the people of Poland, the Balkans, the Ukraine, or European Russia what life under a Nazi occupation was like. To which answer the young scholars respond, we were born during the Khrushchev regime and grew up during the Brezhnev regime and that hardly seems an improvement over a Hitler regime.

In Japan, for another example, some young scholars are asking why the United States opposed the Japanese conquest of China. Had Japan been given a free hand, they say, China today would not be a Communist dictatorship. To the American answer, that the Japanese acted as the occupiers of China in a manner brutal beyond description, the Japanese reply, "Worse than Tiananmen Square?"

In the United States, a question frequently asked by today's college students is "Was there not a way we could have defeated Hitler without supporting Stalin?" Considering that nine out of every ten Wehrmacht soldiers killed in the war were killed by the Red Army, the answer is "Certainly not." But considering that the United States was years ahead of the Germans in atomic research and development, the question appears valid.

We can never know what the consequences of different decisions would have been, while we know precisely what the consequences of a decision made and enforced were. But fiftieth anniversaries lead us to think about what might have been if different paths had been followed, to consider why they were not, and to speculate on the risks involved in setting out on the path that was chosen.

There are some big questions about American entry into the war, and one that many Americans regard as the biggest of all is this: Did President Franklin Roosevelt know that the Japanese were about to attack Pearl Harbor and deliberately keep that information from the commanders in Hawaii in order to suffer a humiliating defeat, so as to unite a badly divided country behind American involvement in the war? Did he take the "back door to war"? The answer is unequivocally no. The charge and its "conspiracy history" of the worst kind is ridiculous. Although widely made and widely believed, it displays a stunning ignorance of how government works, and of Roosevelt's actual policy.

To the more reasonable charge, that Roosevelt maneuvered events in such a way as to leave the Japanese no choice but to strike, the reply is that while he certainly put pressure on them, most of all with his on-again, off-again oil embargo, he did not put a gun to Tojo's head and tell him to attack or die. Nor did he want the Japanese to attack, at least not in December of 1941.

The United States did not voluntarily enter the war. On December 8, 1941, Roosevelt did not ask Congress to declare war on Japan but to recognize that a state of war existed between the two countries. Nor did he ask Congress to declare war on Germany until after Hitler, on December 11, declared war on the United States.

These are fundamental facts, and they force us to examine Roosevelt's policies from an angle other than the Pearl Harbor conspiracy thesis. Roosevelt's supporters, and they are many and learned, praise him for carefully overcoming the strong isolationist sentiment of the American people and bringing them to recognize their duty and self-interest. Much can be, and has been, said in support of this interpretation, but much can also be said against it.

In rethinking American involvement in the war from the perspective of fifty years, what strikes me is the terrible risk Roosevelt and the United States were taking in the fall of 1941, how close we came to catastrophe, not by edging toward war, but by refusing to prepare for it and failing to provide any significant help to the enemies of fascism and militarism in their hour of greatest need. A parallel theme, it seems to me, is how American commentators have concentrated on developments in the Pacific theater while ignoring the really decisive impact of developments in the Nazi-Soviet war inside the Soviet Union. And a third theme has to do with the situation Roosevelt found his nation in on December 10, 1941: the United States was not involved in the war he had been determined to enter, against Germany, but was involved in the war he had been determined to put off until later, against Japan. His foreign policy, right up to December 10, was a dismal failure. What saved him and his policy was nothing he did, but was Hitler's act of lunacy.

I will not go into the details of Roosevelt's failure to provide any semblance of world leadership in the crisis years of 1938 to 1941. He recognized the Anschluss of Austria de facto without a whimper. He was not present at and exerted little influence on the Munich conference. His response to the invasion of Poland and the outbreak of war in Europe was purely verbal. He failed to respond to desperate French pleas for assistance when the Germans invaded in May 1940. He gave no significant aid to the United Kingdom during the Battle of Britain in the summer of 1940. In the fall of 1940, during his campaign for a third term, he gave the Axis powers what amounted to a pledge that they had nothing to fear from the United States when he promised American mothers that "your boys are not going to be sent into any foreign wars." His response to the Japanese conquest of Manchuria and much of eastern China was limited to nonrecognition and a trickle of aid to the Chinese. While war raged around the world, he failed to mobilize the United States. In other words, he fully adopted the twin themes of American diplomacy of the twenties and thirties, neutrality and disarmament.

With millions of men under arms around the world in 1940, the American army numbered 375,000 men, with virtually no tanks or airplanes. Although Roosevelt was the leader of the greatest industrial power in the world, a nation that had colonies in the Pacific and worldwide interests to defend, he had no influence on events because he had no armed forces capable of attacking anyone and only the navy with which to defend the United States. The world was in flames, the United States was vulnerable to winds from both directions, and the nation, having no firefighters, was only dealing out garden hoses.

Of course Roosevelt and his supporters blame this situation on the isolationists, but it can be said with equal justification that Roosevelt's policy had been to appease the isolationists. Perhaps he could not have done more, but we will never know because he did not try. His hesitancy to act reflected a nineteenth-century isolationist America rather than a world power ready to proclaim that the twentieth would be "the American Century."

So, in the spring of 1941, the situation was as follows: Hitler had either conquered or browbeaten into an alliance the whole of non-Russian Europe, and he commanded the greatest and most successful armed force the world had ever seen. Roosevelt had entered into an economic alliance with the only nation then at war with Hitler, the United Kingdom, through the destroyers for bases deal of September 1940, and the lend-lease program (passed in March of 1941), leading him to proclaim that the United States had become the "arsenal of democracy." But it was not much of an arsenal, nor was Britain much of a threat to Hitler—the British were absolutely incapable of mounting an offensive against Germany. Hitler was free to do whatever he chose.

In Asia, the initiative was with Japan. Fully mobilized, with a navy that outclassed the American navy in the critical weapon—aircraft carriers—the Japanese were free to strike north, into Asian Russia, or south, against the French, British and Dutch colonies, whenever they wished. But in Asia, Roosevelt did have the power to influence events, because of Japanese dependence on American oil.

Roosevelt's policy was clear and sensible. He recognized that Germany was the greater threat, that Germany could not be defeated without full American participation, that America was hardly prepared to fight a one-front war, much less one on two fronts, and that it was therefore critical that he get the nation involved in Europe while stalling the Japanese.

But Roosevelt's implementation of this policy was badly muddled and fraught with grave risks. The aid lend-lease provided to Britain was barely enough to keep her going. His reinforcement of the Philippines by stationing B-17s at Clark Field, starting in the spring of 1941, was designed to deter the Japanese from striking south, but it was a classic case of half-measures. The bombers were insufficient as a deterrent, but provoking to the Japanese. His policies left him vulnerable to charges from the isolationists that he was planning for war but left him short of preparing for war.

Consider: in May 1941, the United States had but one combat-ready division, while the Germans had 208 and the Japanese over 100. The United States had a total of 471 military aircraft, while Hitler had 2,700 on his eastern frontier alone. The American army had 200 tanks, while the Wehrmacht was about to invade the Soviet Union with 3,500 tanks. Never in human history has the preparedness gap between potential enemies been greater,

On June 22, Hitler launched Operation Barbarossa. Some thoughtless people in the United States, including Missouri Senator Harry S. Truman, said it was wonderful, this business of Nazis and Communists killing each other, but Roosevelt knew better. The initial German successes put the world in a deadly peril. A quick German victory—and Hitler came awfully close to achieving it—would have made the Nazis self-sufficient in natural and human resources and rendered Britain's only weapon, the naval blockade of Germany's North Sea ports, useless.

We know today that Hitler had made his first major mistake in attacking the Soviet Union, but, at the time, expert opinion, in the United

States and the United Kingdom as well as in Germany, held that the Red Army would be defeated before winter. But what did Roosevelt do to prevent such a catastrophe? It is amazing to look back and realize how limited his response was to Barbarossa. His naval advisor, Admiral Harold Stark, urged him to go to war, now, by providing escort for convoys all the way to Britain and to Russia's northern ports, but he would not.

Nor would he mobilize. Through the first three months of the Russo-German war, American industry produced 115 tanks per month, at a time when Stalin was demanding 500 per month to keep the Red Army in the battle. American war production during those critical months, when much of the rest of the world was waging total war, amounted to only 10 percent of the total output of American industry. In July, when the Russians asked for 3,000 fighter airplanes, Roosevelt promised 200—of which 140 came from British stocks. Stalin wanted 3,000 bombers and got 5. He asked for 20,000 antiaircraft cannon and machine guns and got none, 5,000 antitank guns and got none, 25,000 rifles and got 1,000. As Waldo Heinrichs puts it in *Threshold of War: Franklin D. Roosevelt and American Entry into World War II,* "For waging a battle he regarded as decisive, the president had painfully little to offer besides tokens and promises."

These paltry figures need to be put beside the latent, untapped capacity of American industry. When Roosevelt—who proved to be a magnificent war leader once the nation was committed—called for the production of 50,000 airplanes a year, people thought he was crazy. But within a year of entering the war the United States was producing 4,000 military airplanes per month; by 1944 it was 8,000 per month, or 96,318 for the year. Altogether, the United States built over 250,000 airplanes during the war. There were similar, all-but-unbelievable great leaps forward in the production of tanks, ships, landing craft, rifles, and other weapons. And all this took place while the United States put its major effort into the greatest industrial feat up to that time, the production of atomic weapons (hardly begun in 1942, completed by mid-1945). Had the United States possessed in the fall of 1941 the power the nation was to have by the fall of 1943, the Axis almost surely would have been deterred.

But, as it was, in the fall of 1941 Roosevelt was unable to help Russia, barely able to help Britain, unwilling to try to persuade the American people that their national security was in danger and thus incapable of mobilizing. He was reduced to attempting to goad Germany into declaring war on the United States. He ordered the navy to become ever more active in the Battle of the Atlantic, culminating in his "shoot on sight" orders in September. He evidently thought that such deliberate provocation would force Hitler to declare war. But to Hitler, the American navy was only an irritant. As his armies drove ever deeper into Russia, Hitler ordered his submarine commanders to avoid incidents in the Atlantic involving the Americans.

As Roosevelt tried desperately to get involved in the European war—without ever once telling the American people that they absolutely had to come to grips with the Nazis, who could not otherwise be defeated, indeed promising them, in the face of all logic, that with American tools the British and Russians could do the job—he was trying desperately to avoid war with the Japanese. They were obviously stirring, eager to take advantage of the weakness of the colonial powers in Asia: the French conquered, the Dutch conquered, the British fully involved with Germany, the Americans preoccupied with Germany. Roosevelt wanted to keep the Japanese from striking out; if they attacked to the north, against Siberia, it could well be disastrous for the Soviet Union, and thus for the anti-Axis forces worldwide. If they attacked to the south, neither the Dutch nor the French could do anything about it, the British would have to divide their already hard-pressed fleet, and the United States, as noted, could well be involved in a two-front war when it was not yet ready to fight a one-front war. So Roosevelt played a delicate game with the Japanese, entering into serious negotiations, attempting to use oil as a weapon (by selling them enough to keep them from making a desperate decision to conquer their own sources of oil in the Dutch East Indies, but not enough to allow them to plan for all-out war), buying time.

Roosevelt had gotten himself at cross-purposes with public opinion.

He wanted war with Germany, but many Americans felt that Germany had done nothing to the United States and in any case the Germans were killing Communists; he wanted to avoid war with Japan, but many Americans felt that Japan had violated a bedrock American principle (the Open Door to China), was threatening the American colony in the Philippines, and must be stopped.

We cannot go too far with this in calling attention to the power of public opinion. Roosevelt's supporters cite the polls that indicated most Americans wished to avoid war. When put that way, however, the question almost answered itself. But the polls also showed that a majority supported the lend-lease bill and that 62 percent supported "shoot on sight." What the polls don't show, because it never happened, was the potential effect of presidential leadership. Back in May 1941, as Heinrichs points out in *Threshold of War,* Secretary of War Henry Stimson had warned Roosevelt against relying on incidents instead of leadership to light the path. Roosevelt had nevertheless continued to rely on incidents.

Also according to Heinrichs, in August 1941, Secretary of the Treasury Henry Morgenthau responded to a temporary halt in the German advance into Russia by telling Roosevelt, "We will never have a better chance. Somebody has been looking over this country and the good Lord has been with us, but we can't count on the good Lord and just dumb luck forever." Still Roosevelt refused to attempt to rouse the nation to an all-out effort.

The Roosevelt administration was living in a dream world. The dream was that the Russians would hold out unaided, that the Japanese would wait until the Americans were ready before attacking, and that Hitler would declare war on the United States. That the first and third dreams turned out to be realities doesn't mean that they were not dreams in late 1941; the second dream, or expectation, that the Japanese would wait until the Americans were ready before attacking, turned out to be a costly mistake.

It was based on faulty intelligence as much as wishful thinking. Of all the areas in which the United States was unprepared in late 1941, intelligence stands out. It was simply terrible. In late October, U.S.

Army intelligence told Roosevelt that simultaneous attacks by the Japanese on the Dutch East Indies, Malaya, and the Philippines were beyond Japan's means. The intelligence experts did not even consider the possibility of an attack on Hawaii. In late November, intelligence "lost" the Japanese aircraft carrier fleet. This must rank as one of the great intelligence failures of all time. The Germans were at the gates of Moscow, the Battle of the Atlantic had reached a critical stage, negotiations with Japan had reached an impasse, the Japanese had mobilized and were on the move, the world crisis had reached a white-hot heat, the potential enemies' main offensive weapon, the aircraft carriers, had sortied from their home port, and American intelligence could only guess in which direction they were sailing.

Under the circumstances, one would have thought that every American base in the Pacific, and, for that matter, on the West Coast, would have been on full alert, that airplanes from the Philippines, Wake and Midway islands, Hawaii, Los Angeles and San Francisco would have been flying round-the-clock reconnaissance flights. But they were not, partly because of complacency, mainly because there were not enough airplanes.

Meanwhile, Roosevelt waited for Hitler to declare war on the United States. This, too, flew in the face of logic and ignored recent history. Roosevelt had been a member of Woodrow Wilson's administration; he was determined to avoid Wilson's mistakes. For example, his major policy in World War II, and to my mind his greatest contribution, the demand for unconditional surrender, was designed to escape the trap Wilson had gotten into with the 1918 armistice. He would have done better to try to emulate what Wilson had done right. Wilson had realized that Germany could wage war against American shipping without declaring war, so he had not waited for Germany to declare war on the United States and had convinced the people and persuaded the Congress that the United States had to fight.

By the time America entered World War I, it had long since become a war of attrition. Germany had won that attrition war against Russia, only to have victory snatched from her when the American Expeditionary Force tipped the balance to win the battle of attrition on the Western Front.

But Hitler knew that Germany could not win a war of attrition against the combined forces of the Soviet Union, Britain and the United States. His policy therefore was blitzkrieg, lightning war. It worked in 1939 in Poland and in 1940 in France, but it failed in Russia in the fall of 1941. By November, when the Wehrmacht was halted short of Moscow—only just, but still halted—the war on the Eastern Front had become a war of attrition. That gave Hitler every possible motive to avoid war with America, against whom he could launch no offensive operations of any kind in any case. For Roosevelt, under these circumstances, to pursue a policy of goading Hitler into declaring war was to pursue a hope, not a plan. And the hope was that Hitler was a madman.

In a number of ways Roosevelt had already enjoyed more dumb luck than he could ever have counted on. First, in a tactical sense, although Pearl Harbor was a humiliating defeat, the Japanese had failed to follow up their victory with an offensive to take Hawaii. They had failed to destroy the oil depots and repair facilities. And although they had destroyed America's battleship fleet in the Pacific, they had failed to get any aircraft carriers.

Even more important were their political mistakes. Their objectives were Burma, Malaya, and the Dutch East Indies, where the oil was located. But they had attacked the American bases in Hawaii and the Philippines. The nature of the unprovoked sneak attack united the American people as nothing else could have done, and ensured Japan's defeat. That Japan attacked the United States at all was surely a major mistake. The Japanese leaders assumed that the American air force in the Philippines would cut their line of communication to their targets in the south, but this is one of the biggest "what ifs" of modern history.

What if they had attacked British and Dutch colonial possessions and bypassed the Philippines and ignored Hawaii? In November, Roosevelt had more or less casually told the British ambassador to the U.S. that if the Japanese launched such an attack, he would come to the support of the British. But telling that privately to the British was one thing, persuading Congress to declare war on Japan in defense of European colonialism in Asia quite another. We can never know what might have happened without the attack on Pearl Harbor and the Philippines, but we do know that the American response to the Japanese offensive in China had been mainly verbal; so, too, was the response to the Japanese occupation of the French colony in Indochina. We can assume that Roosevelt's speech to Congress on December 8, 1941,—the "day that will live in infamy" speech—would have been much different without Pearl Harbor. The point is, in Stimson's words, Roosevelt was relying on incidents instead of leadership to light the path.

Despite Pearl Harbor, between midday of December 7 (Washington time) and the morning of December 11, the path was dimly lit. In planning for war, the American military had assumed that American entry into the war would transform the two regional conflicts—one in Europe pitting Germany and Italy against Britain and the Soviet Union, the other in Asia pitting Japan against China—into a world war. In that war, the United States would go on the defensive in the Pacific while undertaking an offensive against the more dangerous enemy, Germany. But that could not happen so long as America was at war with Japan and not with Germany.

What Roosevelt would have done had Hitler not declared war is something else we can never know. He evidently planned to proceed on the assumption that war against Japan also meant war against Germany, but he would have found it exceedingly difficult to persuade the Congress, not to mention the U.S. Navy, to go on the offensive in the Atlantic while maintaining a defensive posture in the Pacific. Once again the point is that the initiative was not his. He could not shape but could only react to events. His foes charged that he was a dictator pushing the United States into war; actually he was a cautious politician who was taking great risks with national security because of his unwillingness or inability to light the path.

So why did Hitler solve Roosevelt's problem for him by declaring war? He was not required to do so by the terms of the Tripartite Pact between Italy, Germany and Japan of September 1940, as that was a defensive alliance that required Germany to come to Japan's aid only if Japan were attacked. Japan had not come to Germany's aid in June 1941, when Germany invaded the Soviet Union. He had little to gain from declaring war on the United States; in no way could he carry out a strategic offensive campaign against American industry or mobilization capacity, nor had he any thought of doing so. On the Eastern Front his armies were engaged in the greatest battle ever fought; that very week the Red Army had launched its counterattack. The United States was making only a minuscule contribution to that battle. The declaration of war did free German submarines to wage all-out war against American shipping, but Hitler could have done as Ludendorff did in 1917 and launched unrestricted submarine warfare without declaring war, thus putting the onus of declaring war back on Roosevelt. It seems probable that Roosevelt would have responded as Wilson did in 1917, but had he asked for a declaration of war against Germany the isolationists would have argued that his policy of supplying Germany's enemies had forced Hitler to sink American ships and invited intense criticism of going to war to support the Communist dictatorship in the Soviet Union.

Well, that is all speculation. What happened is that Hitler did declare war. It was Roosevelt's biggest break, and an inexplicable decision on Hitler's part. The distinguished German journalist Sebastian Haffner, in *The Meaning of Hitler,* calls it "the most incomprehensible of his mistakes," and points out that it was "the most lonely of his lonely decisions." Amazingly, he consulted no one. He threw away his long-range plan for world conquest, in which the final struggle against the United States was left to the next generation, utilizing the resources of the Soviet Union and the rest of Europe. One would have thought he would have at least asked his military leaders what the implications of a declaration of war against the United States were, that he would have at least consulted with his foreign office, that he would have at least talked to Goering, Himmler, Goebbels and his other henchmen about it. But he discussed it with no other person; on December 11, he simply announced it to the Reichstag.

Thank God he did; doing so sealed his fate, and saved Roosevelt.

Morgenthau, it turned out, had been wrong when he warned Roosevelt that "we can't count on the good Lord and just dumb luck forever."

"Enter" is an active verb, implying some positive deed. In that sense, the United States did not "enter" World War II. It was pulled in despite, rather than because of, the actions of the American president.

SIGINT

Deception and the Liberation of Western Europe

On June 6, 1944, the U.S., Britain and Canada launched the largest force of warships in history across the English Channel. It escorted the largest concentration of troops transport vessels ever assembled, covered by the largest force of fighter and bomber aircraft ever brought together, preceded by a fleet of air transports that had carried forty thousand paratroopers and glider-borne troops to Normandy.

Not one German submarine, not one small boat, not one airplane, not one radar set, not one German anywhere detected this movement. As General Walter Warlimont, deputy head of operations of the German Supreme Headquarters, later confessed, on the eve of Operation Overlord the Wehrmacht leaders "had not the slightest idea that the decisive event of the war was upon them."

None of the surprises achieved in World War II—including Barbarossa, Pearl Harbor, Stalingrad, and the Ardennes offensive of December 1944—was more complex, more difficult, more important, or more successful than Overlord. To fool Hitler and his generals in the battle of wits that preceded the attack, the Allies had to convince them not only that it was coming where it was not but also that the real thing was a feint. This was done through a variety of methods, of which none was more important than the use of radio signals.

SIGINT is an abbreviation for Signals Intelligence.

Code name for the deception operation was Fortitude. It was done on a grand scale. As all deceptions must, Fortitude built on German preconceptions and habits. The enemy assumed the Pas de Calais would be the site of the attack because it was the choicest military objective—closest to England, closest to the Allied objective of the Rhine-Ruhr industrial heartland of Germany. The enemy also assumed there would be subsidiary operations and was especially sensitive about Norway, where the submarine pens were located—Germany's only remaining offensive weapon. To convince the Germans to look to the northeast of the Seine River for the main landing, and even farther north to Norway, Supreme Headquarters Allied Expeditionary Force (SHAEF), under the command of General Dwight D. Eisenhower, created notional armies, gathered them together in Kent, Essex, and in Scotland, and got them ready to invade Norway and the Pas de Calais. This was done primarily by radio messages—filling the air with all the signals that would normally accompany the building of an army—carried on a low-level, and thus easily broken, cipher.

In Scotland, the notional army consisted of two dozen over-age officers and their radio operators. They kept up a constant stream of messages about needing maps of Norway, crampons, ski instructors, cold-weather lubricants. A bomber fleet of wooden planes appeared on runways in Scotland. The Germans heard and saw all this and drew the conclusion the Allies wanted them to draw; instead of drawing down the troop strength in Norway to reinforce France, they sent more troops to Norway.

In addition to the radio traffic, there were dummy tanks, made of rubber or papier-mâché by artists from the motion picture industry, and jeeps driven around dragging chains to stir up dust. Phoney gasoline dumps were built. German air reconnaissance got photos of all this. In Kent, an entire notional American army group gathered, under the command of General George S. Patton. It was called First U.S. Army Group, or FUSAG.

Beyond the use of radio signals, Fortitude depended on the Double Cross system. The British Secret Service had managed to locate and turn every German spy in England. Displaying remarkable patience, the

British had held and built this asset until 1944. They sprang the trap in Fortitude, as they had the spies report by Morse code over the wireless to their controllers in Hamburg the existence of notional divisions, heavy train traffic into Dover, and other items that reinforced the deception.

The most important agent was code-named Garbo. He convinced his German controllers that he had a network of spies operating throughout Britain. The information he sent in was good, even excellent, even if it always seemed to arrive too late to use. Garbo convinced the Germans that he had a terrific problem raising enough cash to pay his agents; the Germans arranged to ship gold to him from Spain; the British confiscated the gold and so the German intelligence apparatus paid the expenses of the British Secret Service throughout the war.

Ordinarily in World War II, the side on the offensive wanted to fool its opponent into thinking it was much weaker than was actually the case. In Fortitude, however, SHAEF wanted the Germans to grossly exaggerate Allied strength. The purpose was to convince the Germans that when the real attack came, in Normandy, that it was a feint designed to draw German armor south and west, across the Seine. Once that was accomplished, the main attack would come at the Pas de Calais or so the Allies hoped the Germans would think. This deception could not be turned around; that is, if the Allies attacked north of the Seine, the Germans would immediately pull all their forces south of the river for fear of their being cut off.

Fortitude's success was measured by the German estimate of Allied strength. By June 1, German intelligence believed that Eisenhower had eighty-nine divisions available, when in fact he had forty-seven. They also thought he had sufficient landing craft to bring twenty divisions ashore in the first wave, when in fact he could barely manage five.

Eisenhower, meanwhile, had an almost exact read on the German order of battle. SHAEF intelligence sources included the French Resistance, which used radio signals to send out the best possible intelligence ("I saw it with my own eyes"), and air reconnaissance, but by far the most important source was German radio traffic. From it, Eisenhower knew that Fortitude was working, because he knew the most and best

German divisions, especially the armored divisions, were in the Pas de Calais region—exactly where he wanted them to be.

As is now well known, the British had managed to break the German Enigma code early in the war. The Germans never caught on—they believed right to the end that they had the best encoding machine in the world (they were right about that) and that it was unbreakable (a critical miscalculation).

Not until 1974 did the world know about Ultra, as the British called the operation at Bletchley Park where the Enigma code-breaking machine (sometimes said to be the first computer) was based. When F. W. Winterbotham wrote *The Ultra Secret,* people asked, "If we were reading German radio traffic right through the war, how come we didn't win the war sooner?" To which the answer is, we did win the war sooner.

But before going into how Ultra worked—and didn't work, and sometimes worked to the Allies' disadvantage—let's follow through on Fortitude. On the evening of June 5, Garbo sent a message to Hamburg. He said an attack was coming in the morning, in Normandy. He named the divisions involved. He gave away the best-kept secret of the war. It arrived in Hamburg just before midnight. It was decoded, then sent on to Berchtesgaden, Hitler's headquarters in the Alps, rather than Normandy, because only Hitler could order the panzer divisions into battle. By the time it arrived in Normandy, the battle had already been joined. So Garbo's message did the Germans no good—but it surely raised their already high opinion of Garbo.

Over the next three days, the battle raged. Field Marshal Erwin Rommel demanded that the armored divisions in the Pas de Calais be released to his command—he insisted that Normandy was the main invasion, the only invasion, and time was critical. On D-Day plus four Hitler gave in, partly—he ordered the two best panzer divisions to move to the sound of the guns.

Garbo, meanwhile, sent another message. It read: "The present operation, though a large-scale assault, is diversionary in character. Its object is to establish a strong bridgehead in order to draw the maximum of our reserves into the area of the assault and to retain them there so as to leave another area exposed where the enemy could then attack with some prospect of success." He pointed to the Pas de Calais as the real target, and offered convincing evidence, such as Patton's absence and the failure to commit any of the notional divisions that appeared on the German appreciation of the Allied order of battle.

Garbo's message was in Hitler's hands within the hour. On the basis of it, the Führer made a momentous decision. The panzers had started for Normandy, but now Hitler ordered them back to Calais, to defend against the main invasion. He also awarded an Iron Cross to Garbo.

The panzers stayed in the Pas de Calais region all through June, all through July, while the Battle of Normandy was fought. They were still there in August, after the liberation of Paris, waiting for Patton's FUSAG to attack. Had the Allies not swung east into Belgium, bypassing the Pas de Calais, they would still be there. This was a spectacular payoff for a small investment.

In the Normandy campaign, Ultra made a critical contribution. After the Americans broke out of the beachhead, at St. Lo in late July, Hitler launched a counterattack, at Mortain. Because he controlled the counterattack personally, he filled the air with orders sent over the radio. Ultra picked them up, and General Eisenhower knew the German intentions and strength as well as his opposite number. This knowledge enabled him to hold at Mortain with what appeared to be alarmingly weak forces while continuing to support Patton's U.S. 3rd Army in its drive toward the Seine. Knowing where the Germans were coming, when, and in what strength, made it possible for Eisenhower to win a classic defensive battle at Mortain, even while maintaining his offensive elsewhere.

It was remarkable that Eisenhower would put so much faith in Ultra, because it had let him down earlier in the war. Thereby hangs a tale.

At the end of the war Colonel Telford Taylor, who headed the American Special Liaison Unit (SLU) operation, which relayed Ultra information from Bletchley Park to the field commanders, had all his SLUs file a report on their activities. They almost all stressed, as Taylor put it in his summary, "the need for careful study of all sources of intelligence." As one SLU wrote, "It is most easy for the Ultra representative to allow himself to become isolated from the main stream of the intelligence section, so that he loses awareness of what other sources are producing. Another facile error, induced by inertia, is to permit Ultra to become a substitute for analysis and evaluation of other intelligence. Ultra must be looked on as one of a number of sources; it must not be taken as a neatly packaged replacement for tedious work with other evidence."

Overreliance on Ultra almost led to disaster in Tunisia in February 1943. Eisenhower's chief intelligence officer at the time was British Brigadier Eric Mockler-Ferryman. He relied heavily, almost exclusively, on Ultra. Radio intercepts indicated a German attack in northern Tunisia. Local information, both from natives and from ground patrols and air reconnaissance, supported by POW interrogation, indicated an attack in the south, from Rommel's Africa Corps, toward Kasserine Pass. Eisenhower wanted to reinforce the south, but Mockler-Ferryman insisted that Ultra was correct and, at his bequest, Eisenhower made no changes in his dispositions. Then Rommel disobeyed the orders coming from Germany, the ones Ultra had picked up, and attacked toward Kasserine. The Americans just did manage to hold their ground, after losing almost half an armored division. Eisenhower sent Mockler-Ferryman back to England and replaced him with General Kenneth Strong, "an officer who has a broader insight into German mentality and method." In a message to his superior, Chief of Staff General George C. Marshall, Eisenhower explained that the embarrassment at Kasserine was primarily "due to faulty G-2 estimates. I am provoked that there was such reliance placed upon particular types of intelligence."

In Normandy, in 1944, and in the race across France and Belgium that followed, SHAEF intelligence supplemented Ultra with a variety of sources. Air reconnaissance was important, although it had some severe limitations—for example, the Germans would hide their tanks in woods during the day, and move them after dark. A rich source was local residents, especially those in organized resistance movements. Germany had conducted her occupation of Western Europe so as to antagonize nearly everyone; no matter how much they hated the Communists, most French and Belgian citizens hated the Germans more. As a consequence, when an allied tank column entered a French or Belgian village, the soldiers could depend on the local civilians telling them the exact truth—

when the Germans left, in what strength, in what direction, with what equipment, and other details. One reason that the late summer offensive came to an abrupt halt in September 1944 was that when the Allied armies reached the German border, local sources of information dried up.

A separate problem for SHAEF intelligence was the commander who simply disregarded information given to him. Patton was notorious for ignoring intelligence—he just wanted to fight. For him, it generally worked out all right. For the British 1st Airborne Division in the Battle of Arnhem in mid-September 1944, ignoring intelligence brought on a disaster.

The intelligence came from the Dutch Resistance. On September 11, it got word to General Strong at SHAEF G-2 that there were two panzer divisions refitting in Arnhem, hidden in woods. Field Marshal Bernard Law Montgomery was about to launch operation Market-Garden, of which the leading element was the British 1st Airborne, scheduled to drop into Arnhem. Without tanks of their own, or proper artillery, the paratroopers stood no chance against panzers. Strong went to Montgomery with the intelligence, accompanied by Eisenhower's chief of staff, General Walter B. Smith.

Strong and Smith tried to get Montgomery to change his plans, but, as Smith later related, "Monty ridiculed the idea. He felt the greatest opposition would come more from the terrain difficulties than from the Germans. He was not worried about the German armor. At least I tried to stop him, but I got nowhere. Monty simply waved my objections airily aside."

Strong wrote in his 1979 memoirs, "Our information was sufficient for me to utter a warning—intelligence can seldom do much more than that—of potential danger from armored troops. After that it is up to the decision makers and there is no guarantee that they will heed the intelligence people." At Arnhem, the British airborne troops paid the price—ten thousand casualties and POWs out of a twelve-thousand-man division.

In December, it was the Germans' turn. Once inside their own country, where they had secure telephone lines, the Germans could dispense with the radio, which rendered Ultra useless, and they did not have to worry about local resistance groups getting out word of their dispositions. Thus they were able to hide two entire armies in the Eifel, the wooded area in Germany on the edge of the Ardennes in Belgium, and wait for bad weather to ground the Allied air forces. Meanwhile they went on the radio again, sending out orders to notional units in Holland for a counterattack. SHAEF intelligence fell into the trap and warned Eisenhower to expect an attack on his northern flank. Eisenhower prepared to meet it.

Then on December 16, rain and fog gave them the cover they needed in the Ardennes, and they launched their counteroffensive. It caught the Allies completely by surprise.

But the Germans did not have the manpower or material to follow through in enough force to reach their objective, Antwerp. Indeed, their overall shortcomings played a major role in their achieving surprise. SHAEF intelligence had a good, if not exact, read on the German order of battle. So far as SHAEF could tell, the Germans were not capable of a sustained counteroffensive. And SHAEF was right. Still, to be caught by surprise was an embarrassment, and a costly one to the American troops in the Ardennes. It was also a hard-earned lesson—SHAEF intelligence had come to depend too heavily on Ultra.

What was intelligence worth to the Allies? The man in the best position to know was Eisenhower. He was fulsome in his praise. To General Stewart Menzies, head of the British Secret Service, he wrote in May 1945: "The intelligence which has emanated from you before and during this campaign has been of priceless value to me. It has simplified my task as a commander enormously. It has saved thousands of British and American lives and, in no small way, contributed to the speed with which the enemy was routed and eventually forced to surrender."

Eisenhower was a careful writer who avoided exaggeration or hyperbole. When he used phrases like "priceless value" he meant to indicate that without Bletchley Park and Ultra, without the Double Cross operation, without SHAEF intelligence, the Allies would have been hard-pressed to win the war, and certainly would have taken much longer.

But as a former SLU officer, Adolph Rosengarten, wrote in his postwar report, "The indisputable truth is that intelligence won neither the 'Crusade' nor World War II." Rosengarten quoted an unnamed general who in 1941 told his junior officers, "Wars are won by guts on both ends of this," and held up a Springfield rifle with a fixed bayonet.

The Allies won World War II because of the courage, stamina, and fighting ability of their combat infantrymen, backed by intelligence. Ultra, and intelligence and deception in general, were indispensable, to be sure, but the men who won the war remain the men to whom Eisenhower dedicated *Crusade in Europe*: "The Allied Soldier, Sailor, and Airman of World War II."

Modern wars are won by teamwork. Intelligence and deception operations are integral parts of the team, but by themselves they are impotent.

D-DAY REVISITED

As part of the research for my book, *D-Day,* my wife, Moira, and I spent a summer in Normandy. Staying in small hotels in the seaside villages, we walked along the beaches and swam in the surf. I've been studying this battle since I first went to work for General Eisenhower as editor and biographer in 1964. I have visited Normandy at least a dozen times, for periods ranging from a couple of days to a week or two. I am always startled to find out how much I don't know, and delighted at how much I learn.

One reason for our trip was new source material I had with me, transcripts of oral histories from the men of D-Day. The Eisenhower Center at the University of New Orleans has been collecting tape-recorded memories from Normandy veterans; to date, we have about 1,000 from Americans and another 300 from German, French, Canadian, and British veterans. In most cases they are detailed enough to make accurate guides.

For example, on Omaha Beach, on the shoulder of the bluff looking down on the Colleville draw, there is a series of German emplacements that impressed themselves forever on the minds of a dozen or so of my U.S. 1st Division informants. The Germans built a miniature Gibraltar to defend that draw. There are a dozen or so "Tobruks" of various sizes.

Some are cement silos sunk into the ground, with openings that a mortar crew inside could fire from with all but perfect immunity. Others held machine guns or flamethrowers; some even had tank turrets on top. Climbing down into them, getting into the tunnel system that connected them, I marveled at how well situated they were to cover that draw, and was appalled at the thought of how much fire they could hurl down on it.

Even more impressive are the twin casemates built to hold 75mm cannon. Made of six-foot-thick, steel-reinforced concrete and big enough to hold the cannon and a five-man crew, they are tucked into the bluff, perfectly sited. Through the aperture of the higher casemate, there is a magnificent view of Omaha Beach stretching out to the west, about four miles long: The sand is golden; the sky is blue; the Channel is gray; the surf is white; the bluff is green; the bathers' swimsuits add splashes of color. Altogether, it is a subject befitting an impressionist painting.

For the Germans firing those 75mm cannon on June 6, however, the scene was terrifying—thousands of young Americans coming ashore to kill them. To prevent that, they fired down on the invaders as rapidly as they could load. An American combat engineer who had been down on the beach told me that those two guns probably killed more Americans than any others in Normandy—he estimated more than 200.

The casemates took a pounding in return. I could locate damage from a 5-inch naval gun, or from a rocket—not much damage, just a pockmark in the concrete. Inside the upper casemate, I spotted the hole where an American 75mm shell had scored a direct hit. It had been fired from a Sherman tank on the beach. Following the angle of the hole, I could trace the exact position of the tank when it fired. A French employee at the Omaha cemetery told me that in 1984 the German battery commander met with the commander of the American tank to discuss their duel of forty years past—each had put the other man's weapon out of action.

That tank got ashore thanks to Lieutenant Dean Rockwell, who made a decision to bring his LCT group all the way in, rather than launch them, "swimming," offshore as planned. A crew member on Rockwell's LCT, Martin Waarvick, told me the story. Rockwell mistrusted the rubber inflatable skirts that guided the tanks and had thought the sea too rough for the tanks to swim, so he brought his four right on in. Of the thirty-three tanks launched at sea, only two others made it to shore; the rest sank.

For three decades, those tanks sat on the bottom of the Channel. Local fishermen knew their location; the wrecks were prime fishing areas. The fishermen refused to divulge the spots until embarrassed into doing so by the local mayors, who pointed out to them that the men whose bones were inside had come over to France to liberate them and deserved a proper burial. In the past ten years, all the tanks have been pulled out, the bones buried.

Lieutenant Rockwell saved the day at Omaha. Until he got his four tanks ashore, the Germans in the casemates at the Colleville draw could and did kill everything on that beach. The descending shells from the navy could not put those cannon out of action, but the flat-trajectory shells fired upward by the tanks directly into the aperture did.

What it was like for the first wave, before the tanks came in support, is best described by S. L. A. Marshall. He has come under considerable criticism lately, some of it justified, but I carried his writings with me all summer and found them to be vivid, moving, and generally reliable.

As the first wave approached, the Germans held their fire. Survivors tell me they thought it was going to be an easy assault, that the naval and air bombardments had put the German defenders out of action. But Marshall writes (in *Atlantic Monthly,* November 1960) that at the dropping of the ramps, the beach "is instantly swept by crossing machine-gun fire from both ends." The first men out

are ripped apart before they can make five yards. Even the lightly wounded die by drowning, doomed by the waterlogging of their over-loaded packs. . . . Half of the people [in Boat No. 4] are lost to the fire or tide before anyone gets ashore. All order has vanished from Able Company before it has fired a shot.

The company is part of the 116th Infantry, 29th Division. Within minutes of its landing, "the sea runs red." Wounded men who drag themselves ashore "lie quiet from total exhaustion, only to be overtaken and killed by the onrushing tide." The few who make it to the beach untouched cannot hold, and they return to the water for cover. "Faces turned upward, so that their nostrils are out of the water, they creep toward the land at the same rate as the tide."

To get a better idea of what happened, I spent a dozen afternoons swimming off Omaha Beach. In June the water is still cold, although not bitterly so; by July it is pleasant. The tide is spectacular, alternately covering and uncovering a 1,500-foot-wide beach.

This enormous tide created all kinds of problems for the invaders, the full extent of which can be appreciated only by swimming. When the sea was running at all high—say, two- or three-foot waves—it was virtually impossible for me to stand up, even in waist-deep water, or rather what would have been waist-deep water if the sea were calm. When the waves were up, the surf would be ankle-deep as one wave washed out, over my head when the next one came on. Even on a calm day, I found it difficult to swim because of the powerful current that runs parallel to Omaha just beyond the breakers.

Another difficulty—one that nearly every survivor mentions—is the sharp drop-offs. I would swim out a couple of dozen yards, then start in. My feet would hit bottom and I'd start walking. Suddenly, I'd be over my head again. At least three of the men who have given oral histories to the Eisenhower Center swear that the Germans dug antitank trenches when the tide was out, and that the invaders fell into them. Nothing of the kind was attempted, for the obvious reason that the next incoming tide would have caved in a man-made trench. These depressions are natural, created by the tidal action, and they shift with every tide.

In short, I found it difficult to get ashore from even a short distance out, in a calm sea and wearing only a swimsuit. The men of D-Day had a moderately rough sea to deal with. In addition, their clothing had been treated with an antigas chemical that stiffened the fabric, and they were loaded down with helmets, heavy boots, rifles or mortars, grenades, ammunition, radios, and other tools of war. I now understand better why drowning was a major cause of death at Omaha Beach.

Once ashore, the invaders entered the killing zone. For the first wave, landing at dawn at low tide, it was pure hell. The Germans concentrated their fire on the GIs trying to struggle their way through the thousands of obstacles Rommel had placed on the beach. With rifle and machine-gun fire kicking up the sand, the Americans tried to crouch and run, but the weight of their waterlogged uniforms and equipment plus the wet sand made running impossible. A dozen veterans have used the same image to describe what it was like: the nightmare in which a demon is chasing you but your legs are so heavy you can't run.

Many tried to hide behind Rommel's obstacles. They were of all different types and descriptions, but the most common were six-foot sections of steel rails welded together as a tetrahedron. These only gave the illusion of protection—they were in fact often more dangerous than the open sand because they were topped with land mines. The Germans would wait until a group of GIs were behind such an obstacle, then fire at the mine to set it off.

Combat engineers coming ashore in the first waves had the job of blowing those obstacles before the tide covered them. Sergeant Vince DeNiccio of New York City told me that his toughest job was getting the men away from a tetrahedron so he could blow it up. As I made various runs across the beach, I could hear the surf and the laughter of children playing on the beach, but I had in mind what Vince had told me: The noise on the beach on June 6 was so great that he had to go up to an individual, cup his hands around the man's ear, and shout as loud as he could, "Get the hell out of here—I'm going to blow this thing!"

Shingle runs parallel to and at the edge of the sand dunes. It consists of small round stones piled up about three feet high and fifteen feet wide. Many of the GIs hit the ground on the edge of the shingle, trying to use it for protection. It didn't work; although they were then relatively safe from rifle fire, the Germans hit them with mortars. They clung there anyway, because a swamp lies between the dunes and the base of the bluff, and that swamp was full of barbed wire and land mines—and exposed to rifle fire.

I walked through the swamp with ease—today a raised, all-weather path leads through it. But when I thought of the men who decided that lying on their bellies behind the shingle, their noses in the sand, was only going to get them killed, and who then crossed the dunes, cut through the barbed wire, and started up the bluff—my admiration soared.

Looking up the bluff, I reminded myself that the brush and small trees that today make it such a lovely sight were all cut down in 1944. The bluff was crisscrossed with rifle pits and trenches, machine-gun pillboxes, and Tobruks. Barbed wire was everywhere.

The men who moved up the bluff were charging a replica of a World War I trench system: The rifle fire was intense; the machine-gun fire was interlocking; the mortars were presighted and active; the mines (which were not a feature of World War I) were everywhere. In the face of this, infantry worked their way up the bluff, got into and through the German trenches, and began pitching grenades into the pillboxes or picking off German soldiers in the Tobruks with their rifles.

Taking that bluff was one of the greatest feats in the history of the U.S. Army. The D-Day plan had been to move forward by going up the draws, at Colleville, Vierville, and Saint-Laurent. And in Darryl Zanuck's movie version of Cornelius Ryan's *The Longest Day,* that is the way it was done. In the climactic scene, a bangalore torpedo blows a gap in the barbed wire protecting the cement wall that blocks the draw. Men rush forward to place dynamite at the base of the wall. A plunger sets the explosive off; it blows a hole in the wall; GIs rush forward and up the draw. As Robert Mitchum, playing General Norman Cota, climbs into his jeep and drives up the hill, the music swells.

But climbing the bluff myself, and listening to the veterans' words on the tapes, I made a discovery: That wasn't the way it happened. The victory was won by individuals and small groups struggling up the bluff. German defenses at the draws were too strong to be breached, and had to be outflanked.

In his oral history, Lieutenant John Spaulding told how. He was leading Privates Richard Gallagher and Bruce Buck.

As we climbed, we bypassed a pillbox, from which MG fire was coming and mowing down F Company people a few hundred yards to our left. There was nothing we could do to help them. We could still see no one to the right. We didn't know what had become of the rest of our company. Back in the water, boats were in flames. After a couple of looks back, we decided we wouldn't look back anymore.

About this time Gallagher said to follow him up the defilade, which was about four hundred yards to the right of the pillbox. We were getting terrific small-arms fire. We returned fire but couldn't hit them.

When Gallagher found the way up, I sent Buck back to bring up my men. [Buck returned with four men from the section.] I couldn't take my eye off the machine gun above us, so Sergeant Bisco kept saying, "Lieutenant, watch out for the damn mines." These were a little box-type mine, and it seems that the place was infested with them, but I didn't see them. We lost no men coming through them, although H Company coming along the same trail a few hours later lost several men. The Lord was with us and we had an angel on each shoulder on that trip.

Trying to get the machine gun above us, Sergeant Blades fired his bazooka and missed. He was shot in the left arm almost immediately. Sergeant Phelps with his BAR [Browning automatic rifle] moved into position to fire and was hit in both legs. By this time practically all my section had moved up. We decided to rush the machine gun about fifteen yards away. As we rushed it, the lone German operating the gun threw up his hands and yelled "Kamerad!"

Coming up along the crest of the hill, Sergeant Clarence Colson, who had picked up a BAR on the beach, began to give assault fire as he walked along, firing the weapon from his hip. He opened up on the machine gun to our right, firing so rapidly that his ammunition carrier had difficulty getting ammo to him fast enough.

With the strength of the German defenses at Omaha, and the enemy's natural advantage due to the lay of the land, the question arises: Why on earth did Ike land there? The answer is, because he had to. Between the British right flank at Arromanches and the Carentan estuary, Omaha is the only beach available. Everywhere else, the Channel runs right up to the bluffs and cliffs, most spectacularly at Pointe du Hoc. Had the U.S. 1st and 29th divisions not gone ashore at Omaha, there would have been a twenty-five-mile gap between the British right flank and the American left flank on Utah Beach. I walked on the edge of the bluff the entire twenty-five miles and can testify that there is not a single spot, other than Omaha, where an ordinary soldier could possibly get to the top.

I say "ordinary" because at Pointe du Hoc soldiers did make it from the base of the cliff to the top, but they were Rangers, elite troops specially trained and especially brave. The men of Colonel James Earl Rudder's 2nd Ranger Battalion scaled the cliffs using one of the oldest implements of war, the grappling hook. Looking at the vertical cliff today, with the sea dashing against the base, it just seems impossible that men could get up it under the best of conditions. Indeed, I had the best of conditions: I was determined to experience as much of the physical challenge of D-Day as I could. I wanted to secure a rope at the top of the cliff, then descend and climb back up it. But I didn't make it. I chickened out. Rudder's men did make it, carrying 60 to 100 pounds of equipment on their backs, despite German defenders firing down on them, dropping grenades over the edge, and cutting the climbing ropes attached to the grappling hooks.

For me, Pointe du Hoc is one of the premier World War II battlefields, not because it was the most important but because there is no better place in Normandy to see the scars and destruction of battle. The German fortifications rival the great World War I fortress at Douaumont north of Verdun. The steel-reinforced concrete casemates protecting the 155mm cannon are at least six feet thick. The casemates are connected by extensive tunnels that contain an underground railroad.

These casemates were pounded by 500-pound blockbusters dropped by the bombers and by huge shells from the 14-inch guns on British and American battleships. They were hit by thousands of tons of high explosive, equal to two or three tactical atomic weapons. The results were devastating. The place reminded me of Stonehenge on the Salisbury Plain, except that these stones are fortifications blasted apart, lying at all angles. The bomb craters are huge.

The D-Day veterans are careful to tell me that in many cases the German defenders were inferior troops. That was not so at Pointe du Hoc, where the Germans in the ruins kept fighting for two and a half days, inflicting nearly 75 percent casualties on Rudder's Rangers. In other areas, however, and especially at Utah Beach, the German soldiers surrendered at the first opportunity. In most cases, this was because they were not German but Poles, Russians, French, Belgians, and others forced into the Wehrmacht after capture in 1940 or 1941. There were thousands of such conscripts.

Some German units did fight effectively. Some fought magnificently. At Saint Marcouf, about six miles north of Utah Beach, I found a tremendous German emplacement—four enormous casemates, each housing a 205mm cannon. I had read about the emplacement but had not previously been able to locate it. Those guns got into a duel with American battleships on D-Day and sank one destroyer. American infantry surrounded them on D-Day plus one. To hold the Americans off, the German commander called down fire from another battery some nine miles to the north, right on top of his own position. That, plus the pounding from American ships, kept the Americans at bay for more than a week while the German cannon continued to fire on Utah Beach. The Germans surrendered when they ran out of ammunition.

Walking on top of the fortresses, I could see innumerable direct hits, all from big shells. They made little more than dents in the concrete. Crawling around inside, I marveled at the fortitude of the German gunners: the noise, the vibrations, the dust shaking loose, the terror they must have felt, along with bad water, stale bread, and no separate place to relieve themselves—and for nine days they kept firing.

Sainte-Mère-Eglise, a small village about six miles inland from Utah Beach, rivals Pointe du Hoc for fame, thanks in large part to Zanuck's movie. The director took considerable liberties with the truth here, too, making the firefight in the square at Sainte-Mère-Eglise into a much bigger thing than it was. His most memorable scene, however—the one in which trooper John Steel (Red Buttons in the movie) caught his chute on the church steeple and hung there for hours playing dead—Zanuck underplayed. I know, because I got the full story from trooper Ken Russell of the 82nd Airborne.

Ken was a seventeen-year-old then. As he was coming down, he saw three buddies land on telephone poles around the square: "It was like they were crucified there." Next to him, another trooper had his grenades on his hip. A tracer bullet hit the grenades "and instantaneously there was just an empty parachute coming down."

Standing in the square years later, I listened to Ken on the tape describe what happened next. There was a fire in the hay barn across the street, caused by tracers.

> The heat drew the nylon chutes toward the fire. The air to feed the fire was actually drawing us towards the fire. One guy, I heard him scream, I saw him land in the fire. I heard him scream one more time before he hit the fire, and he didn't scream anymore.

In the middle of the square is a Norman church. Ken jerked his suspension lines to avoid the fire, and as a result came down on the church's steep slate roof. He slid. His chute caught on a steeple. He was hanging there when "John Steele came down, and his chute caught too." Sergeant John Ray floated down past them. Ken says:

> He hit in front of the church. A Nazi soldier, billeted on the next street behind the church, came around from behind, a red-haired German soldier. He came to shoot Steele and myself, hanging there. As he came around, he shot Ray in the stomach. John being a sergeant, he had a forty-five pistol and while he was dying in agony, he got his forty-five out and when this German soldier turned around to kill us, John shot the German in the back of the head and killed him.

Where the barn burned down, there is today the Parachute Museum, run by Phil Jutras, a World War II veteran who was a politician in Maine until 1972, when he decided to leave what he calls the "American rat race" and retire to this quiet Norman village. He married a local widow and began helping out at the small museum. Soon he became director. He has expanded it to include a C-47, a Waco glider, a tank, some artillery, a movie (in French and English), and, at the entrance, a full-scale model of a paratrooper.

Phil introduced me to locals who have filled me in on the events of

1944 at Sainte-Mère-Eglise. Over the years he has also passed on other stories he has heard from the veterans who come to see him and has guided me to many sites, such as General Matthew Ridgway's command post and General James Gavin's foxhole. For this portion of the story, I have also relied heavily on S. L. A. Marshall's *Night Drop*. It is a book full of marvelous maps. A bit fanciful, it has been criticized by paratroopers and scholars. Nevertheless, I recommend it as the best and most vivid account of the action.

Confusion and chaos marked the night drop, and thus the after-action reports and later oral histories are contradictory. I have great sympathy for Marshall in his attempt to put together an authoritative account of a complex series of small actions.

At La Fiere, Captain Ben Schwartzwalder (later famous as the football coach at Syracuse) of the 507th Parachute Infantry Regiment led forty-four men on a maneuver to capture a manor house next to a bridge over the Merderet River. Using football analogies, Marshall details the action minute-by-minute. Following step-by-step, I held my breath—figuratively—as I moved along beside a hedge and turned a corner. The manor loomed before me, the barns and house joined by connecting stone walls higher than a man.

"Held for downs, Schwartzwalder took time out," Marshall relates. On the other side of the road, "Slim Jim Gavin arrived on the scene, in the van of his band of 300." Unable to see through the hedgerow, Gavin was unaware of Schwartzwalder's party, and he moved on.

I was trying to penetrate the hedge, to get a better fix on the positions of the American units, when I got hit by a foe that made further movement impossible. That foe is present in all the hedgerows and is mentioned by nearly all airborne veterans, but it is so commonplace that it makes almost none of the books. Nettles—they sting like fury. They cause a rash that lasts, a burning that is painful and maddening, and there is no remedy but time. In this one instance I had it worse than the men of D-Day, because their bodies were covered except for hands and faces, whereas I was wearing only a T-shirt and Bermuda shorts.

Everyone knows how the GIs cursed those hedgerows, even beyond the nettles, and what a barrier they were to offensive action, but you cannot appreciate why until you have seen them and tried to crawl through one. They dominate the terrain, making each tiny field a minia-ture fortress. They are anywhere from four to ten feet high and have only one gate, too narrow for a tank. The Germans set up their heavy machine guns in the two corners away from the gate, and pre-positioned mortar and artillery fire on the middle of the field. In the first days of the Battle of Normandy, the Germans would let unsuspecting GIs get into the field, then hit them with interlocking machine-gun, mortar, and artillery fire.

One solution was to use dynamite to blast a hole in the hedge, then ram a tank into the hole and fire white phosphorous shells point-blank at the machine-gun positions. Another was to weld short sections of steel rails onto the front of a tank, then drive it into the hedge. The rails kept the Shermans from going belly-up. Here and there I thought I could see where a Sherman tank had penetrated a hedge, but after forty-five years I couldn't be positive.

All along the French coast from Brest to Belgium and beyond, there are extensive German permanent emplacements. They range from small field fortifications to massive blockhouses that brought to my mind the Great Wall of China or the Maginot Line. Built by millions of French slave laborers, they are unpleasant to look at, squat, gray, forbidding, in many cases their cannon still pointed out at the Channel.

The juxtaposition of these fortifications with the lovely Norman sea-side—the villages, the cathedrals, the châteaus, the cattle and horses, and the friendly people—struck us hard. It is a sad and futile thing that the Germans spent four years putting prodigious effort into building projects that are now only symbols of ugliness, fear, and hate.

They paid for their offenses against the French people. We saw the consequences at Longues-sur-Mer, just outside Port-en-Bessin, where the Germans built a four-gun battery, set back about three-fifths of a mile from an observation post on the edge of the bluff. Each 155mm cannon had its own casemate, built of steel-reinforced concrete about nine feet thick. The guns had a range of more than twelve miles and were thus capable of firing on both Omaha Beach to the west and the British Gold Beach to the east. On D-Day, however, they were mainly involved in fighting duels with cruisers and battleships offshore. HMS *Ajax,* already famous for sinking the *Graf Spee* in December 1939 off the River Plate, put three of the guns out of action.

The Royal Navy scored many direct hits on the casemates, but as at Pointe du Hoc and elsewhere, the damage was relatively slight. Even the biggest naval shells could not penetrate the concrete. To do any effective damage, the shells had to come right through the relatively narrow—ten feet at most—aperture, almost impossible with high-trajectory shells. Still, the *Ajax* did it. How?

I got the answer from André Heintz, one of the founders of the new D-Day museum in Caen. At age seventeen in 1944, he was a member of the French resistance. André told me that when the Germans built the battery, they took away a farmer's best field. The farmer wanted to fight back, and figured out a way to do so.

He had a teenage son who was blind. Like many blind people, the boy had a fabulous memory. The farmer filled his mind with details about the location of the guns—so many meters back from the bluff, so many meters from the crossroads, so many meters between the case-mates, and much more. Because the boy was blind, the Germans paid little attention to him, hardly glancing at his papers, allowing him to travel more or less freely.

The boy journeyed to Bayeux, where he relayed the information to André Heintz. With his primitive, handmade radio set (now on display in the Caen museum), André sent the information on to England. From air reconnaissance and local resistance informants, the Allies already knew that there were emplacements on the bluff at Longues-sur-Mer, but they did not have the exact coordinates. Thanks to the farmer and his son, on D-Day they did.

But even with perfect intelligence and brilliant shooting, there was luck involved in the *Ajax*'s victory. Two of the guns were put out of ac-tion by shells that burst on the edge of the aperture, damaging the mounting and making the cannon immobile. With the third gun, the shell came right through the aperture and burst inside.

The Germans were great at conquering, terrible at occupying. They had an opportunity in France to play on traditional anti-British feelings, heightened by the British withdrawal from the Battle of France in June 1940, and on French fears of communism, to bring the French in on the new German order in Europe. Instead, they acted like beasts. The result was the French resistance, without which victory on D-Day would scarcely have been possible. That, at least, was Eisenhower's judgment: He once told me the resistance was worth five divisions on D-Day.

The British and Canadian beaches—Gold, Sword, and Juno—are not so evocative of D-Day as Omaha and Utah, except at Arromanches, where the cement breakwaters for the artificial harbors can still be seen, and where the museum displays models that show how the system worked. The coast from Arromanches to Ouistreham at the mouth of the Orne River is a traditional vacation spot for the French middle class. Small cottages and shops now cover what was the battlefield. But by staying in small hotels or bed-and-breakfast places, we got to meet people who were there forty-five years earlier, and each of them had a story to tell.

On the morning of D-Day, Jacqueline Noel, seventeen years old, pedaled her bike down to the beach at Ouistreham. She wanted to help. Because she was a nurse wearing a red-cross armband, the Germans did not stop her. On the beach, she worked with the medics. She told me a story that made the sheer scope of D-Day vivid for me in a way that little else could.

About midmorning an Allied bomber was hit. Burning, it began descending in circles. "Everybody started watching," she said, "Germans and British alike. It was obvious that the pilot was trying to find some open piece of water where he could safely ditch his plane. I looked at that armada of landing craft, LSTs, and all the rest, and could not see how he could ever find a place to land. The beach was so jammed with men, guns, and vehicles that it, too, was impossible." Sure enough, the bomber crashed into an LCT.

We were sitting on the beach as she told me the story. The Channel was all but covered with French kids windsurfing, hundreds of them. Jacqueline said there were more landing craft on D-Day than windsurfers that day.

On the beach, she had met Lieutenant John Thornton. She got to know him better in the days that followed. After the war, they married; he took a job as a shipping clerk for a British steamship line, and they lived in Ouistreham. I discovered five other couples who met on D-Day, three British and two American, all still married.

John Thornton told a story that gave me a sense of the ferocity of the battle. He was an artilleryman. On D-Day plus five, he was riding a bike past an artillery park in an open field, a few miles inland. The guns had been firing constantly for three days. Suddenly, on signal, they all ceased firing at once. He was so stunned by the quiet—the first he had experienced since June 6—that he fell off his bike into a ditch, where he lay looking up at a clear blue sky. A lark flew over his head and sang.

Praise the Lord, he thought to himself. *Life goes on.*

And so it does. Normandy endures. Except for the military cemeteries and the German fortifications, it is not much different from the way it was a half century ago. The cream, the cheese, the seafood, the cider remain the best in the world. You sense the presence of William the Conqueror and the Normans in every church, in every village square, in every 1,000-year-old farmhouse or manor. Standing on the bluff looking down on Omaha Beach, or among the sand dunes behind Utah Beach, or among the hedgerows around the Sainte-Mère-Eglise, you can also sense the ghosts of the men who died there on D-Day.

VICTORY IN EUROPE

May 1945

V−E Day, 1945, was the occasion for the greatest outburst of joy in human history. Indeed, except for the Japanese and a few fanatic Nazis, everyone in the world was overjoyed. The end of the war was the single best thing that could happen to every person alive in 1945.

Yet this great occasion brought on recrimination, division, and bitterness among the governments and people of the Western Alliance. The reason for this development was the failure of the Anglo-American armies to take Berlin. Many people at the time, from Prime Minister Winston Churchill on down, and including General Bernard Montgomery and General George Patton, urged Allied Supreme Commander Dwight D. Eisenhower to make an all-out effort to take the German capital before the Red Army got there, but he refused.

As time passed, the issue grew rather than receded in importance and divisiveness, because in the first two decades of the Cold War Berlin was the centerpiece in the struggle between East and West. Senator Joe McCarthy and his friends charged that President Franklin Roosevelt had committed treason at Yalta in early 1945 when he gave Berlin and central Europe to the Soviet Union. Less partisan critics charged that Eisenhower had been naive. Most everyone agreed that at a minimum a great mistake had been made.

To say that Eisenhower made a mistake implies that he could have gotten Anglo-American troops into the city before the Red Army got there, and that had he done so things would have been different in the Cold War, meaning that Berlin would have been in West Germany rather than East Germany. Both assumptions are wrong.

It is commonly said that the United States fought World War II in a simpleminded way, that military considerations always overrode political factors. The concentration was on winning the war rather than winning the peace, so while we did a good job of defeating the Germans we did a poor job of establishing our position for the Cold War. That is also wrong.

Politics and diplomacy played a major role in shaping the strategy of the campaign in northwest Europe, 1944–45, for the obvious reason that the attacking force included troops from many nations, each of which had its own self-interest to protect. It is the nature of a coalition command that the members can only agree on the negative—in this case, get rid of Hitler. There was nothing else holding the United States and the Soviet Union together, and really not much more holding together the United States, Great Britain, the Free French, the Poles, the Norwegians and others in Eisenhower's great crusade.

"Give me allies to fight against," said Napoleon.

"The only thing worse than fighting with allies," said Churchill, "is fighting without them."

In the First World War, effective coalition command was not achieved until the crisis of the spring of 1918 and the Ludendorff Offensives, when Marshal Foch was made the supreme commander. In World War II, the British and Americans agreed on unified commands at the outset, giving the theater commander full operational command of all the forces in the theater. It comes very hard to nations to put their troops under the command of a general from another nation, but it was done successfully in the Anglo-American-French-Canadian alliance during 1944–45.

The structure of the situation meant that Supreme Commander Eisenhower became the focal point for every difference in opinion between the nations in the coalition. Because he gave the orders, the political leader of each nation in the alliance, most of all Winston Churchill and Charles de Gaulle, sought to influence Eisenhower's decisions. How this worked out in practice and its effect on the end of the war in Europe is my subject here.

Politics went into Eisenhower's selection as supreme commander, of course. British generals had been at war longer and could claim to know the German enemy better, and Brooke and Montgomery certainly wanted the job, but with the United States making the largest contribution of men and material the commander had to be an American. Of Eisenhower's positive attributes, the two that stood out were his ability to get men of different nationalities to work together on a single team and his own devotion to the alliance.

During the first five months of 1944, as the mighty host planned, trained and otherwise prepared for the invasion, there were few disagreements among the major allies. This was in sharp contrast to the summer of 1942, when they had argued loudly and continuously over forthcoming operations. The British had wanted to go into North Africa and the Mediterranean, while the Americans had wanted to cross the channel and drive through France to Germany. The British thought the Americans were daft; the Americans thought the British were only interested in strengthening their position in the Middle East and maintaining their lifeline to India, and that they were afraid of the Wehrmacht.

But in 1944, the Anglo-Americans were agreed on the scope of the offensive and on the time and place of the opening attack.

That agreement had not come easily, however. Almost to D-Day, the British remained reluctant partners, fearful that their army would be bled white in France for the second time in a generation. In January 1944, Churchill told Eisenhower, "When I think of the beaches of Normandy choked with the flower of American and British youth . . . I have my doubts . . . I have my doubts."

In early May, Eisenhower had lunch alone with Churchill. As they were parting, the prime minister said, with tears in his eyes, "I am in this thing with you to the end, and if it fails we will go down together." On May 15, however, following the final briefing, Churchill told Eisenhower, "I am hardening toward this enterprise." One must say that was a bit late to be getting on the team.

Three weeks later, D-Day was a great success. In the days that followed, however, the battle did not go well. There was no breaking out of the bridgehead; the Germans had imposed a stalemate.

Montgomery was the ground commander under Eisenhower, and the senior British officer on the continent, under General Alan Brooke and Churchill. That divided responsibility put a severe strain on the relations between Ike and Monty. It was inevitable that the two men would have difficulty working together anyway, because their personalities were so different. Monty was a little man, in his actions as well as his stature. Ike was a big man. Monty irritated almost everyone; nearly everyone liked Ike. But more important than personality differences was their fundamental disagreement over strategy and tactics, caused by their different positions.

Eisenhower wanted to attack, all along the line; like Grant in the Wilderness campaign, he knew that if he kept the pressure on the Germans they would have to crack. Monty wanted to get the Germans "off balance." The British had neither the manpower nor the materiel resources to overwhelm the Germans. Their strength was brains, not brawn. Monty proposed to defeat the Germans in France by outthinking and outmaneuvering them; Eisenhower wanted to outfight them.

The British had reached the bottom of the manpower barrel. The U.S. Army was still growing. Monty wanted to avoid casualties at almost any cost ("bring back as many of the chaps as you can"); to the Americans, Montgomery's caution was excessive and sure to cost more lives in the end, because fighting the war his way would take forever.

In July 1944, as the stalemate in Normandy went on, anxious senior members of Eisenhower's staff, including several British officers—most importantly, Eisenhower's deputy, Air Vice Marshal Arthur Tedder—urged him to fire Monty. They argued that he was bogged down and never would mount a serious attack on Caen.

But Eisenhower realized that firing Monty was out of the question. Monty was immensely popular with the British troops and the British public. Anyway, Eisenhower had no right to remove the senior British commander. Only Brooke could do that, and he was a strong supporter of Montgomery. Churchill didn't like Monty all that much, but he would never agree to Monty's removal. Eisenhower sometimes seemed to be the only man at Supreme Headquarters to recognize these obvious truths. He knew he had to put up with Monty, to cooperate with this difficult and exasperating general, because Monty's place in the command structure was secure.

At the end of July, the Americans broke out at St. Lo. The Germans retreated out of Normandy, taking frightful casualties. Even in victory, there was disagreement between the Americans and the British over Monty's failure to close the Falaise gap, but it was Churchill who caused one of the worst arguments between the Allies in the war. It was over Anvil, the landing in the south of France, scheduled for mid-August. Churchill was dead set against Anvil; he wanted to use the troops (about half American, half French) in Italy and the Adriatic. His idea was to advance on Germany through the so-called soft underbelly. When Eisenhower refused, Churchill appealed to Roosevelt. The president supported Ike. He told Churchill, "For purely political reasons over here, I should never survive even a slight setback in Overlord if it were known that fairly large forces had been diverted to the Balkans."

Churchill went after Ike again. On August 4 he asked to shift Anvil (which he had renamed Dragoon, on the grounds that he had been dragooned into it) from Marseilles to Brest. His idea was that Brest would require fewer troops so that offensive operations in Italy and the Adriatic could be continued. Eisenhower said no.

Churchill increased the pressure. A week before Dragoon was set to go, he spent a day with the supreme commander. Ike later described the session as the most difficult of the entire war. Churchill accused the United States of taking the role of a "big, strong and dominating partner." He complained that Eisenhower was indifferent to British interests. Eisenhower denied it.

Churchill tried tears. He tried shouting. He tried threats, telling Eisenhower at one point that if he did not have his way, "I might have to go to the king and lay down the mantle of my high office."

After the war, right-wing critics of the Roosevelt administration charged that the United States had fought in a terribly shortsighted way. They claimed that had the Americans followed Churchill, Allied forces would have gotten into Germany from the Balkans and thus prevented the Red Army from taking over Central Europe. In fact, according to Eisenhower, the opposite would have happened. In 1943 he had told Brooke that if the Allies didn't cross the channel and liberate France, that if they stayed in the Mediterranean and Adriatic, then the Red Army would march across Germany, through France all the way to the English Channel. The Anglo-Americans would end up with Italy and Yugoslavia, while the Soviets would get Western Europe.

In his acrimonious meeting with Churchill, Eisenhower stated the obvious. He said that if Churchill's motives were political, if he thought that abandoning Dragoon would somehow help prevent a Red Army occupation of Eastern and Central Europe, then he ought to lay his case before Roosevelt. Only Roosevelt could make such a political decision.

Churchill knew how much American soldiers disliked admitting to "political" motives, which were somehow construed as tainted, and insisted on making decisions on strictly military grounds, which were thought to be straightforward. He insisted that he had no political objectives. The correct military policy, he said, was to avoid a sterile campaign in the south of France and push on in Italy and the Adriatic. Eisenhower said he was wrong and refused to change the plan.

The distinction between military and political considerations, which Eisenhower made on a number of occasions, was a false one. On the strategic level, with entire armies involved, the two considerations merged into one. Ike never hesitated to use political arguments to support his military decisions. Thus on this occasion he reminded Churchill that the American government had gone to great expense to equip and supply a number of French divisions, that de Gaulle was most anxious to have them fight in France, and that the only way they could be brought into the battle was through Marseilles.

Dragoon went forward. So did the Allied forces in northern France. Paris was liberated and the Germans were on the run.

At the beginning of September, Ike crossed to the continent, set up his headquarters, and took command of the land battle. Monty fiercely resented this and fought against it. Churchill tried to soften the blow by promoting Monty to field marshal, but what Monty wanted was command, not a baton. He thought Ike ought to handle the politics while he fought the war. He was almost contemptuous of Ike's military abilities and had a grossly exaggerated idea of his own.

But he wasn't alone. Nearly all the British press and many of the politicians were equally resentful of the change in command. What they were objecting to was a historic fact they didn't want to face: Britain was no longer an equal partner in the alliance.

There had been a time when she had stood alone and made the sole contribution to the defeat of Hitler. In 1942 and 1943 she had been the senior member of the partnership, providing more fighting forces than the Americans. In the first half of 1944, the contribution from each nation was roughly equal. But by September 1944, the Americans were putting in two GIs for every Tommy, even while supplying the British army and people with weapons and goods, and by November there were three GIs for every Tommy. America had become a superpower, while Britain hardly ranked as even a great power. Eisenhower's taking command of the land battle symbolized the shift.

As the Allied forces approached the German border, Monty presented Ike with a plan that he claimed would ensure a quick victory. He proposed to cut through what remained of the German lines in a single thrust by his 21st Army Group through Belgium, over the Rhine, and straight on to Berlin.

Patton, to the south, also had a plan. He proposed to attack straight east from Paris, cross the Rhine, and drive straight on to Berlin. Each man told Ike that if he were given all the other one's supplies he would guarantee to be in Berlin before Christmas.

Eisenhower, in command, thought they were guilty of badly underestimating German recuperative powers. He believed, rightly, as time showed, that the Germans still had a lot of fight left in them and that so long as Hitler was alive they would stick to their guns. He therefore decided to advance on a broad front, all armies abreast.

The personality and political factors in Ike's decision for a broad front are obvious. Patton was pulling one way, Monty the other; each man was insistent and certain of his own military genius; both were accustomed to having their own way. Behind each man was his nation's adoring public, who had made Patton and Monty into symbols of military prowess. In Ike's view, to give one or the other the glory would have serious repercussions, not just the howls of agony from the press and public of the nation left behind, but in the very fabric of the alliance itself. Ike feared it could not survive the resulting uproar. It was too big a chance to take, especially on such a risky operation. Eisenhower never considered taking it.

The Allied armies closed on the German border. In mid-December, the Wehrmacht launched a furious counteroffensive in the Ardennes. The shock and the initial setbacks put another severe strain on the alliance. In this instance, it wasn't just Monty vs. Patton, or British interests competing with American interests, but also the Franco-American alliance in a classic clash of diplomatic, political and military factors. The dispute is so instructive it deserves a bit of detail.

Eisenhower needed replacements in the Ardennes. To the south, the American and French troops who had come ashore in Operation Dragoon had taken Strasbourg. Ike figured that if he pulled back from Strasbourg and otherwise shortened his line in the south, he could free up troops for the Ardennes. He ordered it done. Since the order involved French troops, de Gaulle found out and immediately protested. He said the French government could not possibly abandon Strasbourg: for one thing, the Gestapo would butcher every member of the Resistance who had come out of hiding after the liberation of the city; for another, French public opinion would not stand for it.

Eisenhower told de Gaulle that he, too, was concerned about the fate of French citizens in Alsace, but added that he was grateful to de Gaulle "for indicating that you share my views from the military point of view." De Gaulle shot back, "Nothing of what you have been told from me can make you think that from the military point of view I approve of your views. I should tell you frankly that the truth is just the opposite."

Ike went to a map to show de Gaulle why the line-shortening was necessary. De Gaulle cut in: "If were at Kriegaspiel I should say you were right, but I must consider the matter from another point of view. Retreat in Alsace would be a national disaster."

The two generals threatened each other. De Gaulle said he would have to remove the French army (now two divisions strong) from Eisenhower's command. Ike countered that if he did so, Supreme Headquarters would stop the flow of supplies to the French.

De Gaulle could escalate, too. He told Ike that if the supplies to the French were cut, then all the British and American lines of communications—which ran through France—would be in jeopardy.

Ike gave in. He canceled the order to withdraw from Strasbourg. Churchill told him, "I think you've done the wise and proper thing."

Eisenhower hated giving in, hated putting politics first, but he was sensible enough to do it. He wasn't happy. "The French continue to be difficult," he complained to Marshall. "I must say that next to the weather I think they have caused me more trouble in this war than any other single factor." Thinking all the way back to the darkest days of December 1941 and putting the French in perspective, he added, "They even rank above landing craft."

The same day that Ike met with de Gaulle and Churchill, January 3, 1945, Montgomery finally launched a counterattack in the Bulge—Eisenhower had wanted to attack a week earlier, but Monty waited until everything was ready. The trouble with Monty's caution was that it allowed the Germans to pull their tanks out of the Bulge and bring them back to the Rhine, to fight another day. Worse, Monty attacked at the tip of the salient, instead of the base; rather than cutting off the Germans, he forced them to fall back—to fight another day.

Patton was furious. Had it not been for Monty, who was claiming credit for a great victory—seen by the Americans as a missed opportunity—Patton wrote in his diary, "We could have bagged the whole German army. I wish Ike were more of a gambler, but he is certainly a lion compared to Montgomery. Monty is a tired little fart. War requires the taking of risks and he won't take them."

Thus did 1945 get off to a bad start for alliance politics. It was going to get worse.

In March, the Allied armies closed to and crossed the Rhine River.

The last campaign was under way; it would bring on the greatest controversy of World War II between the British and the Americans. Eisenhower's last wartime decision, and the one for which he has been most heavily criticized, was the decision to leave Berlin to the Red Army while directing his last offensive toward Dresden, Bavaria, Austria and the Alps.

By the end of March, with the Allies over the Rhine, Churchill, Brooke, Montgomery and the British public wanted to make an all-out effort to take Berlin, with Monty's 21st Army Group leading the way. But Eisenhower resisted their pressure. He refused to get into the race with the Red Army for the honor of capturing Berlin, whether by British or U.S. troops.

His reasons were many. He doubted that either Montgomery or General William Simpson, commanding the U.S. Ninth Army, could get to Berlin before the Red Army overran it. He expected the Germans to fight so long as Hitler was alive, and he anticipated fearful casualties in street-to-street fighting in Berlin. He asked Bradley what he thought the cost would be; Bradley guessed one hundred thousand men and commented, "A pretty stiff price to pay for a prestige objective, especially when we're got to fall back and let the other fellow take over." (Berlin was well within the occupation zone already assigned to the Russians at the Yalta Conference.)

Still, Churchill pressed. On the last day of March he wired Eisenhower, "Why should we not cross the Elbe and advance as far eastward as possible? This has an important political bearing, as the Russian Army of the south seems certain to enter Vienna." He urged Eisenhower to put Simpson under Montgomery so that a strengthened 21st Army Group could attack Berlin. Such an operation, Churchill said, "avoids the relegation of His Majesty's Forces to an unexpected restricted sphere."

What he meant was that while the Americans were taking Bavaria and Hitler's Eagle Nest and the Red Army was taking Berlin, the British would be liberating Denmark—hardly the glorious ending they had hoped for of their greatest war, but still, as Eisenhower told Churchill, an important political objective because it would keep the Red Army out of Denmark. In other words, Eisenhower feared that if Monty went straight east after crossing the Elbe on the direct road to Berlin, the Red Army to the north would take Lubeck and Hamsburg, thus occupying Denmark and controlling access to the Scandinavian countries.

Churchill accepted Eisenhower's decision and the reasons for it, but still grumbled, "I deem it highly important that we should shake hands with the Russians as far to the east as possible."

And Montgomery continued to disagree. When Eisenhower said Berlin had lost its military importance, as the various war ministries had gone south to the mountains, Monty rejoined, "I consider that Berlin has definite value as an objective and I have no doubt whatever that the Russians think the same; but they may well pretend that this is not the case!"

For once Patton agreed with Monty. He thought Eisenhower was passing up a historic opportunity. "Ike, I don't see how you figure this one. We had better take Berlin and quick." So when General Simpson got a bridgehead over the Elbe River at Magdeburg on April 13, there were insistent calls for Ike to let him march onto Berlin.

Eisenhower wouldn't budge. He felt that taking Lubeck in the north and occupying the Alpine redoubt area to the south were tasks "vastly more important than the capture of Berlin." As the Russians had more than a million men already poised to attack Berlin, while Simpson had only spearheads over the Elbe, with no forward airfields to provide air cover, Eisenhower still doubted that the Americans could get there first. In any case the zones of occupation were already established, and the Americans and British were scheduled to have their own zones in Berlin when the shooting stopped.

In its essence the controversy was not so much over how to defeat Germany quickly as it was over postwar attitudes toward the Soviets. Churchill was deeply suspicious of Stalin's intentions; Eisenhower, and above him, Marshall and Roosevelt, were also suspicious but much more hopeful than the prime minister about the possibility of getting along with the Soviets after the war as they had during it.

This became clear in the related controversy over taking Prague. By April 25 Patton's Third Army reached the Czech border. He wanted

Prague. Churchill and his generals wanted him to get it. They felt there would be "remarkable political advantages derived from liberation of Prague and as much as possible of Czechoslovakia by U.S.–U.K. forces."

Marshall passed these views on to Eisenhower, commenting, "Personally and aside from all logistic, tactical, or strategical implications I would be loath to hazard American lives for purely political purposes."

Eisenhower replied, "I shall *not* attempt any move I deem militarily unwise merely to gain a political prize." So when the Red Army generals asked Eisenhower to hold Patton's forces at the Czech border, for fear of a clash between the friendly forces, Eisenhower agreed. He thus left Prague and most of Czechoslovakia to the Soviet forces. He held to this position even when the Czechs in Prague rose up against the Germans and, over captured radios, specifically asked the Western Allies for help.

What on earth was going on here? demanded the British and many Americans. Churchill wanted to get tough with the Russians, not meekly give in to their requests. Montgomery meanwhile was stacking the arms of the Germans surrendering by the droves to him in such a way that the Wehrmacht could be quickly rearmed if it came to a fight between the West and Russia; Patton was talking wildly about using the great American army in Europe, while it was still there, to drive the Red Army back to Moscow, fighting side by side with the Wehrmacht. Herein lay the seeds of NATO, dominated by a German-American military alliance.

Eisenhower, in 1945, regarded such an alliance as irresponsible and self-defeating. He advocated, instead, making every effort to cooperate with the Russians to build a better world.

His reasons were manifold. There was, most immediately, his hatred for the Germans, who had made him destroy their country, whose concentration camps were just being liberated, and which he visited. Never having been to the Soviet Union, he could not in his wildest dreams imagine that anything remotely like the Nazi concentration camps could exist there. In the spring of 1945, he felt that, while the Nazis were beyond redemption, the Communists were not, and that, while one could not conceive of a genuine, working alliance with the Germans, such an alliance with the Russians was both possible and necessary.

Eisenhower believed that war had become too destructive to be acceptable to a civilized world any longer. Another system had to be found. He had seen the destruction; he felt personally involved to the greatest possible degree, as he was the one who gave the orders that sent tens of thousands of young men to their deaths. He desperately wanted a better world to emerge from the ashes, a world without an arms race, without great powers rattling sabers, without hostile alliances directed against one another. He wanted a world of cooperation, not confrontation. It was certainly a utopian view, but, following the greatest war in history, no other attitude made sense to him.

One key to building the world he sought was plain and simple good will on both sides. Eisenhower was eager to do his part. That was the real reason, above all others, that he left Berlin and Prague to the Russians. For all his constant insistence on military rather than political factors, he avoided the two capitals for the most obvious of political reasons—he wanted good relations with the Russians. They wanted the honor of taking Berlin: they felt they deserved it; Eisenhower did not disagree. Nothing, he felt, would have gotten American-Soviet postwar relations off to a worse start than to engage in a race for Berlin. He wanted to work with the Russians, not compete with them.

Six months later, after trying to get along with the Soviets in the Allied Control Council, Eisenhower had changed his position considerably. If he hadn't given up, he was far more pessimistic about the future of U.S.–Soviet relations. By the time he became president, in January 1953, the Cold War was well under way. During his years in the White House, Berlin gave Eisenhower too many problems, too many headaches. So, did he ever regret not sending Simpson to Berlin and Patton to Prague?

No. In his view the only difference it made about who took Berlin was to the men who fought the battle. The Russians lost one hundred thousand men. (When I was at a Soviet-American conference of military historians in Moscow in 1988, the leading Soviet delegates—some of them veterans from the war—were vigorous in their denunciation of

Stalin for ordering the attacks. They felt that if the city had been surrounded, it would have been forced to surrender in a week or two, and they charged that only Stalin wanted the prestige so badly that he sacrificed splendid soldiers in such numbers.)

And for what did the Soviets take such casualties? Less than a month after the battle, they gave up half the city to the British and Americans—who had not lost one man in Berlin. Had the Americans smashed their way into Berlin, those would have been American casualties (during the 1952 campaign, Eisenhower asked for a volunteer to pick the one hundred thousand mothers whose sons would have been sacrificed for Berlin). No one contends that had the Americans, or the British, taken Berlin, they would have gone back on their signed agreements with the Russians and kept them out of the city.

My own conclusion is that Eisenhower was right to stay away from Berlin, and that whatever he said to the contrary, his reasons were political; he acted at least partly to try to get along with Soviets, but mainly to avoid unnecessary casualties—which in the end is a political, not a military reason.

So let us not recriminate over how the war ended. It was a glorious victory. The utter destruction of Nazism was the supreme accomplishment of the first half of the twentieth century.

The supreme accomplishment of the second half of the century was the relegation of Communism in Europe to the ash heap of history. It took a long time, but let us thank God every day that it did not take a shooting war with the Soviet Union—which surely would have surpassed even World War II as the greatest catastrophe of all time.

THE ATOMIC BOMB
AND ITS CONSEQUENCES

From beginning to end the Japanese-American war in the Pacific was waged with a barbarism and race hatred that was staggering in scope, savage almost beyond belief, and catastrophic in consequence. Each side regarded the other as subhuman vermin. They called each other beasts, roaches, rats, monkeys and worse. Atrocities abounded, committed by individuals, by units, by entire armies, by governments. Quarter was neither asked nor given. It was a descent into hell.

Yet literally within days of the end of the war the two sides shook hands and became partners. All had not been forgotten, much less forgiven, but Japanese and Americans alike came to the realization that the other side was human and that cooperation in construction was infinitely superior to demonic destruction.

By contrast, the race hatred that characterized the Pacific war was absent in the German-American war. How could there be racism in a war that pitted German soldiers who had American cousins against American soldiers who had German parents? Fully one-third of the U.S. Army was German in origin. Nevertheless the reconciliation between Germany and the United States took longer than the reconciliation between Japan and the United States.

One reason for this phenomenon was that the wartime stereotypes held by Japanese and Americans broke down immediately upon contact. Americans were not apes, Japanese were not monkeys; Americans were not raping Japanese girls as had been predicted by the desperate Japanese government, and the Japanese people (as opposed to their militarist government) yearned for peace, contrary to the image the Americans had been given from Japanese government-controlled radio.

There was a more important reason. It was the use of atomic bombs. It is ironic that this violently destructive act, which one would have thought would have set race against race more than any other, in fact made two critical contributions to the surrender and the remarkably quick breakdown of racial hatred. The first was to give the Japanese army a way to surrender without shame; the second was to satisfy the American people's rage for revenge. These immediate results are seldom brought into the debate about the decision to use the bomb.

The moral atmosphere in which that decision was made was deplorable. Life came very cheap in the summer of 1945. The fighting on the Pacific islands was of unimaginable ferocity. Japanese troops, underfed, poorly armed, badly treated, without hope of winning, would fight until they had neither ammunition nor food left. Then they would fight with their bayonets or swords, then with their teeth. To keep going, some became cannibals. They would not surrender. Marines did not want prisoners. Thus we have the astonishing statistic that in the whole of the Pacific war, the largest number of Japanese POWs held by Americans at any one time was a mere 5,424.

Meanwhile American POWs in Japanese hands, and especially those captured on Bataan and put through the death march (highly publicized in the U.S.), were treated as slave laborers under conditions as dreadful as those in Hitler's slave labor camps. American prisoners in German camps fared much better; they suffered a 4 percent death rate as compared to a 27 percent death rate in Japanese camps.

At the policy level, President Roosevelt was not immune to race prejudice, and he was bloodthirsty in what he wanted to do to the Japanese—but he was equally bloodthirsty in his order to carry out the bombing of Germany. As much as Hitler, Goering, Churchill, or the Japanese leaders, Roosevelt was responsible for one of the chief legacies of World War II—the civilian as target. But it was almost inevitable that such a break with the past would occur, because, as war moved closer to being total, the civilian, was considered a legitimate target since whatever he or she was doing was helping the war effort.

There were nevertheless moral objections to bombing cities. At the beginning of the war, Roosevelt had distinguished himself as the world leader who spoke out most forcefully on the moral depravity of such action. In 1939 he made an eloquent plea to all belligerents to refrain from this "inhuman barbarism." The bombing of cities, Roosevelt said, "has sickened the hearts of every civilized man and woman, and has profoundly shocked the conscience of humanity." In 1940, he noted "with pride that the United States consistently had taken the lead in urging that this inhuman practice be prohibited." But after Pearl Harbor, Roosevelt succumbed to the passions of war as readily as his peers. He became the strongest advocate of bombing cities and provided the leadership to build a fleet of 250,000 military aircraft with which to flatten the cities of America's enemies.

In the Pacific, Roosevelt relentlessly pressured General Marshall and General Arnold to bomb Japanese cities. He was a strong advocate of night area low-level attacks with incendiaries designed to burn up Japan's cities. This was done with terrifying results: the March 9–10, 1945, raid on Tokyo, during which two kilotons of bombs were dropped, resulted in a holocaust with more casualties than were caused by the atomic bombs.

The United States entered World War I because the Germans were waging unlimited submarine warfare against merchant shipping. In World War II, the American submarine fleet concentrated on the Japanese merchant fleet, waged a relentless and brilliant campaign against it, and by mid-1945 had sunk it completely.

Their cities were burning, their imports were gone, their people were starving, their main armies were now cut off on the Asian mainland, and they were incapable of reinforcing or supplying their men, but the generals running Japan still insisted that the fighting continue. There was no indication whatsoever that they were willing to surrender, on whatever terms. The terrible casualties they inflicted and suffered in the hopeless defense of Okinawa (climaxed by a mass suicide by those who would not surrender) forced Americans to believe that the home islands would have to be invaded, overrun, and forced to submit.

America's military leaders had to assume that the casualties in such a campaign would be unbearable. Colonel Andrew Goodpaster (later general and supreme allied commander, Europe, for NATO) of the War Department was one of the officers working on casualty estimates. He took the number of Japanese troops on Okinawa and compared it to the number defending Japan's home islands, calculated how many Americans on Okinawa the Japanese had killed, took into consideration the better defensive positions and terrain the Japanese had on the home islands, and concluded that American casualties in an assault on the home islands would be twenty times the number suffered on Okinawa. It came to around half a million.

That estimate has been challenged as far too pessimistic, but not by anyone who had been in combat against the Japanese.

In July 1945, Colonel Goodpaster was put to work on a plan for the occupation of Japan, based on the assumption that there would have been a long and bloody battle on the home islands before the Japanese surrendered. Japanese resentment, hatred, and shame would combine with American emotions toward the hated Japanese to create a tinderbox situation that would require 2 million men to carry out a successful occupation. Goodpaster made his own assumption, that the American people would not bear the cost of such an indefinite occupation. Therefore he included Britain, China and the Soviet Union in the occupation. As in Germany, defeated Japan would be split among the four powers.

After the atomic bomb and President Harry Truman's decision that the United States would unilaterally occupy Japan, Goodpaster forgot about his planning paper. Forty-six years later, a Japanese television team doing a documentary on the atomic bomb came to Goodpaster with a copy of the 1945 paper it had unearthed in the army archives. The Japanese wanted to know if this was authentic; Goodpaster assured them that it was. The Japanese thought about what might have happened to Japan if the Soviet Union had occupied one-quarter of their country. One man spoke for the others: "Thank God you used the bomb."

Serious questions about the decision to use the bomb have been asked for the past half-century. Was it necessary to use atomic bombs to force a quick surrender, or were there alternatives? Was the bomb used as an act of revenge or of diplomacy? At the center of all criticism of the decision is an assumption, namely that the Japanese military leaders were rational men who recognized that their cause was hopeless and were looking for a way to surrender with honor. Their only demand was the retention of the emperor. In fact they were ready to fight to the last man. They were driven not by a view of what the objective situation was but by their view of what their code required them to do. To surrender while still capable of fighting one final battle was dishonorable.

They were already disgraced. They had led their country into a war which they could not possibly win and carried it out with brutal disregard for the dictates of decency or the laws of war. And they had fought it stupidly. But at least they could go down fighting bravely. Therefore surrender was not a problem of calculations of men and resources (by that standard the Japanese should have quit after Midway) but of honor and dishonor.

The strongest argument against using the bomb is that the Japanese were ready to quit, that they only wanted a guarantee about the emperor's continued role, that the Americans had already decided the emperor had to be retained, but that they refused to let the Japanese know this. If that sentence is true, there was no need to use the bomb.

But it is not true. The Japanese army was not going to surrender on the basis of a slight modification in the unconditional surrender demand that would retain the emperor. As soon as such a modification was announced from Washington, Japan's leaders would have concluded that the losses they had inflicted on Okinawa had opened the ears of the Americans to the whisper of negotiations. They would have argued that the concession on the emperor would be followed by others.

The Japanese generals had conquered and still held one of the greatest empires in history. It was easily the largest in terms of square miles covered. From north (the Aleutians) to south (Java) it stretched three-quarters of the way around the globe; from east to west it stretched from North America (the Aleutians again) to central Asia (Burma).

The threat of the bloodletting the Americans would have to endure to conquer Japan gave the generals a bargaining position—to trade a surrender in return for serious negotiations.

On the other side, American public opinion was strongly set against any concession. A Gallup poll taken on May 29 and given front page prominence by the *Washington Post* on June 29 revealed that 33 percent of all Americans wanted Hirohito executed as a war criminal, 11 percent wanted him put in prison, and 9 percent wanted him to suffer the kaiser's fate, exile; only 7 percent favored retaining him in a figurehead capacity.

Meanwhile the Japanese wallowed in fantasy. After the fall of Okinawa, Prime Minister Suzuki was willing to negotiate, but only on the basis of terms satisfactory to Japan (which still occupied nearly all of Vietnam, large parts of China, most of Manchuria and all of Korea). No American would have accepted for one minute the proposition that Japan be allowed to keep her conquests or any part of them. But Suzuki was a hard-liner to an extraordinary degree. As late as August 12, he asserted in council that because the Allies were still insisting on Japanese disarmament it was necessary to continue the war.

President Truman's decision to use the bombs was taken after full discussion of the options and full consideration given to the political and moral factors. Though advisors were involved, it was Truman who had to decide and order. It was Truman, and only he, who knew the loneliness and isolation of high command. He was told by the U.S. Navy that it was not necessary to use the bombs or invade; the navy claimed that it could force a capitulation through blockade. At Potsdam in July, General Dwight Eisenhower told Truman he did not believe it was necessary to use "this awful thing" to compel the surrender of an already thoroughly defeated Japan.

General Henry Arnold, commanding the army air force, told Truman the air force could force a surrender with a conventional air campaign (i.e., napalm and massive iron bomb raids) and that thus there was no need to use the atomic weapons. Arnold was not trying to save Japanese lives; he had laid on a conventional bombing campaign of Japan the likes of which the world had never seen.

There were other, conflicting military opinions. General George Marshall and General Douglas MacArthur advised Truman that he could either use the bombs or go forward with invasion plans; nothing short of those options would force a surrender. In June, Truman approved going ahead with the planning for Operation Olympic, the invasion of Kyushu in the fall of 1945, and for Operation Coronet, the invasion of Honshu in March 1946. But no one wanted to go through with such an invasion.

To avoid it if at all possible was clearly necessary. That last climactic battle on the home islands would have been dreadful to a degree impossible to exaggerate. It would have taken decades for Japanese-American relations to recover from such a racial bloodletting. It also would have prolonged the war at a fearful cost to Japanese cities and civilians.

General Hap Arnold wanted "as big a finale as possible" to end the war. On August 14, five days after the second bomb had fallen on Nagasaki and six days after the Soviet Union had declared war on Japan, the army air force launched a thousand-bomber raid on Tokyo. Truman announced Japan's unconditional surrender before all the bombers returned to their base.

Oh, how the two sides hated each other! As late as August 15 the Japanese were still executing American airmen who had fallen into their hands. Until he was informed of Truman's announcement, Arnold was at work on plans for more thousand-bomber raids against other Japanese cities. Thus one of the more important immediate results of using the bombs was to spare other hundreds of thousands of Japanese in the cities on Arnold's target list. And tens of thousands, perhaps many more, American lives were spared.

For the survivors in Japan, the most immediate and important result of the bombs was that their government had finally surrendered and the killing had stopped. For the millions of Americans who were soldiers, sailors and marines in the Pacific in the summer of 1945, the most immediate and important result of the bombs was that there would not be an American invasion. No American who was spared that horror has ever doubted the wisdom or morality of Truman's decision.

The bomb became the symbol of destruction in World War II more because of its drama—one bomber, one bomb—and its unlimited growth potential than because of its actual effects. As noted, the thousand-bomber raids were more deadly, and an invasion would have been a much greater catastrophe.

American policy makers felt that it was necessary to shock the Japanese into surrender. Actually, it was more necessary to give the people who were running Japan, the military, an excuse to quit. That was the great contribution of the atomic bomb.

The generals had no answer to the atomic bomb. They could not evade the fact that they were defeated and could offer no alternative to the government save a suicidal resistance which the emperor refused to contemplate. With Hirohito's decision for surrender the only alternatives open to the military were a revolt against the emperor (which would have proclaimed to the world the hypocrisy of their claim to being his most faithful servants) or mass suicide. A very few contemplated the first course, and some four thousand chose suicide, but clearly the great majority refused either alternative and accepted as the emperor had commanded that they endure the unendurable. The war was over.

With surrender, the army gave up its special position in Japanese life. If not dishonored, it had certainly been discredited. In the course of less than one week, two atomic bombs turned Asia's most militaristic and aggressive nation, with a half-century of expansion by force as its recent history, into Asia's least militaristic nation. There has been no significant military revival in Japan since the end of the war. Formerly a society and a state dominated by the military, it has become a country without one.

Another critical result of the use of the bombs came in the days and weeks after the surrender and the occupation of Japan by American troops. Newspapermen and news cameras came with them. The American press and movie theaters were filled with accounts and photos of Hiroshima and Nagasaki, which had a tremendously powerful impact. People who had been demanding blood and retribution were shocked at what they saw, and they decided—almost all Americans decided—that the Japanese had been punished enough.

Not very many Americans thought that Germany had been punished enough, especially in the wake of the photographs coming out of the concentration camps. It was some years—and the imminent threat from the Red Army in Eastern Germany—before the Americans reached out their hands to the German people. In Japan, the GIs and marines were reaching out their hands as they stepped ashore in September 1945.

Thus it was that the most brutal act of all in that most racist war of all had the surprising effect of bringing the two sides to their senses. The surrender came just in time to prevent the Red Army from overrunning all Korea and possibly Japan; thus it saved Japan from a division into Communist and non-Communist parts. It was the Americans who moved into Japan, where they found they could get along well with their former enemies. With the Japanese military eliminated and the American lust for revenge satiated by Hiroshima and Nagasaki, the military occupation of Japan and the remaking of that country was successful beyond anyone's wildest dreams. That the United States and Japan are allies today is the result.

GENERAL MacARTHUR

A Profile

Newsmen, visiting Tokyo's Dai-Ichi Building, during the American occupation of Japan, were amazed at the things they heard there from members of Douglas MacArthur's staff. These officers, one-, two-, and three-star generals in the army and the air force, were tough, independent-minded men who had made their way to the top of their profession through demonstrated ability. They had, one assumed, a normal amount of skepticism, a certain degree of cynicism, a high level of sophistication, and more than the ordinary share of intelligence.

Yet, when asked about their chief, their eyes lit up and they babbled like Stone-Age men describing the Sun God. "The greatest man alive," Major General Edward Almond said of MacArthur. Lieutenant General George E. Stratemeyer went further: MacArthur was the greatest man since Christ, the greatest general in world history, "the greatest man who ever lived." An operations officer declared, "We look to MacArthur as the second Jesus Christ."

One officer, however, responded that he just could not make a judgment about MacArthur. "He's too enormous . . . I don't really understand him. No one could." There can be no doubt as to the accuracy of the confession. MacArthur was different from other men—in all the vast literature about him, pro and con, he is hardly ever compared to anyone else—and to come to a conclusion about the nature of his character is extraordinarily difficult. One can record events, sayings, decisions, reactions, but they do not constitute a believable portrait. MacArthur simply refuses to fit into any known category, even that of great man, and the human mind finds it difficult to comprehend the unique.

One thing is sure—MacArthur was not the second Christ, nor was he the greatest man who ever lived, or even in 1950 the greatest living American. Neither was he what his detractors said: a fraud, a Fascist general on a white horse, or a threat to the Republic. Most of all he was not what he called himself at the end of his career, a simple old soldier who just tried to do his duty.

If understanding MacArthur is difficult, understanding the public's reaction to him is impossible. He had an enormous following. It would not be an exaggeration to say that in 1951 millions of Americans thought he should be President, even though no one had a clear idea as to his political philosophy. He had not been involved in domestic politics and indeed had not set foot in the United States in fourteen years. When he returned from Japan, in 1951, a crowd estimated at 7,500,000 greeted him in New York City (when Eisenhower returned from a war he had won, in 1945, the crowd was estimated at 4,000,000). Although less than a half-year earlier MacArthur's armies had suffered the most thorough defeat ever inflicted upon American armed forces, although he had been summarily relieved of his command by the President, and although he was advocating a foreign policy which most citizens, to judge by the polls, and nearly all high-level governmental officials regarded as disastrous, the public everywhere welcomed him as the country's greatest hero returning from the greatest conceivable triumph.

Congress invited him to address a joint meeting, an honor rare even for a victorious—unprecedented for a defeated—general. (Can one imagine Congress inviting McClellan to address it after Lincoln sacked him?) When MacArthur finished his speech, Representative Dewey Short, educated at Harvard, Oxford, and Heidelberg, cried out in the House, "We heard God speak here today. God in the flesh, the voice of God."

Everyone seemed to overreact to MacArthur. Something about him encouraged blasphemy, or extremes of a non-religious nature. After Truman fired MacArthur, the Michigan legislature memorialized Congress in a resolution which began, "Whereas, at one o'clock A.M. of this day, World Communism achieved its greatest victory of a decade in the dismissal of General MacArthur. . . ." The Florida and California legislatures passed similar resolutions. The decade, it should be remembered, included the victory of the Communists in the Chinese Cold War, as well as the Communist triumphs in all of Eastern Europe.

Douglas MacArthur was born on January 26, 1880, in Little Rock, Arkansas. His father, a Medal of Honor winner in the Civil War, was a Regular Army general. Young Douglas was thrilled by his stories of the Civil War and his activities in the Far East, where he was the hero of the Philippine Insurrection and the military governor of the islands. In 1899 Douglas, thoroughly steeped in the military life, went up the Hudson River to West Point, where he quickly established himself as an authentic genius. He eventually graduated with the highest marks ever received there. He made a dashing figure in his cadet grey—tall, trim, and handsome. His mother, upon learning that Ulysses S. Grant III's mother had gone to the Point to see to his interests, came up the river, too, in order to manage Douglas's social life. She stayed with him until her death in 1936, dominating his personal life. Those who knew her agreed that the best descriptive adjective was "formidable."

Douglas needed her at West Point. Because his father was a ranking general in the army, upper-classmen singled him out for special treatment. Over and over they made him recite his father's doing at Chickamauga, Lookout Mountain, and Stone's River, but it did not end with that. His special treatment included a full program of exercising at all hours of the day. One night in summer camp, immediately after dinner, he did deep knee bends with arms held rigid at sides for over an hour and was still at it when the other plebes in his tent had collapsed. Suddenly MacArthur lost control of his muscles and fell to the floor, unable to move. Later that year, at a congressional investigation of hazing, he refused to identify the cadets who had hazed him. The congressmen pressed, but at a recess his mother encouraged him not to be a tattletale, and he stood firm.

After graduation, MacArthur served briefly in the Philippines, where he engaged in hand-to-hand combat with brigands. Back in Washington, he was a military aide to President Theodore Roosevelt; and worked in the War Department. In World War I he proposed the formation of an all-American division made up of National Guard units from many states, which became the Rainbow Division. He held various posts in the division, eventually becoming its commander.

MacArthur, a brigadier general when the war ended, was by all odds the best front-line general officer in the war. He was always in or near no-man's land, either leading a charge or reconnoitering. Once, out alone at night on the southern front, he heard the rumbling of German vehicles on the move. He immediately realized that the enemy was pulling back, and that he could hit them before they reestablished their lines and saved their supply dumps. There was no time to consult division or corps; he had to move at once. Gathering up his battalions, he ordered them to "advance with audacity," and he had them moving by 3:30 that morning. They struck out quickly, silently. Suddenly a flare lit up the area and MacArthur saw, just ahead of him, three Germans crouched over a machine gun. He caught his breath and waited for the burst. None came. When someone no longer could stand the tension and turned his flashlight on the Germans, they had not moved. They were all dead.

MacArthur's night attack was a huge success. When he returned to division headquarters the corps commander, Hunter Liggett, was there with his division commander, Charles Menoher. MacArthur had not slept for four days and nights. He briefly explained what he had done, then fell on a cot and went into a deep sleep. Liggett looked down at him and said, "Well, I'll be damned! Menoher, you better cite him." MacArthur got his fourth Silver Star.

Even as a young brigadier, MacArthur did not live as other men did. He got into trouble with GHQ because he refused to wear a helmet, did not carry a gas mask, went unarmed, always had a riding crop in his hand, and was usually in the trenches, seldom in his headquarters. In every case he was violating a specific regulation. Someone at GHQ ordered an investigation; the results were so laudatory that it almost became a joke. One noncom, for example, told the visiting staff officer, "He's a hell-to-breakfast baby, long and lean, kind to us and tough on the enemy. He can spit nickel cigars and chase Germans as well as any doughboy in the Rainbow." Menoher declared, "MacArthur is the bloodiest fighting man in this army." When Pershing heard of the investigation, he bellowed, "Stop all this nonsense. MacArthur is the greatest leader of troops we have, and I intend to make him a division commander."

Following the war, MacArthur came home to assume the superintendent's position at West Point. He was the youngest superintendent in history, and had been out of the academy for only sixteen years, so many of the faculty had been full professors while he was only a plebe. Only one class was present, as all the others had graduated early to go to France. Teaching methods were antiquated—they had not changed since the Civil War. Congress, returning to normalcy, was cutting back the appropriations, even though equipment was worn out and obsolete.

The assignment was a tough one, but extremely important because the Military Academy required inspired leadership to establish a bridge between the traditional and modern. Although most of the instructors were young officers, recent graduates themselves, many of whom had just returned from the war in Europe, much was necessary to liberalize the academic education and to bring the tactical instruction up-to-date. The army itself, always conservative in its policies and methods between wars, was slipping into the routine of preparing for past rather than future wars. Such a trend was inherent in the Military Academy, where the senior professors had held their posts for over thirty years. As MacArthur said, "How long are we going to go on preparing for the War of 1812?" And as one cavalry officer's wife said just recently, "After World War I the cavalry went right on training to fight the Indians."

MacArthur felt that the cadets were too much isolated from the rest of the nation. To do away with cadet provincialism, he gave the cadets more opportunity to see the rest of the service and the outside world. He improved the curriculum, too, placing more emphasis on the humanities and social studies while not neglecting science. In changing the curriculum he offended the old, entrenched professors, and even more the alumni. MacArthur found it difficult to work with the senior members of the faculty, mainly because he was a supreme egotist who could not bring himself to pay proper respect to the professors. He badly hurt their feelings by announcing his intentions without consulting with them or asking their advice. He felt a strong sense of mission and considered his program so obviously necessary and his actions so clearly correct that he never explained himself fully to the Academic Board; the members, consequently, saw him as a brash young man meddling in areas he did not understand.

There was a certain aura about MacArthur that prevented people from getting close or really understanding him or his aims. One cadet of the time remembers, "Neither I nor the vast majority of my class ever saw the general, except when he was walking across Diagonal Walk, apparently lost in thought, his nose in the air, gazing at distant horizons." He shocked everyone with his unconventional uniform, which included a sloppy cap from which he had removed the wire stiffener, and a short overcoat. Pershing had strictly forbidden such dress, so the impression MacArthur gave was that "he was not only unconventional but perhaps a law unto himself."

MacArthur's majestic bearing and his astonishing record of accomplishment intimidated people. He did nothing to dispel this attitude and allowed very few men to get close to him. (Once, when going over a manuscript biography of himself, MacArthur crossed out the word "remote" and substituted "austere.") Indeed, he took such pleasure in his own superiority that not many tried. At an Academic Board meeting one afternoon, a senior professor kept interrupting MacArthur, until finally the superintendent exploded. He banged his fist on the table and shouted, "Sit down, sir. I am the superintendent!" When he ended his tour in 1922, no one doubted it. He had permanently changed the academy, bringing it into the twentieth century and making it into the outstanding military college in the world.

The next decade and a half was an unhappy period for MacArthur, as it was for others of the heroic cast like Winston Churchill and Charles de Gaulle. There were no great issues, no great causes. He had a disastrous marriage to Louise Cromwell Brooks, a bright, giddy, rich divorcée who was very much of the jazz age; there was a great gulf between the interests of General MacArthur and his wife. The divorce was public and loud. His second marriage, in 1937 to Jean Faircloth, was highly successful. She was a Southern belle who had been brought up to be an army wife, and she had the personal qualities that enabled her to live with a genius who cherished himself.

During this period MacArthur served on Billy Mitchell's court-martial, a distasteful assignment since Mitchell was a personal friend. There is a great controversy about how he voted; Mitchell died convinced MacArthur voted guilty. MacArthur's supporters insist that he did not; MacArthur himself, even in his *Reminiscences,* never said.

From 1930 to 1935 MacArthur was Chief of Staff of the Army. He spent most of his time warning about the dangers of war and of the scope it would take, fruitlessly pleading with Congress for more money for the army.

The most famous incident of this period was his rout of the Bonus Marchers from the back lots of Washington on July 28, 1932. The men were veterans who had marched on Washington demanding that Congress pay their bonus in advance. The government had refused to be bullied, and the veterans camped on Anacostia Flats. President Hoover, after a long wait, finally decided to move them out, and had the Secretary of War pass the orders along to the Chief of Staff.

It all could have been done with a minimum show of force (indeed, Hoover would have been wiser to have had the District police do the job), but MacArthur, convinced that the Bonus Marchers represented a Communist conspiracy that aimed to pull off a coup, decided to do the work personally and thoroughly. He called his chief assistant, Major Dwight Eisenhower, into his office and told him to get everything ready. Eisenhower protested that it was highly inappropriate for the Chief of Staff of the Army to become involved in what might turn into a street-corner brawl. MacArthur replied that there was "incipient revolution in the air" and paid no attention.

That afternoon MacArthur, Eisenhower, and Major George Patton led cavalry, infantry, and tanks on the Bonus Marchers. The army won the "battle" and the pitiful shacks in which the veterans had lived were burned down. MacArthur was convinced that he had saved the Republic. Late in life, when he was eighty-four, he declared that because of his routing of the Bonus Marchers he became a "man to be destroyed, no matter how long the Communists . . . had to wait, and no matter what means they might have to use. But it was to be nineteen years before the bells of Moscow pealed out their glee at my eclipse."

When his tour as Chief of Staff ended, MacArthur went to the Philippines, to build there an army for the Commonwealth, one that could provide self-defense for the islands by 1946 when they were to become an independent nation. He took Eisenhower with him. MacArthur had the highest possible opinion of Eisenhower. In personal reports, MacArthur said that Eisenhower was the best staff officer in the army, a man for whom no position was too high. MacArthur expected that Eisenhower would go right to the top in the next war.

Eisenhower never deified MacArthur, but he did have great respect for him. He was, however, a little bemused by MacArthur's habit of referring to himself in the third person. The Chief of Staff would call Major Eisenhower into his office to explain something, saying "So MacArthur went over to the senator, and said, 'Senator . . .' "

The two men worked well together in the Philippines, even though they had practically no money with which to build an army. They finally broke on a small point. MacArthur thought he could improve the morale of the people by showing them their emerging army. He suggested a large parade in Manila, with units brought in from all over the islands. Eisenhower protested that it would cost too much, taking money desperately needed for equipment. MacArthur insisted.

Eisenhower went to work, and soon Commonwealth President Quezon heard of the arrangements. He called Eisenhower in and asked what was going on. Eisenhower, astonished, said he assumed MacArthur had cleared the parade with Quezon. When the President said no, he had not, Eisenhower left the room while Quezon telephoned MacArthur.

When Eisenhower saw MacArthur the next day, MacArthur was furious. He swore he had never ordered a parade, but had only asked

Eisenhower to investigate the possibilities. Now Quezon had heard of it and was horrified at the cost. Eisenhower said he only acted on orders, and MacArthur again denied it. Shortly thereafter Eisenhower left the Philippines; after that he carefully made only guarded, noncommittal comments about MacArthur.

The incident pointed up a central element in MacArthur's character. He had a deeply rooted need always to be right. It increased as he grew older. Henceforth he would hold to his ideas, no matter what any member of his staff might say, and if the event proved him wrong, he would deny, vehemently, that he had ever said or ordered this or that. His monumental egotism allowed him to ignore all contrary documentary evidence—he simply denied its existence. MacArthur had to be right, to be omnipotent, to be MacArthur.

MacArthur lived in the Manila Hotel in isolated splendor. In those days a white man still commanded respect in the Far East, and a white general was akin to a god. He had only to utter a wish to have it fulfilled. Convinced that Orientals were most impressed by the flashy display, he appeared at review dressed in a white uniform of his own design made of sharkskin material, with four stars on his shoulder, a red ribbon at the base of his lapels, his General Staff insignia on his left breast, a gaudy, gold-braided cap on his head and an enormous corncob pipe in his mouth. By resigning from the United States Army after two years in the Philippines (he was reactivated in 1941), he fulfilled a boast he had made as a cadet; Quezon made him a field marshal in the Commonwealth army.

All was not ritual and regalia. MacArthur did what he could to build up the Philippine army. Part of his aim was to boost morale by inspiring awe of the commander in chief. His target date for readiness was 1946; since the Japanese attack came five years early, it is impossible to judge the efficiency of his methods. What is certain is that the half-trained, underarmed Filipinos were no match for the Japanese in 1941.

MacArthur did not think that the Japanese would come. Invasion, he predicted, "would cost the enemy . . . at least a half million of men as casualties and upward of five billion of dollars in money." He thought no enemy, after studying the lesson of Gallipoli, would ever again attempt an attack against a coast defended by modern weapons. In any case, the Philippines held no strategic or economic value for the Japanese. MacArthur felt he was the only white man who understood oriental psychology, and argued that those who feared a Japanese attack "fail fully to credit the logic of the Japanese mind."

Deliberate isolation may have impressed the Filipinos, but there was another side to the coin. MacArthur was also isolating himself from the best military thought of the day. Hardly any officer in the United States Army agreed with MacArthur's estimate of the situation. Most thought that the Filipinos were a long way from creating an effective fighting force, that amphibious landings were possible, indeed probable, and that Japan very much coveted the Philippines. MacArthur's plan for defense of the Philippines seemed to be hazy, and when the war came he was slow in implementing them.

There can be no doubt that MacArthur failed in the Philippines. Six hours before the attack on Clark Field destroyed his entire bomber force of four squadrons on the ground the War Department had informed him of the Pearl Harbor attack and said that the nation was at war. His chief airman, Lewis Brereton, asked permission to attack Formosa, but MacArthur refused. Later MacArthur denied that he had received any hard news about Pearl Harbor, but the messages the War Department sent—along with the acknowledgments from the Philippines—are now in the archives, for all to see. He also denied that Brereton made the request, and implied that Clark Field was Brereton's fault (which in part it was, since the B-17's were lined up wing tip to wing tip, an easy target). The documents bear out Brereton's claim to have made the request. In his memoirs, MacArthur declared that an attack against Formosa would have been disastrous, since he had no fighter planes to protect the bombers. This was a valid reason, but it did not jibe with his earlier assertions that he never heard Brereton's request.

In the ensuing struggle for the Philippines, MacArthur was slow to recognize how badly the battle was going, slow to pull back to Bataan, and slow to stockpile supplies on the peninsula. As a result, the troops went on half rations the day they took up their positions on Bataan; in the end hunger and weakness proved to be more dangerous than the Japanese.

MacArthur set up his headquarters on Corregidor, and visited the front lines at Bataan only once. The local commander, Jonathan Wainwright, described the visit.

" 'Jonathan,' he said, greeting me most cordially as he stepped out of the car, 'I'm glad to see you back from the north. The execution of your withdrawal and of your mission in covering the withdrawal of the South Luzon force were as fine as anything in history.'

"Douglas was a little expansive on some occasions, and I don't mean that unkindly. I just wondered if I deserved such praise.

" 'And for that,' he continued, 'I'm going to see that you are made a permanent major general of the Regular Army.' That was nice, for I was only a temporary one at the time.

"He spoke to the other generals for a few minutes, then came back to me.

" 'Where are your 155-millimeter guns?' he asked.

"I told him where the six of them were, and since two of them were fairly close I suggested that he walk over with me and take a look at them.

" 'Jonathan,' he said, 'I don't want to *see* them, I want to *hear* them!'

"It was our only meeting on Bataan."

On Corregidor, MacArthur, when he was not directing antiaircraft fire and deliberately exposing himself in order to build up morale, was sending a flood of messages to the War Department screaming for reinforcements. The navy, however, refused to risk what was left of the fleet in a desperate attempt to break the Japanese blockade. Washington wrote off the Philippines, and began to build up a base in Australia, from whence the counteroffensive could someday be launched. All the War Department wanted from the men on Bataan was time.

It was a realistic policy, but that did not help the defenders. Chief of Staff George Marshall patiently explained that the navy was doing its best and trying to build its forces for later assaults. As Forrest Pogue puts it, telling MacArthur that was like telling "a man dying of thirst that he must wait for a drink of water until a well could be dug and a water main laid. Thoughts of well-dressed officers sitting in comfortable offices and sleeping in clean beds excited the anger of the battlers of Bataan and deepened their suspicions of a faceless enemy called Washington."

It was at this point that MacArthur began to build up an active persecution complex. It had always been latent; now it became virulent. In 1943 Robert E. Sherwood visited his headquarters. He reported that the general and his staff seemed to think the War Department, the State Department, the Joint Chiefs of Staff, even the White House itself, were "under the domination of 'Communists and British Imperialists.'" In December 1944, MacArthur told Clark Lee, "Yes, we've come a long way since Melbourne, despite the navy cabal that hates me, and the New Deal cabal." He complained that Roosevelt "acted as if he were the directing head of the army and navy."

There was something much bigger involved than MacArthur's personal feelings. They were merely the surface manifestation of a gigantic struggle over the direction of American foreign policy. Roosevelt, Cordell Hull, Harry Stimson, and most of all George Marshall—in short, official Washington—had decided to defeat Germany first in World War II. This was partly a strategic decision forced upon the policy makers. Germany was the more dangerous enemy, Europe was closer than the Far East, and so shipping men and supplies there was easier, and so on. But it was also a foreign policy decision of the highest magnitude, for it meant that in the government's estimation Europe was more important than Asia, at least to Americans living in the middle of the twentieth century.

MacArthur violently disagreed. He believed that Asia was the key to the future, and that it was on that continent and its offshore islands that America should make her major commitment. The split between MacArthur and Marshall could not have been more decisive. Their argument was to dominate American foreign policy discussions for the next two decades. MacArthur had important followers in the United States, led by Robert Taft and the Asia-firsters, while Marshall had the backing of Roosevelt and Truman, and thus the power. In many ways the argument continues to this day.

Marshall stuck to his Europe-first policy, and slowly the forces on Bataan fell back. Roosevelt ordered MacArthur to leave the islands (he had planned to go inland and organize guerrilla warfare activities) to take command of the Southwest Pacific Area, headquarters Australia. Along with his wife and four-year-old son, MacArthur made a dramatic escape on PT boats.

Upon his arrival in Australia, MacArthur committed some of the pettiest acts of his career, things not at all typical of the man, and which must have been caused by his enormous hostility toward Washington and his burning shame at the loss of the Philippines. Marshall had personally seen to it that MacArthur received the Medal of Honor for his heroism on Corregidor. The Chief of Staff then asked MacArthur to forward a recommendation for Wainwright for the same award. Marshall already had plenty of eyewitness accounts of unquestioned heroism on Wainwright's part but he needed a formal o.k. from Wainwright's superior. MacArthur flatly refused. "His animosity toward Wainwright was tremendous," Marshall later recalled. MacArthur said that Wainwright's actions fell far short of those needed to win the award, and claimed that the sworn statements of those who had been with Wainwright on Bataan were false. Wainwright did not get the Medal until 1945 and then only because of Marshall's insistence.

MacArthur did recommend that all units on Bataan and Corregidor receive unit citations—except for the marine regiment and the naval detachments. Hanson Baldwin reported that MacArthur's chief of staff "let it be known that this was no oversight; the marines had gotten their share of glory in World War I, and they weren't going to get any in this one!" MacArthur did his level best to live up to that threat; throughout the war, dispatches from Southwest Pacific barely mentioned the marines, and hardly ever the navy. There was some bitterness in the little ditty that sailors and marines in the Pacific used to sing: "MacArthur got back to the Philippines, with the help of the navy and a few marines."

At a press conference in Australia, held shortly after he arrived, MacArthur announced that "I came through and I shall return." The Office of War Information thought the phrase a good one, but asked MacArthur's permission to change it to "We shall return," since presumably MacArthur would need some help. He refused permission, and "I shall return" it stayed.

The emphasis on "I" became more pronounced as the war went on. MacArthur's headquarters exercised the tightest conceivable censorship on news coming from the area; all communiques emanating from headquarters gave the impression that MacArthur was personally directing the campaigns. In Europe, Eisenhower saw to it that Bradley, Hodges, Simpson, Patton, and the others got their share and more of the glory; in the Pacific none of MacArthur's chief subordinates became known to the American public. He had some good ones, the best being Robert Eichelberger. "If you capture Burma for me," MacArthur once said to Eichelberger, "I'll give you a Distinguished Service Cross and recommend you for a high British decoration. Also," he continued, bestowing the final accolade, "I'll release your name for newspaper publication."

MacArthur's communiques became famous. One newsman computed that between the fall of 1942 and October 1944, the MacArthur communiques reported Japanese losses of from 150,000 to 200,000, while the Allied casualties listed in the communiques amounted to 122 killed, 2 missing, and 529 wounded. The communiques always began, "MacArthur's Headquarters," giving the impression that he was in the field leading the men (in fact he was in Australia, where of course he belonged).

The navy circulated a ballad about the communiques:

> For two long years since blood and tears have been so very rife,
> Confusion in our war news burdens more a soldier's life,
> But from this chaos, daily, like a hospice on the way,
> Like a shining light to guide us, rises Doug's communique.

The marines were bitter, too. Their famous poem concluded:

> And while possibly a rumor now,
> Some day it will be fact
> That the Lord will hear a deep voice say,
> "Move over God, it's Mac."

Whatever anyone thought about the way MacArthur managed his public relations, few could criticize his fighting methods. In a skillful, bold campaign, he made his way back to the Philippines. On New Guinea and at the Admiralties, in some of the toughest campaigns of the war, MacArthur's leadership and strategic policy paid huge dividends. His end runs in the Dutch East Indies cut off enormous numbers of Japanese troops without any major cost to the Americans.

Admiral Chester Nimitz, meanwhile, was advancing across the central Pacific. In the summer of 1944 Roosevelt flew out to Pearl Harbor for a conference with Nimitz and MacArthur. The navy wanted to leapfrog the Philippines and secure bases on Formosa and the Chinese mainland. Roosevelt asked MacArthur for comment. The general eloquently pleaded the military case for taking the islands. It would be at best risky and at worst disastrous to island-hop an enemy base as large as the Philippines. Later, in a private interview with the president, he advanced the moral case. Was the president willing, he asked, "to accept responsibility for breaking a solemn promise to eighteen million Christian Filipinos that the Americans would return?" Roosevelt did not reply, and a disgusted MacArthur turned to leave. The president looked up. "Wait a minute, Douglas," he said. "Come back here." MacArthur, he said, could return to the Philippines. As MacArthur departed, Roosevelt muttered, "Well, Douglas, you win! But I am going to have a hell of a time over this with that old bear, Ernie King!"

The troops went back, and MacArthur waded ashore, to say into a handy microphone, "People of the Philippines, I have returned. . . . Rally to me."

On March 2, 1945, MacArthur set foot again in Corregidor. Five months later, at Yokohama, he accepted the Japanese surrender. He was sixty-five, and had led a life full enough to satisfy any man. But much more was to come; his greatest triumphs and failures, as well as his bitterest controversy, lay ahead.

At sixty-five, Douglas MacArthur had done more than even he, as a cocky cadet at the turn of the century, could have dreamed possible. One of the most decorated heroes of World War I, Superintendent of the United States Military Academy, Chief of Staff of the Army, Field Marshal in the Philippine Army, defender of Bataan, directing genius of the offensives in the Southwest Pacific, and head of the invasion forces that returned to the Philippines—all of this had made his name a household word. The country had given him its love, and only withheld the presidency itself, to which his critics said he aspired, but for which he never actively or directly worked. Since he was obviously too old to be a presidential candidate, he could have no ambitions left. Ordinary men, even great men, would have at this point sought a peaceful retirement. MacArthur, however, was anxious to serve his country, and was delighted when Truman designated him head of the occupying forces of Japan.

In Japan, where he was a virtual dictator, MacArthur revealed a side no one had suspected. His politics, at least in regard to Japan, turned out to be liberal and democratic. While running the fairest and most honest military occupation in all history, he allowed the Japanese to write their own, hopefully new, constitution. When the end product turned out to be a warmed-over version of the old constitution, MacArthur and his staff took the document in hand and completely rewrote it. He then submitted it to the Japanese people who after full deliberation adopted it. The constitution is exactly what MacArthur said it was, "undoubtedly the most liberal in history." It combined the American executive system and the British parliamentary one. The emperor was no longer deified, but became the symbol of the state and of the unity of the people. Supreme power resided in the Diet, elected by universal franchise. MacArthur gave the Japanese, for the first time in their history, a bill of rights. He saw to it that Japanese women got a new status, with equal opportunities in employment, coeducation, marriage, voting and property rights.

Some of his innovations had humorous results. MacArthur introduced to Japan the labor union, with the right to collective bargaining. Labor unrest took forms peculiar to Japan. A chorus line went on half-strike by only kicking half as high as usual. A railroad union protested a government decision by blowing the whistles on all the trains in Japan for one minute at the same time.

MacArthur broke up the combine which held the Japanese industrial system in thrall—ten Japanese families had controlled 90 percent of all industry. The American general cut down on their influence through an anti-trust campaign that outdid the New Deal.

His most important act was to redistribute the land. When he arrived, Japan was still a feudal state. Most farmers were either out-and-out serfs or they worked for exorbitant rentals. MacArthur had the government buy up the land, then resell it to the farmers on generous terms. By 1950 he had redistributed more than 5,000,000 acres of land, and more than 89 percent of the arable land in the country was controlled by the people who lived on it. These actions of MacArthur's were instrumental in meeting the Communist threat in Japan, and were much more effective than any armed response to Communism in Asia could have been.

In June 1950, the peaceful flow of life in Japan came to a sudden end. North Korea invaded South Korea.

The ancient Hermit Kingdom of Korea—Chosen, "the Land of the Morning Calm"—had been the traditional invasion route for Japanese excursions onto the Asian mainland, and for Chinese invasions of Japan. In the twentieth century the growing strength of Russia on Korea's northeastern tip had added another great power to the list of those who would use the country for their own purposes. In the Russo-Japanese War of 1905 the Japanese turned back the Russians and solidified their control.

During World War II the United Nations promised independence to Korea. After the Japanese surrendered, the Russians and Americans agreed, for convenience's sake, that Japanese troops north of the 38th parallel would surrender to the Russians, those south of it to the Americans. The Cold War, beginning just at this time, sounded the death knell of the hopes of the Korean people, for although both great nations continued to proclaim their desire to unite Korea and give it independence, neither was willing to do it on the other side's terms.

Northern Korea became another Communist satellite state and the 38th parallel became a sealed political boundary. The United States had demobilized its army and trusted in the atomic bomb for its defense; the chief result was that it had no force, short of the atomic threat, to use in an area like Korea. Since no one advocated using the bomb in order to unify Korea, the United States did the only thing it could do and turned the whole problem over to the United Nations. That organization decreed that Korea should hold nationwide elections, but the Russians refused to allow U.N. supervisors to cross the 38th parallel. The result was the creation of the Republic of South Korea (August 15, 1949). Shortly thereafter the Russians set up a puppet government, the "Democratic People's Republic of Korea." Both sides claimed authority over the entire country.

On June 25, 1950, less than a year later, the North Korean army, trained and equipped by the Russians, launched a surprise attack across the 38th parallel. President Harry S. Truman immediately authorized General Douglas MacArthur (in Japan) to furnish the South Koreans (ROK) with ammunition and supplies. The United States government and MacArthur had earlier decided that Korea was outside the defense line of the United States in the Far East, primarily because of the difficulty of holding on in the peninsula, but Truman now determined that the Communist challenge had to be met. He told MacArthur on June 26 to use air and naval forces against North Korean units fighting in South Korea and called a meeting of the U.N. Security Council, where he asked the members to give military aid to the young republic. Russia was out of the Council at the time, protesting the U.N.'s failure to admit Red China, and the resolution went through.

Truman had thus met the challenge of clear aggression, but not unilaterally. By bringing in the U.N. he gave to the forces fighting in Korea a moral advantage that was of inestimable value.

The war that resulted was, for the military strategist, one of the most fascinating in history. It was, in reality, two wars. In the first eight months it was a war of movement and maneuver, with troops from both sides moving over the rugged, mountainous terrain as easily as troops move through the desert. Both sides suffered from over-confidence and as a result came face to face with total disaster. There was brilliant generalship both north and south of the 38th parallel. Then, after April 1951, the war came to resemble World War I. Both sides dug extensive trench systems. Artillery took over as the major weapon. Two years of stalemate followed.

The first North Korean attack had driven a panicked and helpless ROK force before it. Korean troops threw away their arms and equipment so that they could run faster. MacArthur rushed in troops from Japan, but these ordinary GIs, grown soft in the occupation delights of Japan, were hardly ready for combat. Still, they did what they could, and they managed to slow the onrushing wave. At enormous cost, they bought time.

It was still an open question as to whether time was worth buying. In comparison to the world situation, the United States had never been more unprepared. It did not have enough troops, enough veterans, enough arms and equipment (and what it did have was in poor condition and badly worn), enough anything. On July 13, Lieutenant General Walton H. Walker took command of all U.S. Army forces in Korea, calling them the American Eighth Army, which was a pretentious name for a force that consisted of an understrength 24th Division and elements of an infantry regiment. Within a week parts of two more divisions arrived, and Walker established a perimeter around Pusan, on the southeastern tip of the peninsula.

During August and September 1950, Walker's men held off determined North Korean attacks. Shifting his limited forces brilliantly, Walker managed to hold on. In Japan, meanwhile, MacArthur was building up a striking force. Walker and his men felt that if MacArthur had given them more of the available force, they could have broken out of the perimeter and dealt the enemy a major, perhaps decisive, blow.

MacArthur was thinking of bigger things. He had made his reputation in World War II with amphibious landings, and now he saw a chance to repeat. He planned to go ashore with his X Corps at Inchon, the port of Seoul, and cut the North Korean supply line. Planners in both the army and navy were opposed. The local commanders were opposed. There were not enough landing craft, the port was small and had to be approached along a narrow channel through a maze of mud banks, and the tides were among the highest in the world.

MacArthur insisted on going ahead. On September 13, 1950, ten

United Nations warships entered the harbor and shot up the floating mines. They then went in closer to draw enemy fire; when it came they blasted away at the port's defenses. The date was the 191st anniversary of the Battle of Quebec, which MacArthur found gratifying. Wolfe's victory on the Plains of Abraham emboldened him to go ahead with Inchon, and he declared that the more he thought about Quebec the more he thought he was right at Inchon. MacArthur put it this way: "I imagine that Wolfe thought to himself, if his brigadiers and his admiral believed his plan unfeasible, then General Montcalm must have reasoned that Wolfe would not try it. And if able American officers think Inchon impracticable, doubtless the Communists do too."

Even MacArthur's own staff was opposed, but by this time he was pretty thoroughly out of practice in listening to advice from anyone. In 1951 he said that he had got more and more into the habit of heeding the advice of only two men. The first was George Washington, who built the country, and the second was Abraham Lincoln, who saved it. Their writings, MacArthur said, contained the answers to "pretty much everything."

Inchon is unique in modern military history. It represents the only battle in which the commander deliberately rejected the results of careful scientific staff planning and decided to follow his intuition.

It worked, magnificently. The marines got ashore, raced to Seoul, broke the siege at Pusan, and drove on to the 38th parallel, the pre-war boundary. MacArthur had won a victory unmatched in American history. Still, it had been hard on the nerves, and the shaken navy declared afterwards that even though it was successful, never again would the United States Navy participate in such an attack.

After Inchon, MacArthur was in an expansive mood. He also had learned something from World War II. This time he did not take sole credit (although he might have been justified), nor did he neglect the army's sister services. He wired back to the States, "The navy and marines have never shone more brightly than this morning," and when he went ashore he stayed away from personal references. He told Admiral Struble, "I've lived a long time and played with the navy a long time. They've never failed me."

When MacArthur's troops reached the 38th parallel, a basic political decision had to be made. Contrary to the usual story, MacArthur did not make it. The United Nations, reaffirming its previously stated purpose of unifying Korea and holding free elections, implicitly gave him permission to drive north to the Yalu River and inflict total defeat upon the North Koreans.

The advance went well. On October 15 Truman flew to Wake Island to confer with the general (it was their first meeting) and to set a future course. MacArthur, whose abilities as a prophet were somewhat suspect after his 1941 statements about Japanese intentions in the Philippines and about the efficiency of the Filipino Army, said the war would be over by Thanksgiving. Truman asked about the prospects for Russian and Chinese intervention.

"Very little," the general replied. "Had they interfered in the first or second month it would have been decisive. We are no longer fearful of their intervention. We no longer stand hat in hand. The Chinese have 300,000 men in Manchuria. Of these probably not more than one hundred to one hundred and twenty-five thousand are distributed along the Yalu River. Only fifty to sixty thousand could be gotten across the Yalu River. They have no air force. Now that we have bases for our air force in Korea, if the Chinese tried to get down to Pyongyang, there would be the greatest slaughter."

Later, when the Chinese did come and drove MacArthur back past Seoul, he denied ever having made such a statement. On another occasion he hedged by saying that when he made the prediction, he assumed he could bomb the Chinese across the Yalu. In a third version MacArthur explained that he was dependent upon the C.I.A. for his intelligence, the implication being that he had received the wrong poop. The record is clear enough that, whatever the reason, he did say the Chinese would not come in, and that if they did he would wipe them out.

The lightly armed Chinese came, hit MacArthur's widely scattered forces, and inflicted a crushing defeat. There was an outcry in the American press, with journals like the *Washington Post* and the New York *Herald Tribune* demanding MacArthur's recall. The *Herald Tribune* roundly declared, "Unsound deployment of United Nations forces and a momentous blunder by General MacArthur helped insure the success of the enemy's strategy."

Truman stuck with MacArthur, partly because Matt Ridgway was conducting the actual operations and was able to stiffen the resistance, mainly because the president did not want to face the political repercussions. MacArthur spent most of his time in Japan now, issuing public letters and giving exclusive interviews to nearly every correspondent who showed up.

His theme was always the same. He should be allowed to bomb beyond the Yalu, and he should be authorized to use the Chinese forces on Formosa against the Reds on the mainland. MacArthur argued that there was no substitute for victory, and he said flatly and honestly that he could not understand Truman's policy. With deep sincerity and great eloquence, he described the horrors of the war, and declared that in all conscience he could not subscribe to a policy that aimed toward a stalemate (after MacArthur's defeat near the Yalu, Truman changed his policy from one of forced reunification in Korea to one of the *status quo ante bellum*). The sacrifice of the United Nations troops and of the people of South Korea had to be made meaningful, and this could only be done by achieving victory in the war (meaning reunification under the South Korean government).

The real issue was not the use of troops in Formosa or the bombing across the Yalu—these were tactical matters. MacArthur was again questioning the fundamentals of American foreign policy, and arguing for the adoption of an Asia-first attitude. Hoyt Vandenberg, Chief of Staff of the Air Force, explained to MacArthur that American power was not unlimited, and that if he committed the air force across the Yalu as MacArthur wanted he would be unable to meet a Soviet threat in Europe. The argument did not impress MacArthur. He contended that if Asia fell to Communism, so would Europe.

Every member of the Joint Chiefs of Staff disagreed. During the Senate hearings which followed his dismissal, MacArthur said they supported him, and implied that Truman and the State Department were rejecting the advice of all their professional military advisers. This imposed upon the Joint Chiefs the painful duty of saying publicly that

MacArthur was mistaken. Bradley put the Chiefs' position best. "So long as we regarded the Soviet Union as the main antagonist and Western Europe as the main prize," he explained, the strategy advanced by MacArthur "would involve us in the wrong war at the wrong place at the wrong time and with the wrong enemy."

In December 1950, and again in early 1951, Truman issued general orders that no one in government service should make a statement on foreign policy without clearing it with the State Department. They were obviously aimed at MacArthur. It was, to a certain extent, a muzzling, but nearly every member of the armed forces thought MacArthur had gone too far in his public disagreements. As a professional soldier, he obviously had a duty to disagree with the administration when he thought it was wrong, but his criticism—most felt—would have been more effective and listened to more closely if he had made it privately.

In April 1951, MacArthur sent a letter to Republican Representative Joseph Martin, who read it in the House. In the letter MacArthur raised all the basic points again. As MacArthur saw it, he was explaining to a confused and bamboozled public what a ruinous course their civilian leaders had chosen—he was, in short, doing his duty. As Truman saw it, MacArthur had issued a direct and unavoidable challenge.

Harry Truman was not a man to back down. He also was not the man to handle a situation like this with any subtlety or grace. Like a bludgeon, he used his powers and fired MacArthur. "I could do nothing else," he explained, "and still be president."

MacArthur returned for his hero's welcome, while Truman's popularity sank to the lowest point possible. The president was confident, however, that the public would, upon reflection, back him, and the indications are that it did. MacArthur toured the country repeating his message, but rather quickly he began to fade from the center of the public's conscience. By 1952 the people were glad enough to elect Eisenhower and get the war over on Truman's original terms—the restoration of South Korea. The Europe-first policy remained in force throughout the fifties.

MacArthur took up residence in the Waldorf Hotel in New York, where he lived a quiet life and wrote his memoirs. He still lived in isolated splendor, still baffled visitors with his astonishing memory and forthright views. On occasion he went out into the public, where he could still move people to deep emotion. Once he visited President John Kennedy and out-quipped one of the best ad-libbers ever to live in the White House. He had not lost the capacity to surprise—no one had expected MacArthur could be a humorist. With all of his many sides he remained true to his central characteristics. Looking over his eighty-odd years as he wrote his memoirs, he could not find a single major mistake to confess. He remained independent, relied on no one, did not allow people to get close to him, and defied understanding.

He was not immune to all the laws of human nature. As an old man his thoughts more and more returned to earlier, happier days, to baseball games on the Plain, to battles of World War I. In May 1962, he delivered one of his last public addresses. It was to his first and most lasting love, the cadets of West Point. He ended by saying, "Today marks my final roll call with you. But I want you to know that when I cross the river my last conscious thoughts will be of the Corps—and the Corps—and the Corps.

"I bid you farewell."

A FATEFUL FRIENDSHIP

Eisenhower and Patton

They never had much in common. George Patton was a conceited, spoiled child from an extremely wealthy, snobbish family. He dressed as he pleased, said what he liked, and did as he wished. He cursed like a trooper and told off his inferiors—and sometimes his superiors—with profane eloquence. Although he moved easily in America's highest society, many people, soldiers included, thought Patton vulgar. Dwight Eisenhower came from the wrong side of the tracks in a tiny midwestern town. He had to support himself while in high school by working nights in a creamery; he wanted to be well liked, and he obeyed his superiors. The only thing he did to attract attention was to do his duty quietly and efficiently.

Patton was an erratic genius, given to great outbursts of energy and flashes of brilliant insight. He was capable of sustained action, but not of systematic thought. A superstitious man, he was much taken by his own *déjà vu* and his sensations of having been somewhere before; he devoutly believed that he had fought with Alexander the Great and with Napoleon, among others. Eisenhower had a steady, orderly mind. When he looked at a problem, he would take everything into account, weigh possible alternatives, and deliberately decide on a course of action. Patton seldom arrived at a solution through an intellectual process; rather, he *felt* that this or that was what he should do, and he did it.

Patton strutted while Eisenhower walked. Both were trim, athletic, outdoor types; but Eisenhower was usually grinning, Patton frowning. Patton indulged his moods, while Eisenhower kept a grip on his temper.

Despite the differences, the two soldiers shared a friendship that survived two decades and (according to Eisenhower) "heated, sometimes almost screaming arguments . . ." Their common West Point training—Patton graduated in 1909, Eisenhower in 1915—helped hold them together; other factors were, however, more important. Both had a deep interest in tanks and armored warfare. Patton, five years Eisenhower's senior, had led tanks in battle during World War I; Eisenhower had trained tank crews in Pennsylvania. After 1918, when the War Department almost ignored the new weapon, Patton and Eisenhower, like those junior officers in England, France, and Germany who believed that the tank would dominate the battlefield in the next war, naturally drew together. But beyond this mutual interest, they respected each other. Patton's dash, courage, and recklessness complemented Eisenhower's stubborn, straightforward caution. Each admired the other and benefited from the relationship.

The two young majors met in 1919, and almost immediately they began an argument that would last until Patton's death. Patton thought the chief ingredient in modern warfare was inspired leadership on the battlefield. Eisenhower felt that leadership was just one factor. He believed that Patton was inclined to indulge his romantic nature, neglecting such matters as logistics, a proper worldwide strategy, and getting along with allies.

A letter Patton wrote to Eisenhower in July 1926 illustrated the difference between the two men. "Ike" had just spent a year at the Command and General Staff School at Fort Leavenworth. He had applied himself with almost monastic diligence to his studies and had graduated first in his class. Patton, fearful that his friend had concentrated too hard on such subjects as transportation, staff functioning, and how to draft a memo, decided to set him straight. After congratulating Eisenhower on his achievement, Patton declared, "We talk a hell of a lot about tactics and stuff and we never get to brass tacks. Namely what is it that makes the poor S.O.B. who constitutes the casualty list fight." Leadership was Patton's answer. Officers had to get out and inspire the men, keep them moving. One or two superheroes would not do; Patton thought any such notion was "bull." Finally, he concisely summed up the difference between his and Eisenhower's approach to battle. "Victory in the next war will depend on EXECUTION not PLANS." By execution, Patton said, he meant keeping the infantry advancing under fire.

Eisenhower disagreed. Plans, he said, meant that food and ammunition and gasoline would continue to reach the men at the front lines, that pressure would be applied where it hurt the enemy the most, that supreme effort would not be wasted. The most difficult tasks in the next war, Eisenhower believed, would be raising, training, arming, and transporting the men; getting them ashore in the right places; maintaining good liaison with allied forces. Execution would matter, of course, but it was only one part of the total picture.

During the thirties their army assignments kept the two men apart, but they stayed in touch. It was a bad time for armor advocates: the army had practically no tanks. Patton, disgusted, joined the cavalry, where he could at least play polo, while Eisenhower worked patiently through a series of staff jobs. Patton lived expensively—entertaining, racing around in sports cars, keeping his own string of polo ponies, and traveling by private yacht and private plane. This was in an army that was, for most practical purposes, poverty-stricken. During the Depression, Congress cut officers' salaries and introduced annoying economy measures on army posts. Most career men tightened their belts, entertained frugally, and associated only with their fellows. Patton's ostentatious display of his wealth was offensive to most of his colleagues, especially his superiors; they could not begin to compete with him.

Eisenhower, meanwhile, kept begging for assignments with the troops, but his superiors, most notably General Douglas MacArthur, liked to have the hardworking, efficient major around. He lived according to the accepted pattern and was one of the best-liked officers in the army. While Patton disported himself outside the system, Eisenhower worked from within. In 1940, for example, Patton—who had finally become a colonel in 1938—took command of a tank brigade of the 2d Armored Division. He found that most of his tanks were not working because of an absence of spare parts. When a mechanic pointed out that many usable parts were available from Sears Roebuck, Patton ordered them and paid out of his own pocket. He kept the bill a secret, but it probably ran into many thousands of dollars. As chief of staff of a division, Eisenhower often faced similar problems. His solution was to write a friend in the War Department and, with this extra prodding, get the material he needed through the proper channels.

When World War II began in Europe, Patton quickly forgot about polo and his active social life. Eisenhower was certain that Patton would go straight to the top when America got into the war, and in September 1940 he wrote his friend: "I suppose it's too much to hope that I could have a regiment in your division, because I'm still almost three years away from my colonelcy." Still, he thought he could do the job.

Patton may have had his doubts, and in any case he had a better idea about what Eisenhower could do for him. Apply for armor, Patton advised, and join up with me as my chief of staff. "He needs a brake to slow him down," General George C. Marshall once said of Patton, "because he is apt to coast at breakneck speed, propelled by his enthusiasm and exuberance." Patton himself understood this, and he thought Eisenhower would be the perfect brake.

They did not get together, however, until two years later. Eisenhower, by 1941, had become a temporary colonel and was chief of staff for the Third Army. His son, John, was considering whether to go to West Point or to study law, and he asked his father's advice. Eisenhower said that the army had been good to him, although he expected to retire as a colonel and admitted that his hopes had once been higher. Still, he had to be realistic; he warned John that he would never get rich or famous in the army. He could get instead the satisfaction of knowing he had made a contribution to his country. John took West Point.

Patton, meanwhile, continued to move ahead in armor. He did so because of his abilities, of course, but more to the point because the Army Chief of Staff, General Marshall, was a remarkable man, able to overlook idiosyncrasy and to judge by performance. A rigid soldier and old-fashioned gentleman himself, Marshall had seen the impetuous Patton in action at Saint-Mihiel in World War I. He had marked him favorably in his famous little black book, a book he used ruthlessly after he became chief of staff to weed out the unfit and to jump men like Patton over their superiors. Marshall moved Patton up to temporary brigadier general in 1940 and, in April 1941, to major general.

When America entered the war in December 1941, Marshall called Eisenhower to Washington; he did not know Eisenhower, but he had read his efficiency reports and observed his brilliant staff work in maneuvers in Louisiana in 1941. Within three months Eisenhower was head of the Operations Division of the War Department. Marshall was so favorably impressed that three months later he sent Major General Eisenhower to London to take command of the European Theatre of Operations. In July 1942 Great Britain and America decided that their first joint offensive of the war would be an invasion of French North Africa. Eisenhower had pleased the British as much as he had Marshall, and they agreed that he was the ideal Supreme Commander for the invasion. He could choose his own assault commanders; the first man he picked was Patton. It was an ironic reversal of what Eisenhower had hoped for two years earlier.

Eisenhower gave his old acquaintance the potentially toughest assignment, that of hitting the beach at Casablanca. Shortly after Patton arrived, however, the French quit fighting, as a result of Eisenhower's deal with Admiral Jean Louis Darlan, Vichy's chief of state in French Africa. This brought the North African French into the Allied camp, and Patton lost his chance for glory. He compensated by competing with the local sultans in lavish living during three months as head of United States occupation forces in Morocco, and by hobnobbing with upper-echelon Vichy Frenchmen so convivially that it struck some Americans as aid and comfort to the enemy.

In March 1943, following the Battle of Kasserine Pass, Eisenhower brought Patton to Tunisia to take command of the II Corps, which had been badly battered. He told Patton to restore morale, raise the image of American troops in British eyes by winning a victory or two, and take care of himself. Patton, Eisenhower said, did not have to prove to him that he was courageous.

Patton had always been a martinet when it came to morale. He himself indulged in gaudy uniforms, but he insisted that his enlisted men dress meticulously according to regulation, even in the front lines. He worked them hard, subjecting them to twice as many drills and training exercises as most generals. His insistence on spit and polish was so great that he once tried to get Bill Mauldin's famous "Stars and Stripes" cartoons banned from his area because Mauldin's GIs always looked like the sloppiest soldiers in the world. (Eisenhower, incidentally, overruled Patton on the issue, after Patton called Sergeant Mauldin into his headquarters and raked him over.) It is doubtful that Patton's men ever loved him—that notion was mainly journalists' copy—but they did respect him, and they respected themselves as a result. He used his techniques with the II Corps, and they worked. He made the man shave regularly and stand straight, and then scored a tactical victory over the great German tank commander, Erwin Rommel. A grateful Eisenhower gave Patton the most coveted combat position in the army—command of the invasion of Sicily.

Patton did well. His Seventh Army sent the German and Italian opposition reeling across Sicily past Palermo. It was a campaign that left the British, especially General Bernard Montgomery, awestruck. Patton had proved himself to be a master of pursuit, a general who could keep the troops going under all conditions. He was not so good at a set-piece battle. When he turned his army east for the drive to Messina, across from the Italian toe, the Germans were waiting. Progress was exasperatingly slow. The narrow roads, winding through the mountains, gave the Germans every advantage. Patton was almost beside himself.

On August 3, while he was in this mood, he tried to make himself feel better in a way that had often worked well before: visiting an evacuation hospital near the front and talking to brave soldiers who had recently been wounded in action. This time it backfired. The general had gone around the tent and chatted with a number of bandaged men, asking them how they got hit, where they were from, and so on, when he came to Private C. H. Kuhl, a young infantryman from Mishawaka, Indiana. Kuhl was sitting on a box, and he had no visible sign of wounds. To Patton's query, the soldier said simply, "I guess I can't take it."

As Patton admitted later, he "flew off the handle." In his opinion, most cases of "shell shock" or "battle fatigue" were just plain cowardice, and he proceeded to say so to Kuhl in a high, excited voice and with an appropriate selection from his rich selection of profanity. Then he slapped Kuhl across the face with his gloves and turned to the medical officer in charge, shouting: "Don't admit this son of a bitch. I don't want yellow-bellied bastards like him hiding their lousy cowardice around here, stinking up this place of honor!" Patton then stalked out. Kuhl, who had indeed been admitted to the hospital on a diagnosis of psychoneurotic anxiety, was found upon examination to have a chronic diarrhea, malaria, and a temperature of 102.2°F.

This slapping incident, although it shocked those who witnessed it, was not widely reported. Patton felt that he had done the right thing; he dictated a brief account of the episode for inclusion in his diary, and added in his own hand: "One sometimes slaps a baby to bring it to." He then issued a memorandum to the officers of his command directing that any soldiers pretending to be "nervously incapable of combat" should not be sent to hospitals but, if they refused to fight, should be "tried by court-martial for cowardice in the face of the enemy."

Having rehearsed his hospital scene with Private Kuhl, Patton repeated it a week later with added flourishes. Early on the hot Monday afternoon of August 10, while on his way to a military conference with General Omar Bradley (who was then Patton's subordinate), his command car passed a sign pointing the way to the 93rd Evacuation Hospital. Patton told his driver to turn in. A few minutes later he was going from litter to litter, talking to the battle casualties and commending them for doing a good job against the Germans. Then he came to a man who, like Private Kuhl, was fully dressed, unbandaged, and apparently in good health. "What's the matter with you?" the general asked.

When the soldier said the trouble was "my nerves" and began to sob, Patton exploded. "Your nerves, hell, you are just a goddamn coward, you yellow son of a bitch," he screamed. He then struck the soldier twice, knocking his helmet liner off so hard that it rolled into the next tent; Patton even pulled out one of his famous pearl-handled revolvers and waved it in the man's face. "You ought to be lined up against a wall and shot," one witness reported the general as shouting. "In fact, I ought to shoot you myself right now, goddamn you!"

The commanding officer of the hospital was incensed. Private Paul Bennett, the victim of Patton's outburst, was a regular-army soldier with a good fighting record; he had begun to show signs of unusual nervous tension only after receiving from his young wife a picture of their new-born baby. Moreover, he had gone to the hospital reluctantly, insisting that he did not want to leave his unit. Within a week a detailed report of the incident had worked its way from the hospital through channels to Eisenhower's headquarters in Algiers.

It was 10:30 A.M., August 17, and Patton's men had just triumphantly entered Messina. Eisenhower was feeling friendly toward Patton, and after reading the report he said mildly, "I guess I'll have to give General Patton a jacking up." He then praised Patton for the "swell job" he had done in Sicily. Eisenhower did order Brigadier General Frederick Blessé, his surgeon general, to go to Sicily and conduct a full investigation, but he warned him to keep it quiet. "If this thing ever gets out," Eisenhower told Blessé, "they'll be howling for Patton's scalp, and that will be the end of Georgie's service in this war. I simply cannot let that happen. Patton is *indispensable* to the war effort."

Eisenhower then sat down and wrote a personal letter to Patton. By now he was beginning to feel the seriousness of Patton's offense and to realize that more than a "jacking up" was required. "I clearly understand that firm and drastic measures are at times necessary in order to secure desired objectives," Eisenhower wrote, "but this does not excuse brutality, abuse of the sick, nor exhibition of uncontrollable temper in front of subordinates." Eisenhower said he did not intend to institute any formal investigation, or put anything in Patton's official file; but he did warn that if the reports proved true he would have to "seriously question your good judgment and your self-discipline." This would "raise serious doubts . . . as to your future usefulness."

In conclusion Eisenhower declared, "No letter that I have been called upon to write in my military career has caused me the mental anguish of this one, not only because of my long and deep personal friendship for you but because of my admiration for your military qualities." But, Eisenhower warned, "I assure you that conduct such as described in the accompanying report will *not* be tolerated in this theater no matter who the offender may be."

But by this point the press corps in Sicily had got hold of the story. The reporters had conducted their own investigation and were prepared to make it public. "If I am correctly informed," one reporter noted, "General Patton has subjected himself to general court-martial by striking an enlisted man under his command." They wanted to know, a committee of correspondents told Eisenhower's chief of staff, what Eisenhower was going to do to punish Patton.

All of Eisenhower's famous abilities as a mediator were needed now. He called the reporters into his office and frankly confessed that he was doing all he could to hold on to Patton. He asked them to keep the story quiet so that Patton could "be saved for the great battles facing us in Europe." The effort worked. The correspondents entered into a gentleman's agreement to sit on the story.

Patton, meanwhile, tried to make amends. He apologized, although somewhat curtly, to Private Bennett and to the nurses and doctors of the 93rd Evacuation Hospital. He wrote Eisenhower, "I am at a loss to find the words with which to express my chagrin and grief at having given you, a man to whom I owe everything and for whom I would gladly lay down my life, cause for displeasure with me." The incident was closed, or so Eisenhower hoped.

Three months later Drew Pearson learned of the Patton slapping incident and gave it full treatment in a radio broadcast. Eisenhower's chief of staff made matters worse when, in a press conference, he admitted that Eisenhower had not officially reprimanded Patton. Since there was a shortage of battlefront news at the time, the story received front-page treatment everywhere. Eisenhower, the War Department, and the White House each received hundreds of letters, most of them demanding that any general who would strike a private in a hospital be summarily dismissed from the service. The letter writers were especially upset because Eisenhower apparently had done nothing to censure Patton.

Eisenhower made no public defense of his actions. Nor was he willing to throw Patton to the wolves. He did answer a number of the incoming letters of criticism, carefully pointing out that Patton was too important to lose. In each case he asked that the letter be regarded as strictly personal. He advised Patton to keep quiet, since "it is my judgment that this storm will blow over." In the end, it did.

In the late fall of 1943 Eisenhower received his appointment as Supreme Commander for Overlord, the invasion of France. One major factor in his selection was his ability to get British and American officers to work together, something that would be even more important in Overlord than it had been in the Mediterranean. For this reason he was tempted to leave Patton behind. "Georgie" was something of an Anglophobe and loved to tweak sensitive English noses, especially Montgomery's; and Montgomery would be one of the chief commanders in Overlord. But despite this, and despite the slapping incident, Eisenhower decided to bring Patton along. He told Marshall, who had doubts, that he thought Patton was cured of his temper tantrums, partly because of "his personal loyalty to you and to me," but mainly because "he is so avid for recognition as a great military commander that he will ruthlessly suppress any habit of his own that will tend to jeopardize it." Marshall, remembering his own earlier admiration for Patton, and bending to Eisenhower's insistence, agreed.

Eisenhower's most important responsibility as Supreme Commander was the defeat of the German armies. He felt that whatever trouble Patton caused him in other ways, he would make a tremendous combat contribution to victory. Without accepting Patton's contention that execution was more important than planning, Eisenhower recognized that "the first thing that usually slows up operations is an element of caution, fatigue or doubt on the part of a higher commander." Patton was never affected by these.

So Patton, who had been in the doghouse without a real command since Sicily, went to England to prepare for the great invasion. On April 25, 1944, he went to the opening of a Welcome Club that the people of

Knutsford had organized for the growing number of American troops in the town. About sixty people were there, sitting on hard-backed chairs in a cold, damp, depressing room, listening to insipid speeches on Allied unity. Patton was thoroughly bored. When asked to speak, he ad-libbed: he thought Anglo-American unity important "since it is the evident destiny of the British and Americans to rule the world, [and] the better we know each other the better job we will do."

Patton thought the meeting was private; but a reporter was present. The statement went out over the British wire services, and the next morning the British press indignantly featured it. Some editorial writers were angry because Patton had omitted Russia from the list of ruling powers; others cited the implicit insult to the smaller nations. The next day Patton's remarks were widely circulated in the United States, where he was denounced by both liberal and conservative congressmen. All agreed that generals ought to stay out of politics.

Patton, in short, had put his foot in his mouth. Eisenhower was disgusted. In his small office at SHAEF headquarters in Bushey Park, on the Thames River near London, he dictated a letter to Patton. "I have warned you time and again against your impulsiveness in action and speech and have flatly instructed you to say nothing that could possibly be misinterpreted. . . ." Then he sent General Marshall a cable expressing his disgust over the incident. He added, "I have grown so weary of the trouble he constantly causes you and the War Department to say nothing of myself, that I am seriously contemplating the most drastic action"—namely, sending Patton home.

Marshall told Eisenhower to do what he thought best, and on April 30 Eisenhower replied: "I will relieve him unless some new and unforeseen information should be developed in the case." Eisenhower felt Lieutenant General Courtney H. Hodges would be satisfactory as Patton's replacement—and Hodges had no record of getting his superiors in trouble. Eisenhower admitted that he had about given up on Patton: "After a year and a half of working with him it appears hopeless to expect that he will ever completely overcome his lifelong habit of posing and self-dramatization which causes him to break out in these extraordinary ways."

At 11 A.M. on May 1, Eisenhower met with Patton at Bushey Park. An old hand at getting out of a fix, Patton let out all the stops. He told Eisenhower that he felt miserable, but he would fight for his country if "they" would let him. Alternatively, he dramatically offered to resign his commission to save his old friend from embarrassment. He seemed on the verge of tears. The outpouring of emotion made Eisenhower slightly uncomfortable; he did not really want Patton on his knees begging. He ended the interview by dismissing Patton without having made a decision.

For the next two days Eisenhower mulled it over. He finally decided that Patton was too valuable to lose and sent a wire informing him that he would stay on. Patton celebrated with a drink, then sent a sentimental letter to Eisenhower expressing eternal loyalty and gratitude. To his diary, however, he confessed that his retention "is not the result of an accident" but rather "the work of God."

Eisenhower's aide, Harry Butcher, noted that Patton "is a master of flattery and succeeds in turning any difference of views with Ike into a deferential acquiescence to the views of the Supreme Commander." But if Butcher saw something that Eisenhower missed, there was a reverse side to the coin. Patton bragged that he was tolerated as an erratic genius because he was considered indispensable, and he was right. The very qualities that made him a great actor also made him a great commander, and Eisenhower knew it. "You owe us some victories," Eisenhower told Patton when the incident was closed. "Pay off and the world will deem me a wise man."

Patton paid off. On July 30, 1944, eight weeks after the invasion of Normandy, his Third Army began to tear across France in a blitzkrieg in reverse. Eisenhower used Patton's talents with the skill of a concert master, giving him leeway, holding him back when necessary, keeping him away from Montgomery's throat (and vice versa), and making sure that Bradley kept a close watch on his movements. It must be added that Patton showed small appreciation of Eisenhower's peculiar responsibilities. To hold the alliance together, Eisenhower had to humor Montgomery on a number of occasions. When he learned that Eisenhower had given more supplies to Montgomery than to the Third Army, Patton is said to have mumbled, "Ike's the best damn general the British have got."

Patton had something of the boy in him. He liked to believe that he was putting something over on his superiors, that he was getting away with mischief. On a number of occasions Patton thought he was fooling both Bradley and Eisenhower. When he received orders to carry out a reconnaissance in force at the German border, for example, he turned it into a full offensive. He thought neither Bradley nor Eisenhower realized what he was up to; but of course they did, and had counted on it.

Aside from his drive through France, Patton's two great moments came during the Battle of the Bulge and when he crossed the Rhine River. On December 19, three days after Hitler's last offensive began, Eisenhower and his chief subordinates at SHAEF met at Verdun with Bradley, Patton, and other field commanders. The Germans had caught the Allies by surprise and were making significant gains. Sitting around a potbellied stove in a damp, chilly, squad room, Eisenhower opened the meeting by announcing that he only wanted to see cheerful faces at the table. "The present situation is to be regarded as one of opportunity for us and not of disaster," he said. Patton grinned and declared, "Hell, let's have the guts to let the —— —— —— go all the way to Paris. Then we'll really cut 'em off and chew 'em up." Eisenhower grinned back, but said that the Germans would never get across the Meuse River.

When the Germans struck, Patton had been preparing an offensive of his own, headed east. Eisenhower ordered him to switch directions, attack north, and hit the Germans in the Bulge on their left flank. In three days Patton got all his divisions turned and was on the road. By December 26 he had battered his way through to Bastogne and, along with Montgomery's forces on the German right flank, he stopped the German thrust.

In March 1945 Patton's Third Army reached the Rhine. A few American troops had already made a surprise crossing at Remagen, where they had found a bridge intact, but the main crossings were yet to come. The big effort was to be made in the north, near the Ruhr industrial concentration, by Montgomery's British and Canadian troops. Ever since Sicily, Patton had been in keen competition with Montgomery, and he was determined to get his men across the historic river first. The British general's preparations were detailed and meticulous. On March 24, after a massive artillery barrage, Montgomery started to cross. To his astonishment, he learned that Patton and his men were already over. Patton had been carrying bridging equipment and a navy detachment with landing craft close up behind his infantry ever since the liberation of Paris, for just this moment. With less than half Montgomery's strength, he beat the British to the east bank. While he himself was going over one of the Third Army's pontoon bridges, Patton paused and deliberately undid his fly. "I have been looking forward to this for a long time," he said.

Six weeks later the war was over. Peace highlighted the contrasting personalities of Eisenhower and Patton. Eisenhower moved smoothly into his new job as head of the occupation. He faithfully and without question carried out his superiors' orders. Patton chafed. He talked about driving the Russians back to the Volga River. He got chummy with German generals. As military governor in Bavaria, he kept former Nazis and even some SS officials in the local administration because, he argued, no one else was available. Actually, there were others available, men of Konrad Adenauer's stamp; but it was easier for Patton to work with the old hands. In any case Patton's policy ran exactly counter to national policy, and Eisenhower ordered him to get rid of the Nazis. But except for a few prominent officials, Patton did nothing. He was sure that, before long, German and American generals would be fighting side by side against the Russians.

His area soon gained a dubious reputation, and the press waited for a chance to bait Patton into damning the de-Nazification policy. It came on September 22, when he called a press conference and asserted that the military government "would get better results if it employed more former members of the Nazi party in administrative jobs." A reporter, trying to appear casual, asked, "After all, General, didn't most ordinary Nazis join their party in about the same way that Americans become Republicans or Democrats?"

"Yes," Patton agreed. "That's about it."

The headlines the next day screamed that Patton had said the Nazis were just like Republicans and Democrats back home.

Eisenhower phoned Patton and told him to get over to headquarters in Frankfurt right away. Patton arrived wearing a simple jacket and plain trousers rather than his fancy riding breeches, and he left behind the pearl-handled pistols he usually wore. The generals were together for two hours. When Patton walked out he was pale: Ike had taken the Third Army away from him.

Eisenhower gave Patton a meaningless paper army to command. He stayed in Germany, spending most of his time hunting. In December, on a hunting expedition, his neck was broken in an automobile accident. Eisenhower, who had returned to Washington to become chief of staff, wrote him on December 10. "You can imagine what a shock it was to me to hear of your serious accident," the letter began. "At first I heard it on the basis of rumor and simply did not believe it, thinking it only a story. . . . I immediately wired Frankfurt and learned to my great distress that it was true."

Eisenhower told Patton he had notified Mrs. Patton and had given orders that everything possible should be arranged, including the fastest transportation available to fly Mrs. Patton to his bedside. "By coincidence, only the day before yesterday," Eisenhower continued, "I had directed that you be contacted to determine whether you wanted a particular job that appeared to be opening up here in the States. The real purpose of this note is simply to assure you that you will always have a job and not to worry about this accident closing out any of them for your selection."

Eisenhower confessed that "it is always difficult for me to express my true sentiments when I am deeply moved," but he wanted Patton to know "that you are never out of my thoughts and that my hopes and prayers are tied up in your speedy recovery. If anything at all occurs to you where I might be of some real help, don't hesitate a second to let an aide forward the message to me."

Mrs. Patton arrived at her husband's bedside the next day, and she read Eisenhower's letter to him. When she reached the end, he asked her to read the part about the job again.

Nine days later, George Patton died.

THE WAR ON THE HOME FRONT

For millions, World War II was the greatest catastrophe in history. Those who suffered most were the Jews, Russians, Germans, Japanese, Poles, Yugoslavs, Filipinos, and Chinese. Altogether, nearly 50,000,000 people were killed; millions more were terribly scarred, either physically or mentally. Trillions of dollars worth of property was destroyed, including art works and other irreplaceable cultural and historical treasures.

For other millions of people, Word War II was a boon. Those who benefited most were the yet-unborn Germans and Japanese. Among contemporaries, the people who benefited most, by far, were Americans.

The first thing that stands out about America in the war is that although the United States made a decisive contribution in Europe, and played *the* critical role in the Pacific, the cost of victory was relatively low. Fewer than 300,000 American soldiers, sailors, and airmen were killed, out of an armed force of some 16,000,000; as compared to most other belligerents, this was a low ratio. Although some American property in Hawaii, and a great deal in the Philippines, was destroyed, the forty-eight states suffered no damage. These two facts—a low casualty rate and almost no damage to property—meant that the American experience of war was far different from that of other nations.

Around the world, the most common emotion in the period 1939–45 was fear, the most common sensation was hunger. In the United States, fear and hunger were nearly absent. During the six-year war, no elections were held in Europe, Asia, Africa, or the Middle East; even Great Britain and France put democracy on hold. But in the United States during those six years, two presidential, three congressional, and hundreds of state elections were held, all of them hotly contested. Throughout the world freedom of speech was extinct—except in the English-speaking democracies.

These contrasts between America and the rest of a world at war are matched by the contrasts between prewar and postwar America. In countless ways it was a unique time; the half-decade, 1940–45, did more to shake America out of her past and to shape her future than any comparable period except the Civil War.

The biggest single difference between America in the 1930s and America mobilized for war was that everyone had jobs. Unemployment during the Depression averaged 15 to 20 percent, and sometimes reached 30 percent, in a work force that was almost exclusively male. But during the war, unemployment averaged only 1 percent in a greatly expanded work force, and that 1 percent consisted of people moving from one job to another. People who would have loved to have had a thirty-hour-per-week job in the Depression suddenly found they could work fifty, sixty, seventy hours if they wished, with time-and-a-half for all hours over forty.

Many good things flowed out of this employment boom. Between 1939 and 1945, per capita income doubled, rising from $1,231 to $2,390. Judy Litoff and David Smith, in their book, *Since You Went Away: World War II Letters from American Women on the Home Front,* show the human side of the situation. Polly Crow's husband was in the army; they had an infant son; she worked the swing shift at the Jefferson Boat Company outside Louisville, Kentucky, a company making big, ocean-going landing craft. "We now have about $780 in the bank and 5 bonds," Polly wrote to her husband, "which sho looks good to me and as soon as I get the buggie in good shape I can really pile it away."

Thanks to effective wage and price controls, inflation was moderate, so that most of the gain was real. With no new cars, new homes, washing machines, or other durable consumer goods for sale, most of the income went into savings. Personal savings increased tenfold, from $2,600,000,000 in 1939 to $29,600,000,000 in 1945.

A steady job and money in the bank meant financial security, something most Americans under thirty-five years old had experienced only as children, if ever. Another new experience was travel. Most Americans in 1940 had never been out of their home state, many of them never out of the county of their birth. Only a handful had been abroad. But between 1940 and 1945, some 12,000,000 young American men went overseas—not necessarily to the country or continent of their choice, but still into a different culture. Within the United States, more than 15,000,000 civilians moved during the war, more than one-half of them to new states. With 17 percent of the population on the move within a four-year period, this was a mass migration that dwarfed even the westward movement of the nineteenth century.

Nearly all those who left home were in their late teens, twenties, or thirties, which means that nearly everyone in those age groups moved at least once. This had a tremendously broadening effect on American politics and culture.

The internal migration helped break down regional prejudices and provincialism. Yankees and westerners who moved south, where most of the army bases were located, or southerners who moved west or north, where most of the war industries were located, learned to tolerate or understand if not actually approve of the different mores they encountered. The army helped in this process. Unlike the Civil War, when army units were recruited from a single state, in World War II men in most cases were thrown together willy-nilly—so much so that a war-spawned cliché of film and fiction is the squad made up of the hillbilly from Arkansas, the Jew from Brooklyn, the coal miner from Pennsylvania, the farmer from Ohio, the lumberman from Oregon, the Italian from Chicago, the Pole from Milwaukee, and the Cajun from Louisiana.

At first they hate each other; training draws them together; combat welds them into a band of brothers; they emerge by the final scene as just plain Americans with a strong sense of nationalism. And the truth is that this happened in life before it happened in art.

To sum up this string of generalizations, the American people in 1945 were far better off financially than they had been in 1940, with a broader and more tolerant and sophisticated outlook, and a deeper and more meaningful nationalism.

The differences between the war years and the Depression were no greater than those between the war years and the 1950s and 1960s. The generation that fought the war, those between fifteen and thirty-five years of age in 1940, transformed America in the decades after the war. A few examples will illustrate the point. City dwellers during the war went shopping "downtown" in solid masonry buildings of two or three stories. Small town and rural people shopped on "Main Street." Shopping centers, malls, drive-ins, and suburbs were undreamed of. Americans had more cars in 1940 than anyone else in the world, but, as historian William O'Neill points out, "the rule was the same as for bathrooms, one to a family." Almost no four-lane roads existed; businessmen traveled by train. Nearly everyone had a radio—again, one to a family (in 1945 there were 34,000,000 households; 33,000,000 of them had a radio, more than had indoor plumbing).

For entertainment other than the radio, local dances, concerts, private parties at home and the like, people went to the movies, some 85,000,000 people each week in 1945. Almost everyone saw the popular movies, such as *Casablanca, Thirty Seconds Over Tokyo, Bambi,* and *Guadalcanal Diary.* Patriotism was profitable for Hollywood, and the movie industry cashed in on the war in its typical shameless fashion. A few good movies were made, one or two of them classics, along with hundreds of stinkers.

Daily life was much different during the war than it would be only a decade or so later. Most clothes were made of cotton or wool; few buildings were air-conditioned; by mid-afternoon everyone looked a bit wilted. People dressed formally: middle-class men always wore a coat and tie in public; women wore a dress or suit. Except on the tennis court, no man ever appeared in shorts. Milk was home-delivered early in the morning, the mail twice a day. O'Neill remarks that "people could smoke all they wanted to and did. Wine was an affectation. Real Americans drank beer out of long-necked returnable glass bottles," and lots of it. Soft drinks were loaded with sugar. Again quoting O'Neill, "Good girls did not have sex before marriage. Good boys weren't supposed to but often fell on account of their animal nature, which they could not help. Thus all colleges locked female students in at night for their own protection."

Despite the New Deal reforms, the government did little for people. Social Security was brand new, offered limited benefits, and did not cover large parts of the work force. No medical help whatsoever was available for anyone from any agency of government.

But wartime government expanded far beyond anything even the most ardent New Dealer had thought possible in the 1930s. A bewildering variety of government agencies set prices, fixed wages, allocated resources, rationed gasoline and food and much else, and established priorities for military production. Almost none of these agencies survived the war, but the idea of big government did. The GIs (the very name, standing for Government Issue, bespoke the new role of government in everyday life) and their wives grew accustomed to government services and to a certain degree of government paternalism. Servicemen's wives received a government allowance of $28 per month, plus $12 for the first child and $10 for each additional child, and they were served by a national day-care program. Enlisted men were encouraged to allot $22 from their monthly pay of $50 to their wives.

Far more important was one of the wisest pieces of legislation Congress ever passed: the GI Bill of Rights of 1944. It provided support for college education as well as for home and business loans for veterans. Almost 8,000,000 veterans got educational assistance from the GI Bill. Other millions got loans. The total cost to the government was about $30,000,000,000, which was an even better investment than the purchase of Alaska, as the money was recovered many times over in taxes from the recipients. The effect on America's colleges and universities was simply staggering; the home loans got the suburbs started; business loans spawned a boom in small businesses.

The war dramatically changed political attitudes. In the 1930s most Americans felt that entering World War I had been a big mistake. Neutrality and disarmament were the themes of American diplomacy in the 1930s. Those policies, thought to be a means of avoiding war, had failed. In the 1940s people came to believe that the mistake had not been entering World War I; rather it had been failing to join and support the inter-war League of Nations. The new common wisdom was that collective security and military preparedness could have prevented World War II, so collective security and military preparedness became the keystones of postwar diplomacy, along with magnanimity toward the defeated, another hard-learned lesson of the Versailles settlement.

The overseas experience of the young men helped break down isolationism in America. Men who had fought and lived in North Africa, Europe, the Pacific, and Asia could not believe that what happened in the rest of the world was of no concern to Americans. People came to realize that no great nation could be isolationist in an age of long-range bombers, atomic weapons, and V-2 rockets.

One of the ways in which America during the war was different from what went before and what came after was the role of women, especially young women. And the first thing that was different for them was that, unless they lived near an army or navy base, few young men were around. This fact had many repercussions, the first of which was that the young women spent much more time with each other—providing support, entertainment, working together—than their mothers had or their daughters would. The housing shortage, especially around the bases and the industrial plants, forced them to share homes, not infrequently five or more to one home, with one bathroom and one kitchen. Gasoline was rationed—three gallons per week—not to save fuel, which was abundant, but to save rubber, which was impossible to obtain after the Japanese overran Southeast Asia. With a national speed limit of 35 miles per hour (also to save rubber), it hardly mattered, as long trips were too time-consuming; for driving around town to shop or getting to work, women formed car pools or rode buses.

Women also entered the work force in record numbers, something that is so well known that one need only mention "Rosie the Riveter" to make the point. Perhaps less well known is the way servicemen's wives with young children coped with the war. My mother's experiences, if not typical, were at least commonplace enough to provide an example. My dad, a doctor in a town of one thousand people in central Illinois, joined the navy the day after Pearl Harbor. I was six years old when the war began; I had a brother two years older and another two years younger. Mother, then thirty-one years old, was determined that we would stay together as a family as long as possible—so she and my brothers and I became camp followers. We lived in Chicago, Iowa, Florida, and Wisconsin. When Dad went to the Pacific in 1944, she went by train to San Francisco to see him off; we boys stayed with various relatives.

Ardent patriotism was rampant during the war; everyone pitched in. Mother ran a Cub Scout troop; we had our victory garden; she sent her boys out gathering milkweed pods (for making life jackets) and collecting old newspapers and tin cans; she worked an eight-hour day in the local pea cannery (alongside German POWs captured in North Africa). She made a hot meal for us every night, and she insisted on a clean plate—my sharpest memory of those meals is groaning at the sight of another meal of tuna fish and noodles with stale potato chips crumbled on top, only to hear Mother say, "Think of the poor starving children in Europe." She wrote to Dad every day, and she did volunteer work for the Red Cross.

How she did it, I don't know. But I know that she did. So did millions of other American women. As much as the men, they made victory possible; more than the men, they held the American family together.

They were helped by the women's magazines, which were full of exhortations. "Now is the time to prove to your husband (and to yourself) that you have the stuff in you that our pioneer ancestors had," one writer remarked. "You'll be on your mettle to prove that you are every bit as good a manager as you are a sweetheart." And Max Lerner wrote, rightly, "When the classic work on the history of women comes to be written, the biggest force for change in their lives will turn out to have been war. Curiously, war produces more dislocations in the lives of women who stay at home than of men who go off to fight."

Many of these young wives and mothers were teenagers. "Quickie" marriages were the norm—there were a million more marriages during the war than would have been expected at prewar rates. Teenagers got married because, in the moral atmosphere of the day, if they wanted to have a sexual experience before one of them went off to war, they had to stand in front of a preacher first. Many worried that such hasty marriages, followed by long separations, would never work, but most of them did. The girls became women. They traveled alone—or with their infants—to distant places on hot and stuffy or cold and overcrowded trains. They became proficient cooks and housekeepers, managed the finances, learned to fix the car, and wrote letters to their soldier-husbands that were consistently upbeat. "I write his dad everything our [baby] does," one young mother explained, "only in the letters I make it sound cute."

They were tough. Edith and Victor Speert of Cleveland, Ohio, were married in June 1942, just before he went off to the army. She went to work. At the end of the war, before he returned from Europe, she wrote to warn him, "I'm not exactly the same girl you left—I'm twice as independent as I used to be and to top it off, I sometimes think I've become 'hard as nails'—hardly anyone can evoke any sympathy from me. I've been living exactly as *I* want to and I do as I damn please. You are not married to a girl that's interested solely in a home—I shall definitely have to work all my life—I get emotional satisfaction out of working; I don't doubt that many a night you will cook the supper while I'm at a meeting. Also, dearest—I shall never wash and iron—there are laundries for that!"

One of the ironies of our history is that we fought our greatest war against the world's worst racist with a segregated army while maintaining, either by law or custom, a system of racial separation at home. The army assigned the overwhelming majority of its blacks to menial, rear-area tasks—they were not allowed into combat units, and their officers were lily white. In the capital of the nation leading the worldwide struggle for democracy and freedom, blacks got their water from separate drinking fountains, used segregated toilet facilities, could not eat in white restaurants, sat in the balcony in their own section in movie theaters, sat in the back of the bus, could not enter public parks, and otherwise were degraded in public in every way possible.

The extent of the racism that prevailed in wartime America cannot be exaggerated, or excused, but only marveled at. As the propaganda extolling democracy swelled, the subjugation of blacks continued. Throughout the South, and in much of the North, blacks could not vote. As another example, black servicemen were sometimes put to guarding German POWs who were employed in harvesting crops; in effect, the prisoners were migrant workers. They moved from one state to another by bus. They were fed at restaurants along the highway. The Germans sat down to eat; their black guards were not allowed inside.

Still, many blacks did improve their financial situation, most of them by moving out of the rural South to the urban North and West and taking jobs in war industries. There was tension on the job—although everyone understood that the shortage of labor made it necessary to hire blacks, many whites (and their political leaders) objected to blacks receiving equal pay—and even greater tension outside the workplace, because of the shortage of housing around the industrial plants. The result was race rioting, a euphemism for roving white gangs beating up on blacks. The worst was in Detroit in June 1943; twenty-nine blacks were killed, hundreds injured, thirteen hundred arrested. That one was well-publicized; fights, and sometimes riots, between white and black soldiers at army bases at home and overseas were not.

There were hints of progress. In April 1944 the Supreme Court ruled that blacks could not be barred from voting in the Texas Democratic party primaries. In December 1944, confronted with a severe shortage of front-line infantry, General Dwight Eisenhower allowed blacks to volunteer for such duty, promising that they would be integrated into combat units. Black sergeants had to give up their stripes to get the army to let them go into combat to fight for their country. Thousands did so. When the crisis was over, they went back to their segregated labor units, but they had fought so well that senior officers began to question the wisdom of keeping 12 percent of the army's troops out of the army's combat units. By 1950 the army was well on its way to becoming what it is today, the most successfully integrated organization in the United States. Two months after the war, there was a symbolic breakthrough for blacks: Branch Rickey, owner of the Brooklyn Dodgers, signed Jackie Robinson to the first contract ever for a black player in the major leagues.

While Americans deplored Hitler's racism, they fought an openly racist war in the Pacific. Official propaganda depicted the Japanese as beasts, vermin, subhuman. Treachery was their chief characteristic, it was felt, an attitude greatly strengthened by Pearl Harbor. Some 127,000 people of Japanese ancestry lived in the United States in 1941, 80,000 of them native-born citizens, or Nisei. Most of the Nisei were simple California truck farmers. This tiny group caused the greatest panic. They were suspected of sabotage—every forest fire on the West Coast was blamed on them—of sending signals by bonfires or automobile headlights to Japanese submarines, and of espionage. A demand arose, fed by politicians, including California Governor Earl Warren, to evacuate them to camps in the interior. Yet, in Hawaii, where Japanese-Americans made up one-quarter of the population, and where at least a few *had* engaged in espionage, there was no demand to remove them, because to do so would have disrupted the economy and thus the war effort.

In February 1942 President Roosevelt ordered the war department to move the Nisei away from the West Coast. General John DeWitt, who oversaw the evacuation, defended the policy with a curious logic: "The very fact that no sabotage has taken place to date is a disturbing and confirming indication that such action will be taken." The Japanese-Americans were rounded up, forced to sell their property at outrageously low prices, and shipped off to camps in the Western desert, or as far away as the Arkansas Delta, where they were put to work harvesting crops by day, living in camps surrounded by barbed wire at night. Two years later the Supreme Court ruled the evacuation was constitutional. Forty years later Congress condemned the relocation policy as a product of "war hysteria, racial prejudice, and failure of political leadership," and compensated internees with a payment of $20,000 each—too little, too late.

Private Herrett Wilson, in a letter to his mother written from the Pacific, put it in context. "I fought and killed so that the enemy might not invade our land," he said, "and I ask is it all for naught when red, white and blue fascists drive Nisei about like coyotes and plague the fathers, mothers, and relatives of our colored comrades that fight by our side."

Despite the treatment of Japanese-Americans and blacks, American hubris during World War II ran very high. Americans congratulated each other on living in the best, the freest, the richest, and most democratic country in the world. This was the other side of the deeper, more meaningful nationalism: it often became chauvinism, an overstated belief in American "exceptionalism," a conviction that this was the "American Century," an assumption that everything that came out of America was good, while what came out of the other 94 percent of the world was bad.

Americans claimed to be number one in everything, especially in science and technology. The development of the atomic bomb—perhaps the greatest single feat of industrial production in history—seemed to prove the point. But in fact, Americans took credit for many scientific achievements that actually originated elsewhere. The proximity fuse, radar, and sonar were British innovations. Penicillin was discovered in England, sulfa and DDT in Germany. America was badly behind the Germans in jet propulsion and solid-fuel rocketry. And the basic theoretical work on the atomic bomb was done by European scientists who had fled Hitler's Germany to come to the U.S.

What America did best was to take other people's ideas and research and improve the designs, then develop techniques for mass production. The atomic bomb is but one example. The heart of the story of America at war was engineering skill plus mass production. A nation that had been stuck in the doldrums of the Great Depression for ten years, unable to figure out how to put people to work or to utilize its industrial plant at even half capacity, responded to the stimulus of the war with an industrial mobilization that was staggering in scope and stunningly successful.

The raw figures from just one industry give some idea. In 1939 American factories produced a grand total of 5,856 aircraft of all types, 921 of them for the military. When President Roosevelt called for the production of 50,000 airplanes a year, people thought he was crazy. But in 1944 American factories produced 96,318 aircraft, all of them for military use. The total produced in the war was more than 250,000. The figures were roughly similar for trucks, jeeps, and tanks, all of which came off the assembly line in a never-ending stream. Shipyards built aircraft carriers faster than the Japanese or Germans could build patrol boats, even as they simultaneously turned out thousands of landing craft and Liberty ships. In 1945 one-half of all the ships afloat had been built in the United States.

The U.S. Army, at 175,000 men, hardly existed at the beginning of 1940. It was virtually without equipment. Five years later, at more than 8,000,000 strong, it was far and away the best-equipped army in the world, especially in tanks, artillery, and other heavy weapons. American industry accounted for one-half of all the world's 1945 weapons production.

Close cooperation between government and industry, which had been almost at war with each other during the New Deal, made this miracle possible. Government built war plants, then leased them to private industry on favorable terms. "Cost-plus" contracts guaranteed profits, as did liberal tax write-offs. Government suspended the enforcement of antitrust laws, but did enforce wage controls and all but forbade strikes. The great corporations benefited most, but small manufacturers also prospered.

One of the most persistent and worst problems of the Depression had been overproduction on America's farms. During the war this situation completely reversed. Farmers could not grow enough food; they greatly expanded the acreage under cultivation and used their profits to buy new tractors and other farm machinery; America became the granary of democracy, as well as the arsenal.

Government intervention in the economy was pervasive and went far beyond anything ever before dreamed of. Government agencies decided which manufacturers got the steel and aluminum, critical to all weapons; who got workers; who got gasoline and food; and more. People cheated on the rationing systems; there was an active black market; fortunes were made; but in general the system worked. Sometimes it even provided a bit of humor. A classified advertisement in San Diego read: "Gentleman would like to meet attractive young lady with four good tires." Another in New York read: "For sale—four almost new deluxe white wall tires and tubes for $450. Throw in '38 Lincoln convertible."

In every way possible, government tried to make each individual feel that he or she was an integral part of the war effort. The most obvious, easiest, and most widely practiced method was to encourage people to invest in war bonds. Children put in pennies, workers and soldiers had payroll deductions, movie stars sold bonds for kisses at rallies. The bonds helped curb inflation by sopping up excess purchasing power.

Everyone signed up for the war effort, many to their great profit. Songwriters turned out tunes such as "Praise the Lord and Pass the Ammunition," "You're a Sap, Mr. Jap," and "We're Gonna Find a Feller Who Is Yeller and Beat Him Red, White and Blue." Hollywood cashed in with shallow and simplistic war movies in which brave, blond, clean shaven, always optimistic GIs performed improbably heroic deeds against overwhelming odds. Private firms used advertising to trumpet their patriotism. Newspaper and magazine ads showed smiling servicemen and defense workers drinking Coke to keep them going, chewing their favorite gum to relieve tension, smoking cigarettes to reward themselves for shooting down a Jap plane or turning out a record number of artillery shells. Those who had nothing to sell to the public— Ford, General Motors, General Electric—placed ads showing soldiers in foxholes dreaming of the cars they would buy when it was all over, or beaming housewives lost in fantasy about the new refrigerators and stoves they would get.

Wartime propaganda, on the whole, was about as bad as official propaganda usually is, and little need be said about it, other than that it depicted a world in which all the good was on our side—the Russian Communists were transformed into agrarian reformers, Stalin into Uncle Joe—while the enemy had no redeeming trait of any kind. But having said that, it needs to be noted that our propaganda was mild compared to that coming out of Berlin and Tokyo. If Frank Capra's famous "Why We Fight" propaganda series, made in Hollywood at government expense and shown to almost all the servicemen, was grossly oversimplified in its presentation of the causes of the war and the aims of the Allies, it should be added that the U.S. Army distributed hundreds of thousands of paperback books (thus starting a revolution in publishing) to the troops. Authors ranged from Homer to Shakespeare to Hemingway. German troops got copies of *Mein Kampf.* To my mind, right there one sees the difference in the two sides.

For a majority of Americans, the theme of the war was teamwork. "We are all in this together" was a phrase heard almost as frequently as "Don't you know there's a war on?" In the Depression people felt isolated, alone, fearful. In the war people felt a sense of belonging. Obviously in the armed services, but also on the home front, there was a commitment to the notion that society's needs come before individual desires. We were faced with a great challenge, we met it, we overcame all obstacles, and we won.

Another feature of the war experience was deferred gratification. The theme of almost all advertising and much government propaganda was the rewards that were coming after victory was attained. The message to those sharing a kitchen and bathroom with three other families, to mothers and children living in a single room, to workers driving in a beat-up, ten-year-old car, to GIs shivering in a foxhole outside Bastogne, was that all these hardships of today would disappear once the job was done. Tomorrow was worth saving for and delicious to dream about.

In the ads the dream was about material prosperity, but Rose McClain of Washington state had the best dream of all. On V-J Day she wrote her husband, serving in the Pacific, "Today I cried and thanked God for the end of this war and I prayed that this shall be the end of war for all time. That our children will learn kindness, patience, honesty, and the depth of love and trust we have learned from all of this, without the tragedy of war."

And Marjorie Haselton of Massachusetts wrote her husband, stationed in China, the same day: "You and I were brought up to think cynically of patriotism by the bitter, realistic writers of the twenties and thirties. This war has taught me—I love my country and I'm not ashamed to admit it anymore. I am proud of the men of my generation. Brought up in false prosperity and then degrading depression, they have overcome these handicaps. None of you fellows wanted the deal life handed you—but just about everyone of you gritted your teeth and hung on. You boys proved that you had a fighting spirit and team work that couldn't be beaten."

In these days of the "me" generation and instant gratification, it is no wonder that those of us over fifty-five years of age look back with a certain nostalgia and think of it as "the good war."

MY LAI

Atrocities in Historical Perspective

This is a painful task—to examine a side of war that is hard to face up to but is always there. When you put young people, eighteen, nineteen, or twenty years old, in a foreign country with weapons in their hands, sometimes terrible things happen that you wish had never happened. This is a reality that stretches across time and across continents. It is a universal aspect of war, from the time of the ancient Greeks up to the present. My Lai was not an exception or an aberration. Atrocity is a part of war that needs to be recognized and discussed. It is not the job of historians to condemn or judge but to describe, try to explain, and, even more so, attempt to understand.

In the case of My Lai, the question is who was responsible. Was it one person? Was it a bad platoon leader who was inadequately trained all of his life, including by the army and by his society? Was it that he just could not handle the responsibility, and he broke? Maybe it is as simple as that. I know a lot of Vietnam War veterans who would take very extreme action if they could get Lieutenant Calley in their hands. They blame him for besmirching their reputation and the reputation of the United States Army and the reputation of the American armed forces in Vietnam. Then there are others who say: "No, no, you can't blame Calley. What you need to do is look at the U.S. Army as a whole, the army as an institution, the way the army was fighting that war, and the things that Westmoreland was demanding from his platoon leaders. There's the explanation for what happened in Vietnam." The problem here is that you have the whole U.S. Army going berserk. Yet others would argue: "No, no, the army is but a reflection of the society. Although it is one of the greatest of all our glories in this republic that the army is a reflection of the society, it was American society that made this happen. The racism that permeates all levels of American society is where you look for the cause of what happened at My Lai. It is America's sense of exceptionalism, America's self-appointed task of cleansing the world, that made My Lai happen." In this view, responsibility rests with the society as a whole.

I would like to take a slightly different perspective on what happened at My Lai, beginning with some reminders about other American soldiers, in other situations and countries, at other times. The first thing we should recognize is that those of us who have never been in combat have no right to judge. I have never had other men shoot at me, and I have never had to shoot at other men, but I have spent my life interviewing people who did both. Combat is the most extreme experience a human being can go through. There is little in civilian life to compare to it, and for the vast majority of people it is mysterious. Most people in human history do not go through combat. It depends on when you were born. If you were born between 1890 and 1900 and you were a white male, you were almost certainly going to be in combat. If you were born in the 1830s in Europe and were white, you almost certainly were not going to be in combat. And so it goes. Most people never have to face the questions raised by combat: Could I stand up to the rigors of combat? Could I kill? Could I charge an enemy who is trying to kill me? Would I be brave? Would I be cowardly? Would I hide? Would I lead?

There is nothing worse than combat. What can the combat soldier be threatened with if he does not stay in the line—that he will be thrown into the stockade? It is warm in the stockade; there is hot food, and a bed, and nobody is shooting. Anyone there knows that the president is going to give a blanket pardon when the war is over. Men stay in the line because they are doing their duty. They stay in the line even more so because their buddies to the right and to the left of them are counting on them. One of the things that went wrong in Vietnam was that a sense of comradeship was hard to build up when men were rotating constantly and were not shipping over as units. Divisions did not train together, go over together, and fight together; thus the comradeship was not present.

Most of us see war through the movies. In the movies a man gets shot, and he dies. He never knew what hit him, and the commanding officer can write home to the widow or to the family: "He was going great and everything was going fine. Then he got one right through the middle of the eyes. He never knew what hit him, and he was gone." But it does not happen like that. What happens to men in combat is that they see their buddy with his brains oozing out of a hole in his head. It has not killed him, and he is begging for water and for a cigarette and for morphine simultaneously. They see a man trying to stuff his guts back into his stomach. They see a man carrying his left arm in his right hand. They see men who have lost their manhood to a piece of shrapnel. They see farm boys who have lost a leg. None of these people are dead. They all have to be dealt with. They have to be comforted, they have to have some kind of medical assistance, and they are there. If they all died the way they do in Darryl Zanuck's movies, war would be a lot less horrible than it is, and there would be fewer atrocities.

A feature of the contemporary experience which seems to apply to My Lai is that men seldom see their enemy. In the nineteenth century that was not so true. Surely General Meade's troops saw George Pickett's men coming across that open ground at Gettysburg. But later the range of the weaponry increased. Rifled bullets appeared in the late nineteenth century, and so the distance at which the killing took place increased. Artillery got more accurate. The airplane became part of combat. I know a man who went through World War II, and twice in eight months he saw and aimed and fired at an enemy. Most casualties in twentieth-century war do not come as a result of someone being fired on at close range. They come as a result of booby traps or snipers. They come as a result of that invention of the devil—the land mine. (I would like to see land mines banned, just like gas warfare. They are not that effective militarily, and they are still causing problems in Vietnam today. In fact, they are still losing farmers to World War I mines in France.) In combat, soldiers are always afraid, always enraged, and very often seeking revenge.

Some of the army case studies that I want to discuss did not end up in massacres, while others did. The first is from a biography of Meriwether Lewis, *Undaunted Courage: Meriwether Lewis, Thomas Jefferson, and the Opening of the American West,* which I wrote with my wife. This may seem a long way away from My Lai, but I believe that there are some genuine connections.

The expedition's sentinel had detected an old man, an Indian, trying to sneak into the camp site. The soldier threatened the intruder with his rifle, and, Lewis writes, "gave the fellow a few stripes with a switch and sent him off." So the men's tempers were running very high, just as Lewis's was. Never before had they hit an Indian, but never before had they been so provoked. One party of warriors tried to wrest a tomahawk from Private John Colter, but they had picked the wrong man. Colter was the original mountain man and the discoverer of Yellowstone National Park. "He retained it," Lewis dryly recorded. Still, as the expedition worked its way upriver, whether dragging the canoes through the rapids or portaging them, the Indians were always there, ready to grab anything left unguarded for one instant. There are various accounts of their stealing knives, kettles, and other items.

In the evening, three Indians stole Lewis's dog, Seaman, a wonderful black Newfoundland. That sent Lewis into a rage. He called together three men and snapped out his order: "Follow and find those thieves, and if they make the least resistance or difficulty in surrendering my dog, shoot 'em." In my mind, Meriwether Lewis was one of the greatest soldiers the United States Army ever produced, yet he was sending men out with orders to shoot people if they did not give his dog back. He was under direct orders from the president to avoid hostilities with the Indians if at all possible; he wanted to build a trading empire with these Indians. But he was so provoked that he was ready to kill to get his dog back. Fortunately for him, when the Indians realized they were being pursued, they let Seaman go and fled.

Back at camp, meanwhile, an Indian stole an axe and got caught; after a tussle, he gave it up and ran. Lewis told those at the camp that "if they make any further attempts to steal our property or insult our men we should put them to instant death." After several days and more thefts, his pent-up fury burst forth. He caught a man stealing, cursed him, beat him severely, and then "made the men kick him out of camp." His blood was up. He informed the Indians standing around "that I would shoot the first of them that attempted to steal an article from us, that we were not afraid to fight them, that I had it in my power at that moment to kill them all and set fire to their homes."

The next morning the Indians stole a saddle. Lewis's blood rose past the danger point. He swore he would either get the saddle back or would burn their houses. "They have vexed me in such a manner by such repeated acts of villainy that I am quite determined to treat them with every severity. Their defenseless state pleads forgiveness so far as respects their lives." He ordered a thorough search of the village and marched there himself to burn the place down if he did not get the saddle back.

That was the closest Lewis came to applying the principle of collective guilt. Fortunately, the men found the stolen goods hidden in a corner of one of the houses before Lewis reached the village. He had been wonderfully lucky. Had those goods not been recovered, he might have given the order to put the houses to the torch. The resulting conflagration would have been a gross overreaction, unpardonably unjust, and a permanent blot on his honor. It would have turned every Chinookan village on the lower Columbia against the Americans, and thus made impossible the fulfillment of the plan Lewis was developing for a cross-continent American-run trading empire. He had a lot at stake, but he had been ready to allow his anger to override his judgment. He had come close to being out of control.

Regarding the period after the Civil War, the United States Army has been unjustly maligned for its record in the wars with the Plains Indians. It is accused of starting most, if not all, of the wars, and then of blundering once hostilities broke out and committing various atrocities. The army was badly served by its political masters, however. It was given conflicting orders and hardly ever knew from one month to the next what the policy of the government might be. It was poorly equipped and inadequately supplied. It was the clear duty of the army to protect the advancing frontier and the transcontinental railroads, and the Indians were in the way. They had to be removed. There were two ways to do this: force them on to reservations or bribe them there. The government never made the bribe attractive enough, so the army got the dirty job of removing them. In the process, though the army contributed its share of blunders, stupidity, and cruelty, and initiated its share of hostilities and atrocities, it also fought with great skill and bravery.

Near dawn on November 28, 1868, Major General George Armstrong Custer led his Seventh Cavalry to a Cheyenne encampment on the banks of the Washita River in what is now Oklahoma. (The following account is from my book *Crazy Horse and Custer: The Parallel Lives of Two American Warriors.*) The village contained certain young men who had been guilty of hitting frontier outposts, probably guilty of some murders and certainly of some theft. Custer was acting under orders from Major General Philip H. Sheridan to wipe them out. He attacked at first light with the band playing "Garry Owen." Warriors rushed from their tepees, confused, disorganized, unbelieving. Custer's men shot them down. Some Indians managed to get their weapons and flee to the safety of the river, where they stood in waist-deep freezing water, behind the protecting bank, and started returning fire. Others got into some nearby timber and began to fight. But that first assault was overwhelming, and Custer had control of the village. His men were shooting anything that moved.

Many of the troopers had been fruitlessly chasing Indians for two years, and they poured out their frustrations. Everyone was extremely tense after the nightlong approach to the village, and the indiscriminate killing relieved the tension. In any event, the soldiers said later, it was hard to tell warriors from squaws, especially because a few of the squaws had taken up weapons and were fighting back, as were Indian boys ten years of age. The troopers shot them all down. Still, according to George Bird Grinnell, who got his information from the Indians, "practically all the women and children who were killed were shot while hiding in the brush or trying to run away." Within an hour, probably less, resistance was minimal. A few warriors kept up a sporadic firing from the banks of the river, but for all practical purposes the battle was over. Looking around, Custer could see dead Indians everywhere, one hundred and seventeen of them, their blood bright on the snow. He was in possession of fifty-one lodges and a herd of nearly nine hundred ponies. He burned the village, destroying several hundred pounds of tobacco, enormous quantities of meat, and more than one thousand buffalo robes. Before leaving, Custer detailed four of his ten companies and ordered the men to shoot the ponies. Within minutes, more than eight hundred ponies lay on the ground, neighing and kicking, in their death throes.

At Sand Creek in Colorado, six hundred to seven hundred Cheyenne gathered in November 1864 to camp for the winter. Without warning or provocation, volunteer soldiers commanded by Colonel John Chivington charged the camp and brutally murdered and mutilated about a third of the Cheyenne, mostly women and children. In the Philippines from 1899 to 1902, U.S. troops waged a bloody conflict with Filipinos, whom they called "gooks," who were resisting American colonization. Torture of captives and destruction of villages, including the killing of all inhabitants, punctuated the American conduct of the war.

The incident that came to most people's minds when My Lai was revealed, however, was the massacre at Wounded Knee in December of 1890. These Indians, Big Foot's band, were Oglala Sioux. They had been out on the prairie engaging in the Ghost Dance, which was a religious phenomenon that swept through the Plains Indian tribes in the late 1880s. Many of the Indians west of the Mississippi River were participating in this type of Ghost Dance; they believed that if they continued it long enough the buffalo would come back and the whites would disappear, and they could have the old life back. These activities caused great consternation and even panic in areas where whites were and in the War Department of the United States government. So orders went out to the army to round up the dancers and bring them back into the reservation, where they could be watched.

A detachment from Custer's old regiment, the Seventh Cavalry, rounded up Big Foot and his band of Sioux up in the Badlands in Dakota and was bringing them back to the reservation near Crawford, Nebraska. They were camped overnight at a place called Wounded Knee. In the morning, Colonel James W. Forsyth, who was in command, decided to disarm the Indians before proceeding. It was a foolish decision. They were causing no trouble, were moving exactly as ordered, and were outnumbered and heavily outweaponed by the white soldiers. The process of disarmament stirred emotions on both sides. The Indians refused to produce what weapons they had, which were hidden in blankets and in their tepees. The soldiers went inside the tepees and threw off the blankets, digging under other material, looking for weapons. We may assume that this indiscriminate search was leaving a lot of damaged goods behind and was creating chaos. Tempers rose. A medicine man named Yellow Bird pranced about performing incantations and calling for resistance. There was a scuffle between a soldier and an Indian, and a shot rang out.

How many atrocities in the world's history have started with a shot ringing out? And nobody knows who fired it. One can think also about Lexington and the origins of the American Revolution. Who shot first? We do not know whether at Wounded Knee it was a soldier or an Indian. Instantly the young Indian men threw off their blankets, pulled out their rifles, and sent a volley toward the nearest formation of soldiers, or so the soldiers reported. The Indians told a different story, which is also typical of what happens in atrocities. In a murderous face-to-face melee, Indians and soldiers shot, stabbed, and clubbed one another. Women and children scattered in panic as bullets laced the tepees. The close-range action ended abruptly, and the combatants broke from the council square. On the hilltop the artillery jerked their lanyards. A storm of exploding shells leveled the village. At least 150 and perhaps 300 Sioux, about half being women and children, died. Twenty-five soldiers were killed, many by friendly fire.

Later testimony showed conclusively that the troops, with several exceptions, had made efforts to avoid harming noncombatants, but a lot of questions were raised as to how strenuous those efforts were. The testimony also supported Forsyth's placement of his units for the task of disarming the Indians, although here the judgments were less persuasive, especially in light of Major General Nelson Miles's repeated injunctions to his subordinates never to let their units mix with Indians, friendly or not. He had told them not to go into the village, not to go into the tepees and try to carry out searches there, but to keep a distance and always be aware that the possibility of hostilities existed. Forsyth got off, although Miles branded him guilty of incompetence, inexperience, and irresponsibility, and basically his career came to an end.

Another example comes from World War II. This happened in the 506th Parachute Infantry Regiment of the 101st Airborne Division on the tenth day of June in 1944. As a man named Captain Spears was walking back to his command post, he went by a ditch that a group of German POWs were digging, where there was one sergeant guarding them. Spears had by now been in four days of combat and probably had not slept in all that time. He had seen buddies killed, and he himself had killed and been slightly wounded. Spears stopped beside the twelve German soldiers who were digging and then jumped into the ditch with them, pulled out his Luckies, and shook the pack. With each one of them saying "danka, danka, danka, danka, bitte, bitte, bitte, bitte," they got cigarettes, which Spears then lit with his Ronson lighter. As they were inhaling the first cigarettes they had probably had since the sixth of June, Spears got back up on the outside of the trench, took his carbine off his shoulder, and shot all twelve of them, in cold blood, while the sergeant looked on horrified. Spears walked on to complete his mission for that day, went on to become company commander and to stay in the army, where he had a very good career. What seems like an entirely irrational act just happened. He just broke and lost all control.

An awareness of atrocities such as these is part of the discussion about what happened at My Lai.

For me, My Lai was the single most shocking thing to come out of the Vietnam War. I had a very hard time watching those young men on television describing to Mike Wallace what they had done at My Lai. I had been a student of military history, was teaching at the Naval War College, and had spent eight years with General Eisenhower, but it was beyond my understanding that American boys could do this. I have spent a lot of time since trying to comprehend how it could happen—how American boys could do what SS boys did, how Boy Scouts could act like Nazi Youth.

In one way, what happened at My Lai was a logical development from what happened in the Second World War. In that war, the civilian became a legitimate target. This was a new thing, and it was very deliberately done at the highest levels by the German government, by the British government, and by the American government. In the period from 1939 to 1941, Franklin Roosevelt had taken the lead in denouncing the bombing of cities and rejecting any attempt to turn civilians into targets. He called on the nations of the world to treat the bombing of cities as they had the use of poison gas, that is, to make it a war crime and eliminate it. Then the United States got into war, and Roosevelt became the most enthusiastic advocate of strategic bombing. By late 1944 and into 1945, he was pushing General Hap Arnold, the air force chief, to burn Japanese cities to the ground. He wanted Arnold to go in there with high incendiary bombs and napalm and burn down homes built of sticks and wood. I see a direct link from there to My Lai.

It seems to me that the fundamental problem in Vietnam from the military's point of view was that they were trying to win a war on the strategic defensive. This was an army that had a tradition from World War II of going after the enemy, going to his homeland, and forcing an unconditional surrender. Although the army had not quite achieved that in Korea, they had accomplished a great deal there. Vietnam was certainly the kind of action that any World War II commander would have taken one look at and said, "We go for Hanoi."

There was, however, left from the Korean War, the fear that the Chinese would enter. We did cross into North Korea. We almost liberated North Korea in the late fall and early winter of 1950, and the result was that we brought the Chinese hordes down on us. Later we presumed that the Chinese would never allow us to invade and hold North Vietnam. We did not want to get into a war with the Chinese army, so we were not going to invade North Vietnam and take Hanoi. Whether those who made the decision were right about what the Chinese might have done, I do not know. Having made that decision, that we were not going to go over to the offensive, every effort should have been made, and was not, to shut the war down right then, on whatever terms we could get. (It is a lot easier to say now than it was to see how to do it then.) The United States should also have abandoned the fiction that worked altogether to the advantage of the North Vietnamese, and altogether to our disadvantage, that this was a war in South Vietnam, and that Laos and Cambodia were neutrals. The arguments for not going into North Vietnam were very strong and were persuasive to the president.

Because Westmoreland was on a strategic defensive, those above him either agreed to or suggested to him the idea of body count. Using the body count as a way to measure progress in the war was a terrible idea, and it had all kinds of awful repercussions. In the first place, in war what does body count mean? It means that the soldier has fought until you had to kill him. There would never come a point in the enemy's experience in which he would put down his weapon, throw up his arms, and say "I'm yours, I quit, I surrender." If you had to kill him, he never said that. That means that he was being fed well enough to stay in the line, that enough ammunition was reaching him, that his morale was high enough so that he would continue to fight until you had to kill him. Progress in a war is measured by how the enemy soldiers react; POWs are counted, men coming in with their hands up in surrender. Those are men who are demoralized, who are out of ammunition, who are not being fed. When you have the enemy in that situation, you are making progress. When the situation is that you cannot dispose of an enemy until you have killed him, you have the opposite of progress. Also, let us say it out loud, the problem with the body count above all else was that every body counted as long as it was dead and Vietnamese. In far too many cases, promotions depended on the body count that was reported.

Some people have posed this question: Was it not true that the American army over there had just given up on the war, that they were all on drugs, that there was no discipline left? First of all, that is an exaggerated assumption. Insofar as it is true, it has to be remembered that in February 1968 Lyndon Johnson decided we were going to retreat. He refused Westmoreland's request for reinforcements to follow up the Tet victory, and in fact they began drawing down in the summer of 1968. Nixon won the presidential election that fall, and, shortly after taking office, he announced publicly that the United States was getting out. We were retreating. In effect he was saying: "We can't win this war, and my aim is to turn it over to the Vietnamese and pray God that they'll hold on until I get reelected." That left the young men in Vietnam, the soldiers, fighting a rearguard action. Who wants to be the last man killed in a retreat? Insofar as there was a breakdown in discipline in Vietnam, and there was, it occurred because of a political decision made in Washington, not because of what was happening in the field.

Lieutenant Calley lost control, as did his men. Meriwether Lewis did not, although he came close. Forsyth lost control, as did Chivington. And Custer certainly lost control, if he ever had it. There were hundreds of other officers in the wars against the Plains Indian tribes of the latter part of the nineteenth century who never did lose control. They were as provoked as Lewis had been, or Forsyth or Custer or Chivington. The great bulk of them did not lose control. There were hundreds and hundreds of platoon leaders in Vietnam who were as provoked as Calley, as scared and as poorly trained, and who were leading kids fresh out of American high schools who were also inadequately trained, and they never lost control. One of the things that stands out about My Lai in my mind and makes it not only possible for me to live with it but to be once again proud of the institution that I have spent most of my life studying, the United States Army, was that the army itself investigated the incident, made that investigation public, and did its best to punish the perpetrators of this outrage. I would defy anybody to name another army in the world that would do that.

THE CHRISTMAS BOMBING

Of the many controversies that swirl around the American role in the Vietnam War, one of the most contentious centers on the Christmas bombing of Hanoi in December 1972. This event followed Henry A. Kissinger's October news conference in which he said, "Peace is at hand," and President Richard Nixon's triumphant reelection in November. It preceded the signing of the armistice in January 1973 and the release of the American POWs.

According to Nixon and his supporters, the Christmas bombing forced the North Vietnamese to make concessions, accept an armistice, and release American POWs. It was a great U.S. victory that brought peace with honor.

According to Nixon's critics, the armistice agreement signed in January 1973 was identical to the one reached in October 1972. The bombing brought no concessions from the enemy, nor was it intended to; its purpose was to persuade the South Vietnamese to go along with an armistice to which they were violently opposed. The bombing ended not because the enemy cried "enough" but because American losses of B-52s were becoming intolerable. In addition, conservative critics called the bombing an American defeat that brought a temporary cease-fire at the cost of a free and independent South Vietnam.

Like so much else in the Vietnam War, the issue of the Christmas bombing was divisive and remains so. To the prowar hawks, it was done with surgical precision, sparing civilian lives; to the antiwar doves, it was terror bombing, pure and simple. These differences in view cannot be reconciled or settled, but they can be examined.

For three years, Kissinger, as national security adviser, had been engaged in secret talks with Le Duc Tho in Paris, seeking a negotiated peace. In the spring of 1972 the Communists had launched their largest offensive ever and had almost overrun South Vietnam. Nixon had responded by bombing Hanoi and mining Haiphong Harbor. The offensive was stopped. In October, Kissinger and Le Duc Tho finally reached an agreement. Its basic terms were a cease-fire in place; the return of POWs; total American withdrawal from South Vietnam; and a National Council of Concord and Reconciliation in South Vietnam to arrange elections, its membership to be one-third neutral, one-third from the current government in Saigon, one-third Communist. Nixon was satisfied that this agreement met his conditions for peace with honor.

President Nguyen Van Thieu of South Vietnam, however, felt betrayed. He perceived the agreement as a surrender: it gave the Communists a legitimate role in the political life of his nation; it allowed the Vietcong to hold on to the territory it controlled in South Vietnam; worst of all, it permitted the North Vietnamese Army (NVA) to continue to occupy the two northern provinces and retain more than 150,000 troops in his country. Thieu absolutely refused to agree to the cease-fire. In early December, Kissinger went to Paris to persuade Le Duc Tho to remove the NVA from South Vietnam; Le Duc Tho adamantly insisted on going through with the October agreement.

On December 13, 1972, Kissinger flew back to Washington to meet with Nixon and an aide, General Alexander Haig, to discuss the options. The doves urged them to make a separate deal with Hanoi for the release of the POWs in return for total American withdrawal, leaving Thieu to sink or swim on his own. This proposal had no appeal to Nixon or his aides. To abandon South Vietnam now, after all the blood that had been shed, all the money that had been spent, all the uproar that had overwhelmed the American political scene, would be wrong, cowardly, a betrayal. To abandon Thieu would amount to surrendering the fundamental American goal in the war: the maintenance in power of an anticommunist government in Saigon.

To get Thieu to sign the agreement, and to force Le Duc Tho to give just a bit more, some dramatic action by the United States was necessary. With fewer than 25,000 U.S. troops remaining in South Vietnam, down from a high of 550,000 when Nixon took office, there was no possibility of escalating on the ground. The only real option discussed was to expand the bombing campaign against North Vietnam.

There were, however, powerful arguments against that course. Sending B-52s over Hanoi meant risking those expensive weapons and their highly trained crews, because the Soviets had been rushing SA-2 SAMs (surface-to-air missiles) to North Vietnam. The SAMs fired a ten-meter-long missile that U.S. airmen ruefully called "the flying telephone pole." Each missile carried a 286-pound warhead with fuses that could be set to detonate close to a target, on impact, or on command. Guided by a radar tracking beam that honed in on its target, they traveled at a speed of Mach 1.5. The range was up to thirty horizontal miles and about eleven miles up. Fighter-bombers could evade the missiles by diving toward them and then veering off sharply, but that technique was not possible for B-52 pilots.

There were other technological problems for the big bombers. Built in the 1950s, they had been designed to drop nuclear weapons over the Soviet Union. They had only four 4.5mm tail guns—and, in any case, the SAMs came on too fast to be shot down. The B-52s' best defense was altitude: They usually dropped their bombs from 30,000 feet. But the SAMs were able to reach almost 60,000 feet.

And there were political as well as technological problems. Because of the strength of the antiwar movement in the United States, the government—under both Lyndon Johnson and Nixon—had imposed many restrictions on targets in the air war, which, naturally, infuriated the airmen. This policy had little effect on public opinion—the doves and foreign critics still charged that the U.S. Air Force was carrying out a barbaric, terrorist campaign—but it was a great help to the North Vietnamese. They knew what was off-limits and could concentrate their SAMs around such predictable targets as railroad yards and radar sites.

The technological advantage was with the enemy; for this reason, Secretary of Defense Melvin Laird, his deputy Kenneth Rush, and the chairman of the Joint Chiefs of Staff, Admiral Thomas Moorer, were opposed to using B-52s over Hanoi, and they so advised the president. Many of Nixon's political advisers were also opposed, because to escalate the bombing after Kissinger's "peace is at hand" statement would drive the Nixon-haters in Congress, in the media, on the campuses, and among the general public into a frenzy.

But something had to be done to convince Thieu that, whatever the formal working of the cease-fire agreement, he could count on Nixon to come to the defense of South Vietnam if the NVA broke the cease-fire. And Le Duc Tho had to be convinced that, despite the doves in Congress, Nixon could still punish North Vietnam.

That made the bombing option tempting. Although the B-52s were relatively slow and cumbersome, they packed a terrific punch. They carried eighty-four 500-pound bombs in their bomb bays and twelve 500-pound bombs on their wings. They could drop those bombs with relative accuracy, much better than World War II bombers. (The Seventh Air Force commander, General John Vogt, complained that the internal radar systems of the B-52s were "notoriously bad" and that "misses of a thousand feet or more were common." However, in World War II, misses of 1,000 meters—three times as much—had been common.) They flew from secure bases in Guam and Thailand. They had been used with devastating effect in the Battle of Khe Sanh in 1968 and again to stop the NVA spring offensive of 1972. The temptation to use them against Hanoi was great, and growing.

Kissinger tried to resist it. He recommended more bombing south of the 20th parallel, against NVA units that were not as well protected by SAMs as Hanoi was, and reseeding the mines in Haiphong Harbor. On the other hand Haig, always a hard-liner, argued forcefully for an all-out bombing campaign by the B-52s against Hanoi itself.

Nixon later said that ordering the bombing was "the most difficult decision" he had to make in the entire war. But, he added, "it was also one of the most clear-cut and necessary ones." He issued an order on December 14 to reseed the mines, from the air—and also to send the B-52s against Hanoi. He told Kissinger he was prepared "for new losses and casualties and POWs," and explained, "We'll take the same heat for big blows as for little blows."

To Kissinger, the president seemed "sullen" and "withdrawn." Nixon "resented" having to do what he did, because "deep down he was ready to give up by going back to the October draft" of the armistice agreement. His bombing order, according to Kissinger, was "his last roll of the dice . . . helpful if it worked; a demonstration to the right wing if it failed that he had done all he could."

Once Nixon set the policy, public relations became his obsession. John Scali, White House adviser on foreign affairs information policy, put the problem succinctly to Nixon's chief of staff, H. R. Haldeman, in a telephone conversation: "We look incompetent—bombing for no good reason and because we don't know what else to do." On May 8, 1972, Nixon had gone on television to explain his reason for bombing Hanoi and mining Haiphong: It was in response to the Communists' spring offensive. Scali had thought the television appearance unnecessary in May, as the justification for Nixon's strong action was obvious then. But in December, when his critics and even some of his supporters could not figure out his reasons, Nixon refused to go on television to explain his actions.

Kissinger badly wanted Nixon to make a broadcast; he had been urging it for days. But Nixon, according to Kissinger, "was determined to take himself out of the line of fire." Nixon feared that any attempt to rally the people to support more bombing after "peace is at hand" would fall flat.

On the evening of December 14, four days before the bombing was set to begin, Nixon told Kissinger to hold a news conference to explain the status of the negotiations. The president followed up with a five-page, single-spaced memo on December 15 and another of two pages on December 16, instructing Kissinger on what to say. He told the national security adviser to "hit hard on the point that, while we want peace just as soon as we can get it, that we want a peace that is honorable and a peace that will last." Kissinger should admit the U.S. goals had been reached "in principle" in the October agreement, but add that some "strengthening of the language" was needed "so that there will be no doubt on either side in the event that [the agreement] is broken." He should accuse Le Duc Tho of having "backed off" some of the October understandings.

Kissinger should emphasize that with the Christmas season coming on, the president had a "very strong personal desire to get the war settled." But he should also point out that the president "insists that the United States is not going to be pushed around, blackmailed or stampeded into making the wrong kind of a peace agreement." Finally, he should say that "the president will continue to order whatever actions he considers necessary by air and sea"—the only reference to the bombing order, which had already gone out.

In his memos, Nixon was repetitious to a degree unusual even for him, an indication of the strain he was under, due perhaps to the difficulty of his position. As an example of his dilemma, it was the Americans—in response to demands from Thieu—who had backed off the October agreements, not the North Vietnamese. But Nixon could not have Kissinger straightforwardly tell the American people his administration was bombing Hanoi to convince Thieu to sign. Thieu was increasingly seen in the United States as the sole obstacle to peace and thus was increasingly unpopular. On December 15 Senator Barry Goldwater, an Arizona Republican and one of the toughest hawks, said that if Thieu "bucks much more" the United States should proceed with its withdrawal and "to hell with him."

Kissinger held his briefing on December 16 and said what he had been told to say. He stressed the president's consistency, unflappability, firmness, patience, and farsightedness. He mentioned Nixon fourteen times (he had been criticized by Haldeman for referring to the president only three times in his October news conference).

By this time the tension in the Nixon-Kissinger relationship was threatening to lead to an open break. Kissinger was unhappy with his boss because of his interference, and his back-and-forthing, on the negotiations. Nixon was furious with Kissinger for his "peace is at hand" statement, which had raised public expectations to a high level, expectations that were going to be dashed when the bombing began. Nixon also resented the way Kissinger had thrust himself onto center stage, his constant leaks to reporters, and the way the reporters responded by giving Kissinger credit for the huge margin of the election victory. Further, earlier in December *Time* magazine had named Nixon and Kissinger "Men of the Year," with their pictures on the cover; Kissinger correctly feared that Nixon resented having to share the honor.

On December 17, Nixon wrote a letter to Thieu. Usually the president signed drafts of letters to foreign heads of government prepared by Kissinger; in this case, he wrote the letter personally. Nixon had Haig fly to Saigon to hand-deliver it. In the letter Nixon made a threat: Unless Thieu accepted the agreement, the United States would go it alone. "You must decide now whether you want me to seek a settlement with the enemy which serves U.S. interests alone."

Although Nixon himself would do anything possible to avoid a break, the threat was not meaningless because, as Goldwater's statement indicated, Congress might carry it out regardless of the president's wishes. Thieu knew that, and he also knew how to read between the lines of Nixon's letter. After reading it, he told Haig it was obvious he was being asked to sign not a peace agreement but rather an agreement for continued American support.

On December 18, the air force launched its B-52s and fighter-bombers against Hanoi. The orders were to avoid civilian casualties, at all costs; for example, a missile-assembly plant manned by Russian technicians in the heart of Hanoi was off-limits, partly because of fear of Soviet casualties, partly to avoid near-misses that would devastate residential areas. Still, Linebacker II, as the operation was code-named, greatly damaged railroads, power plants, radio transmitters, and radar installations around Hanoi, as well as docks and shipyards in Haiphong.

It was not Nixon but Johnson who had imposed the restrictions on targets; in fact, they frustrated him. The day after the bombing began, he read a report about targets that had been avoided for fear of civilian casualties, and he called Admiral Moorer. "I don't want any more of this crap about the fact that we couldn't hit this target or that one,"

Nixon said. "This is your chance to use military power effectively to win this war, and if you don't, I'll consider you responsible." But the armed forces, concerned about their reputation and perhaps doubtful of the effectiveness of area bombing, continued the restrictions.

Nevertheless, a French reporter in Hanoi referred to "carpet bombing," a line repeated by Radio Hanoi. As a result, there was an immediate worldwide uproar and many expressions of moral revulsion. There had been no presidential explanation or announcement of any kind. People everywhere had taken Kissinger at his word, that only a few t's needed to be crossed and a few i's dotted and the negotiations would be wrapped up. The shock when the bombing was announced was even greater than that following the Cambodian incursion of 1970.

The adverse congressional and editorial reaction was unprecedented. Senator William Saxbe, an Ohio Republican, said Nixon "appears to have left his senses." Democratic Senate leader Mike Mansfield of Montana called it a "Stone Age tactic." Democratic Senator Edward Kennedy of Massachusetts said it was an "outrage." In an editorial, the *Washington Post* charged that the bombing caused millions of Americans "to cringe in shame and to wonder at their President's very sanity." James Reston, in the *New York Times*, called it "war by tantrum."

Nixon did have supporters, including Governors Nelson Rockefeller of New York and Ronald Reagan of California and Republican senators James Buckley of New York, Howard Baker of Tennessee, and Charles Percy of Illinois. John Connally, former governor of Texas and treasury secretary, called Nixon daily to encourage him and assure him that, regardless of what politicians and the media said, the people were behind him.

That was probably an exaggeration, but not as gross as the exaggerations of Nixon's critics. They charged that he had ordered the most intensive bombing campaign in the history of warfare. That was nonsense. In comparison to the human costs at Dresden, Hamburg, Berlin, and Tokyo—not to mention Hiroshima and Nagasaki—in World War II, the bombing of Hanoi during the Christmas season of 1972 was a minor operation. Under the severe targeting restrictions followed by the air force, civilian casualties were only around 1,500, and at least some of those were caused by SAM missiles falling back on the city after missing their targets. In World War II, a bombing raid that killed fewer than 2,000 German or Japanese civilians was not even worth a minor story in the newspapers, not to mention expressions of moral outrage from opinion leaders and prominent politicians. The Christmas bombing of Hanoi was not terror bombing, as the world had come to know terror bombing in the twentieth century.

Nixon's private response was to personalize it and assign to his critics the lowest possible motives. In his diary he wrote that they "simply cannot bear the thought of this administration under my leadership bringing off the peace on an honorable basis which they have so long predicted would be impossible. The election was a terrible blow to them and this is their first opportunity to recover from the election and to strike back."

That was by no means the whole truth. The most basic cause for the moral revulsion was the nature of the war itself. Few in the United States had protested the firebomb raids of World War II, which set out deliberately to kill civilians. Why the difference three decades later, especially when the air force was doing its utmost to avoid killing civilians? Because from 1942 to 1945, the United States was fighting for its life against a foe who was not only pure evil but also powerful enough to threaten the entire world. In World War II there had been no ongoing negotiations with the Germans and Japanese, only a demand for their unconditional surrender. In 1942–45, the Americans were bombing in order to hasten that surrender.

But in 1972, no one believed that the United States was fighting for its life, or that the NVA could conquer the world, or that there could be no end to the war until Hanoi surrendered; and few believed that more bombing would bring a quicker end to the war.

Despite the protest, Nixon continued to send the B-52s and fighter-bombers, and the battle raged in the sky above Hanoi. If Hanoi was far from being the most heavily bombed city in history, it certainly was one of the best defended. The SAMs shot down six of the ninety B-52s that flew missions on December 20; the following day, two of thirty were destroyed. The air force could not long sustain such losses; on the other hand, the Soviets could not long continue to supply SAMs in such quantity to the North Vietnamese (they were shooting a hundred or more per day at the attackers).

Nixon felt his resolve was being tested; he was determined to prevail. Kissinger, however, broke under the pressure of the protest and began leaking to reporters, especially Reston, word that he had opposed the bombing. This infuriated Nixon. He instructed his aide Charles Colson to monitor all Kissinger's telephone calls and contacts with the press. The president, according to Colson, "was raving and ranting about Henry double-talking." Colson did as instructed and discovered that Kissinger was calling Reston and others, "planting self-serving stories at the same time he was recommending Nixon be tough on Vietnam."

When Haldeman confronted Kissinger, the national security adviser simply denied the facts. "I have never given a personal opinion different from the president's," he claimed, and said he had not given an interview to Reston. Haldeman got him to admit he had called Reston on the telephone, just before Reston wrote a column stating that Kissinger had opposed the bombing and implying that Kissinger was the one moderate, sensible man among Nixon's advisers. Kissinger concluded his conversation with Haldeman by suggesting that it was time for the president to give him a vote of confidence: a letter from Nixon giving Kissinger backing and credit for the progress in the negotiations.

Nixon went to his home in Key Biscayne, Florida, for Christmas. He ordered a twenty-four-hour halt in the bombing for the holiday. In his diary he complained he was "more and more" a lonely individual. "It is a question not of too many friends but really too few—one of the inevitable consequences of this position." He received very few Christmas salutations, even from Republicans on Capital Hill and members of his cabinet. As a result, he told interviewer David Frost four years later, "it was the loneliest and saddest Christmas I can ever remember, much sadder and much more lonely than the one in the Pacific during the war." He did make some telephone calls, including one to Ronald Reagan, who complained about CBS News coverage of the bombing and said that under World War II circumstances the network would have been charged with treason.

The day after Christmas, despite urgings from some of his aides and much of the media that he extend the Christmas Day truce, Nixon ordered the biggest bombing raid yet, 120 B-52s over Hanoi. Five were shot down, but that afternoon Nixon received a message from Hanoi. The Communists, who had evidently exhausted their supply of SAMs, proposed that the talks resume in Paris on January 9. Nixon replied that he wanted technical talks resumed on January 2, and he offered to stop the bombing of Hanoi if the Communists agreed. Hanoi did so.

General Haig was furious. He did not want to stop the bombing when Hanoi was all but on its knees. He was incensed when he discovered that "every single adviser of the president . . . [was] calling the president daily, hourly, and telling him to terminate the bombing." But even Haig realized that Nixon had little choice, because if he continued the bombing after the congressional session began on January 3, "there would have been legislative restrictions which would have been national suicide from the standpoint of ever negotiating a settlement."

Nixon decided to call off the bombing. On December 29 he announced that he had suspended offensive operations north of the 20th parallel and that the Paris talks would resume.

So who won the eleven-day battle? The North Vietnamese had shot down fifteen B-52s, and eleven fighter-bombers had gone down. Ninety-three American airmen were missing—thirty-one became known POWs. The enemy had fired 1,200 missiles and lost three MiG jets to achieve these results. Some 40,000 tons of bombs had fallen on Hanoi—40 kilotons, or the equivalent of two Hiroshima-size bombs. However, visitors to Hanoi soon after the battle ended, including Americans, all testify that although great destruction was done to military and industrial targets—such as the airfields, railroad network, and factories—residential areas were mostly untouched.

There was no clear-cut winner. Thus the last American action in the Vietnam War was characteristic of all those that had come earlier—cursed by half measures. From 1964 to 1969 Johnson's actions, as described by Nixon were always "too little, too late." That had also been true of Nixon's ultimatum in November 1969; of his Cambodian incursion of 1970; of his Laotian operation in 1971; of his May 8, 1972, air offensive; and now of his Christmas bombing. He had taken the heat for an all-out offensive without delivering one. It was not that he did not want to, but rather that it was overwhelmingly obvious the American political system would not allow him to do so.

Nixon called Hanoi's willingness to resume the talks a "stunning capitulation," one presumably brought about by the bombing. But it had been Saigon, not Hanoi, that had created the stalemate in the talks. In his message to Hanoi, Nixon had referred to the October agreements; going back to them represented an American, not a North Vietnamese, concession. Kissinger's reference to "normalization" of relations continued the hints he had been secretly making to Le Duc Tho that when peace came the United States would aid in the reconstruction of North Vietnam, just as it had helped Germany and Japan after World War II.

On December 30 Senator Henry Jackson, a Democrat from Washington, called Nixon to ask the president to go on television and explain that "we bombed to get them back to the table." Nixon passed the message along to Kissinger with a note: "He is right—but my saying it publicly would seriously jeopardize our negotiations."

Nixon had another reason to hesitate to make the claim that Jackson wanted him to make. It would have been extremely difficult to get informed observers to believe that Nixon had bombed Hanoi in order to force North Vietnamese acceptance of terms they had already agreed to. It was much easier to believe that Nixon's real target was not Hanoi but Saigon. And as 1972 came to an end, there was no indication that Thieu was prepared to sign.

On January 2, 1973, the House Democratic Caucus voted 154 to 75 to cut off all funds for Vietnam as soon as arrangements were complete for the withdrawal of American armed forces and the return of the POWs. On January 4 the Senate Democratic Caucus passed a similar resolution, 36 to 12.

Nixon passed the pressure on to Thieu. Initially he tried to do so through Anna Chennault, the widow of General Claire Chennault, whose influence on the right wing of the Republican party was considerable. He had her friend John Mitchell, his former attorney general, ask her to use her influence with Thieu, but the "Dragon Lady," as she was commonly called, refused. There was irony here. In 1968 Mitchell had persuaded Mrs. Chennault to intervene with Thieu to get him to refuse to help Johnson in his election-eve bid for peace, which if successful might have given Hubert Humphrey the presidency. Now Nixon wanted her to persuade Thieu to cooperate with the president and accept an unsatisfactory peace. She would not.

Nixon again wrote directly to Thieu. The letter, dated January 5, was less threatening than previous ones and contained a more explicit promise: "Should you decide, as I trust you will, to go with us, you have my assurance of continued assistance in the post-settlement period and that we will respond with full force should the settlement be violated by North Vietnam."

Nixon was not in a position to give such a promise. Without congressional appropriations, he could not come to Saigon's aid.

That same day he had a meeting with the leaders of both parties. The atmosphere was cold. He spoke briefly about Vietnam. He said he knew many of the men in the room disagreed with his policies but added that he was determined to persist.

Nixon concluded, "In any event, you have indicated your own positions—some of you—which is in direct opposition. I understand that. I have the responsibility. Gentlemen, I will take responsibility if those negotiations fail. If they succeed, we all succeed."

On January 6 Nixon went to his retreat at Camp David, where he met with Kissinger, who was flying to Paris the next day. The president said that if Kissinger could get Le Duc Tho to go back to the October 8 agreement, "we should take it." Kissinger demurred, but Nixon insisted. He did want Kissinger to get some wording changes so that "we can claim some improvement," but the point was that the war had to end, on whatever terms, in this round of negotiations; otherwise the Ninety-third Congress would force the administration to end it on even worse terms.

The president did agree that Kissinger could threaten the North Vietnamese with a resumption of the bombing of Hanoi if they did not cooperate, but Nixon then warned him that "as far as our internal planning is concerned, we cannot consider this to be a viable option." As for

Thieu, Nixon referred to Haig's report of his December visit to Saigon: Thieu was saying that "it is not a peace agreement that he is going to get but a commitment from the United States to continue to protect South Vietnam in the event such an agreement is broken." Nixon said that was exactly right.

January 9 was Nixon's sixtieth birthday. In an interview, he gave his formula for living: "Never slow down." He admitted that he had many problems "but boredom is the least of them."

He also wrote by hand a piece of self-analysis: "RN approaches his second inauguration with true peace of mind—because he knows that by his actions, often in the face of the most intense sort of criticism, what he is bringing to the world is 'peace of mind'—that is, a peace formed by the exercise of hard reason and calm deliberation, and durable because its foundation has been carefully laid." Nixon instructed Haldeman to pass the piece along to the staff and called it "an excellent line for them to take" when talking to the press about the president.

That afternoon Nixon got what he called "the best birthday present I have had in sixty years." Kissinger cabled from Paris that there had been "a major breakthrough in the negotiations. In sum, we settled all the outstanding questions in the text of the agreement."

Le Duc Tho had accepted Kissinger's revised wording on the demilitarized zone. But it made no practical difference; the accord that had been reached was basically the same as in October. Kissinger aide John Negroponte was disappointed. He told friends, "We bombed the North Vietnamese into accepting our concession."

Getting the Communists to accept the accord had never been the problem; the problem was Thieu, and that remained. Nixon was eager to have the situation resolved before Inauguration Day, January 20, but he worried that Thieu would refuse to cooperate.

On January 13 Kissinger returned from Paris. He flew down to Key Biscayne to brief the president. They talked until 2 A.M. Nixon walked out to the car with Kissinger to say goodnight and to tell him that the country was indebted to him for what he had done. Nixon later wrote that "it is not really a comfortable feeling for me to praise people so openly," but "Henry expects it, and it was good that I did so." Kissinger replied it was only Nixon's courage that had made a settlement possible. In his memoirs Kissinger wrote that he felt "an odd tenderness" that night toward Nixon.

The next morning they turned their attention to Thieu. Nixon wrote him another letter and told Haig to fly to Saigon to deliver it. The letter was full of threats: "I have therefore irrevocably decided to proceed to initial the Agreement on January 23, 1973, and to sign it on January 27, 1973, in Paris. I will do so, if necessary alone." There were also promises. If Thieu would sign, Nixon would make it "emphatically clear that the United States recognizes your government as the only legal government of South Vietnam; that we do not recognize the right of any foreign troops to be present on South Vietnamese territory; that we will react strongly in the event the agreement is violated." Of course, there was a big difference between not recognizing the right of the NVA to stay in South Vietnam and requiring the NVA to leave the country when the American armed forces left. Nixon concluded, "It is my firm intention to continue full economic and military aid."

Nixon feared that his words would not be enough, but he was determined to prevail. "Brutality is nothing," he told Kissinger. "You have never seen it if this son-of-a-bitch doesn't go along, believe me." To add to the pressure on Thieu, Nixon had Senators John Stennis, a Mississippi Democrat, and Goldwater warn publicly that if Thieu blocked the agreement he would imperil his government's chances of receiving any further aid from Congress.

Still Thieu would not yield. He sent a letter to Nixon raising the same complaints he had made in October—naturally enough, since it was the same agreement. Nixon replied on January 20 with an ultimatum.

On the public relations front, meanwhile, Nixon was also busy. On January 19 he told Haldeman, "We need to get across the point that the reason for the success of the negotiations was the bombing and the converse point that we did not halt the bombing until we had the negotiations back on track." He instructed Kissinger to brief the staff on the settlement: "The key to this briefing will be to get a lot of people out selling our line." Nixon wanted "an all-out effort with inspired leaks, etc."

On January 20 Nixon was inaugurated for his second term. He had hoped to be able to announce that peace had been achieved, but Thieu's intransigence made that impossible. Under the circumstances, the hoopla that ordinarily occurs at inaugurations was distinctly absent, and Nixon's inaugural address was short and somber.

The parade following the ceremonies was marred by small groups of demonstrators chanting obscenities and throwing eggs and debris, but it was nowhere near as bad as four years earlier. If Nixon had not quite yet brought peace, he had gone a long way toward achieving that objective. The madness and hatred that had been so prominent in 1969 had abated in 1973. Sadly, in part it had been replaced by a bitterness because of the Christmas bombing and a suspicion because of the growing furor over the Watergate break-in. If Nixon deserved credit for the gains, he also deserved blame for the bitterness and suspicion.

On January 22 word arrived that Thieu had finally bowed to the inevitable and consented to the agreement. The following evening Nixon went on television to announce that on January 27 the formal signing ceremonies would be held in Paris. A cease-fire would begin at midnight that day.

After this announcement Nixon met with Kissinger. Nixon said he did not want to have any hatred or anything of that sort toward "our enemies"—by which he meant the American doves, not the Vietnamese Communists. "On the other hand," he continued, Nixon's foes had to recognize that they "are disturbed, distressed, and really discouraged because we succeeded."

Nixon later wondered whether commentators would appreciate what he and Kissinger had accomplished; he decided "probably not." He told Kissinger that every success was followed by a "terrific letdown," and he urged Kissinger not to let it get to him. There were many battles left to fight; he should not be discouraged.

For his part Nixon wrote later that he had expected to feel relief and satisfaction when the war ended, but instead was surprised to find himself with feelings of "sadness, apprehension, and impatience."

Kissinger was struck by Nixon's being "so lonely in his hour of triumph."

Beyond the letdown he always felt after a crisis, Nixon had reasons for his negative feelings. In the weeks that followed, he often and vehemently maintained he had achieved peace with honor, but that claim was difficult to sustain. Seven years earlier, when pressed by reporters to explain what kind of settlement he would accept in Vietnam, he had held up the Korean armistice of 1953 as his model. What he finally accepted was far short of that goal.

The Korean settlement had left 60,000 American troops in South Korea; the Vietnam settlement left no American troops in South Vietnam. The Korean settlement left no Communist troops in South Korea; the Vietnam settlement left 150,000 Communist troops in South Vietnam. The Korean settlement had established the 38th parallel as a dividing line, and it was so heavily fortified on both sides that twenty years later almost no living thing had crossed it; the Vietnam settlement called the 17th parallel a border, but the NVA controlled both sides of it and moved back and forth without interference. The Korean settlement had left President Syngman Rhee firmly in control of his country, to the point that the Communist party was banned; the Vietnam settlement forced President Thieu to accept Communist membership on the National Council of Concord and Reconciliation.

Small wonder that Thieu regarded the settlement as little short of a surrender, and feared that the cease-fire would last only until the Americans got their POWs back and brought their armed forces home. Small wonder, too, that he worried about his future, as his army was woefully inferior to Rhee's army (not to mention the NVA).

Thieu did have one asset to match Rhee's: a promise from the American president that if the Communists broke the agreement the United States would come to his aid. But in South Vietnam, in the spring of 1975, that promise proved to be worthless, because by then Nixon had resigned to avoid impeachment. In some part the resignation was brought on by the Christmas bombing. Kissinger's "peace is at hand" promise, followed by Nixon's triumphant reelection, and then by the bombing, creating feelings of bitterness and betrayal and led many

Democrats to want to punish Nixon. Nixon gave them their excuse with Watergate.

Nixon's defenders assert that had it not been for Watergate, the North Vietnamese would not have dared to launch their offensive in 1975. Or, if they had, that Nixon would have responded with the fury he showed in the spring of 1972, and the American bombing support would have made it possible for the South Vietnamese to turn back the invaders once again.

Nixon's detractors call this scenario nonsense. They assert that all he ever wanted or expected from the cease-fire was a "decent interval" before the NVA overran Saigon. That decent interval was until Nixon had successfully completed his second term. They argue further that Congress was never going to give Nixon the funds to resume bombing in Vietnam and that he knew it, even as he made his promises to Thieu.

No one can know what might have been. Everyone knows what happened.

EISENHOWER AND NATO

"I consider this to be the most important military job in the world," General Eisenhower told his son John in December 1950, as he prepared to leave Columbia University to go to Europe to take up his duties as the Supreme Allied Commander, Europe. He went on, "I am going to do the best I can in what I definitely believe to be a world crisis."

He told his childhood friend Swede Hazlett, "I rather look upon this effort as about the last remaining chance for the survival of Western civilization."

The challenges he faced were all but overwhelming. The tension, worldwide, was tremendous. In Korea, the Chinese had entered the war and inflicted a stinging defeat on U.N. forces. In Europe, NATO was under way, but it had a long way to go. Across the Elbe River, the Red Army was 175 divisions strong and aggressive. From Moscow, Stalin was hurling threats.

The only firm decision NATO had made was that Eisenhower should be the Supreme Commander. But of what? A multinational force? Independent national armies joined together in a loose alliance? How many troops? Where would they come from? Without German troops, NATO would never be able to match the Red Army. Eisenhower felt that "the safety of Western Europe demands German participation on a vigorous scale," but West Germany was not yet sovereign, was not a member of NATO, and in any case the French, Dutch, Belgians, and others were horrified at the prospect of rearming the Germans only five years after they had been liberated from the Nazis.

German rearmament, European rearmament, was going to be a hard sell. To the Europeans, NATO meant a guarantee that the United States would not desert them, that they could count on the atomic bomb to deter the Red Army. They could see little reason to rearm themselves. Rearmament would merely provoke the Russians, they reasoned, without creating sufficient strength to repel them—at least without using atomic bombs—and if they were going to use atomic bombs, why rearm?

To succeed as Supreme Commander, Eisenhower would have to persuade the Europeans that the Germans were their allies, not their enemies; that they could build ground and air forces strong enough to hurl back the Red Army; that a genuine military alliance of the NATO partners was, even if unique in history, nevertheless workable.

Eisenhower felt the job he was about to undertake was so important that he was ready to renounce the possibility of his becoming president in order to make NATO a success. Just before leaving, he had a meeting with Senator Robert Taft. Taft had opposed NATO. Eisenhower wrote out a statement repudiating any and all "Eisenhower for President" activities; he intended to make it public if Taft would agree to support NATO. But Taft equivocated. When the senator left, Eisenhower tore up his statement. At that instant, Taft lost his only real chance to realize his life's ambition and become president.

On January 1, 1951, Eisenhower returned to Europe. On arrival in Paris, he made a Europe-wide radio broadcast. He used the opportunity to assert his great love for Europe: "I return with an unshakable faith in Europe—this land of our ancestors—in the underlying courage of its people, in their willingness to live and sacrifice for a secure peace and the continuance and the progress of civilization." He said that he had no "miraculous plans," and that he brought with him no troops or military equipment, but he did bring hope.

And his name, the power of which he knew. At the initial NATO planning session, General Lauris Norstad of the U.S. Air Force recalled, "I've never heard more crying in my life." All the staff officers from the various countries said they did not have this, they did not have that, how weak they were. "And I could see General Eisenhower becoming less and less impressed with this very negative approach, and finally he just banged that podium, got red faced, and said in a voice that could have been heard two or three floors below that he knew what the weaknesses were. 'I know there are shortages, but I myself make up for part of that shortage—what I can do and what I can put into this—and the rest of it has to be made up by you people. Now get at it!' And he banged the podium again and he walked out. Just turned around, didn't say another word, just walked out. And believe me there was a great change in the attitude. Right away there was an air of determination—we *will* do it."

He immediately set out to visit all the capitals. His goal was to get from the Europeans positive commitments to NATO that he could use back in the States to counter Taft and others who were charging that since the Europeans were unwilling to rearm, the United States should not bear the burden and the cost. In Lisbon, Eisenhower told Prime Minister Salazar that the Europeans would have to develop "the same sense of urgency and desire for unity and common action to preserve peace as existed in the United States," and asked Salazar to give him "concrete evidence to take back to the American people that the Europeans are giving their defense effort chief priority." He repeated these demands at every stop, and he could be blunt and direct in doing so. He told the Danes that the 4 percent of their national product they were spending on defense was entirely inadequate. He told the Dutch that The Hague was not "showing a sense of urgency, readiness to sacrifice, and determination to pull its full share of the load." In every capital, he urged the leaders to be an example to the others, and insisted that "there is no time to lose."

He was at his most dramatic in Paris, where he told Premier Pleven "that the French do not have enough confidence in their own potentialities; that, after all, they have only been defeated once and that the public officials in a country of such glorious traditions should be constantly exhorting the people to again rise to the height of which the French people are capable." He urged Pleven to "beat the drums to reaffirm the glory of France." Colonel Andrew Goodpaster, taking notes, recorded that "the impression Eisenhower made on M. Pleven was very noticeable. M. Pleven said, 'I thank you; you have aroused new confidence in me already.' " When Eisenhower's chief of staff, Alfred Gruenther, told him he had been "superbly eloquent," Ike grunted, "Why is it that when I deliver such a good talk it has to be an audience of one!"

Part of the pep talk included urging the Europeans to get along with one another. He asked Prime Minister de Gasperi of Italy, for example, if it was not possible "for the Italians to think in friendly terms about Yugoslavia," as he had high hopes of eventually including Yugoslavia in NATO in order to strengthen his southern flank. De Gasperi, citing the struggle between Italy and Yugoslavia for control of Trieste, noted that "it was a sad fact that in Europe nations were usually friendly with other nations which were not their neighbors."

Two neighbors who shared a long frontier and deep hatreds were France and West Germany. When talking with the French, Eisenhower avoided the delicate subject of German rearmament, but he did begin to lay a basis for the creation of a German army by making a trip to the U.S. Rhein-Main air base in West Germany, where he held a press conference. He opened by saying that when he had last come to Germany, "I bore in my heart a very definite antagonism toward Germany and certainly a hatred for all that the Nazis stood for, and I fought as hard as I knew how to destroy it." But, he added, "for my part, bygones are bygones, and I hope that some day the great German people are lined up with the rest of the free world, because I believe in the essential freedom-loving quality of the German people." When a German reporter pointed out that many Frenchmen wanted a permanently neutralized Germany, Eisenhower replied that "in this day and time to conceive of actual neutrality is an impossibility."

In late January, Eisenhower flew back to the States, where he spent four days at the Hotel Thayer at West Point, writing a speech for delivery to Congress. He found it one of the most difficult of his entire career to prepare, because of the number of seemingly contradictory themes that he had to expound. He had to simultaneously convince the American politicians that the danger was great and imminent, but that it would not cost much to meet it; that the West Europeans were too weak to defend themselves, but that they had the spirit and dedication to do so if given American help; that he needed American troops in Europe, immediately, but that he would not need too many of them nor for too long a duration. As he told Robert Lovett, "NATO needs an eloquent and inspired Moses as much as it needs planes, tanks, guns and ships," and he intended to be that Moses.

In his speech, he assured a joint session of Congress that the United States, by itself, would not be responsible for defending Europe from the Russians; that with forty divisions, NATO could mount an effective defense; that only six of those divisions need be American; that the most urgent need was not U.S. troops but an immense flow of American military equipment for the Europeans; that he was fully aware of the worldwide nature of the Communist threat, which meant he recognized that "we cannot concentrate all our forces in any one sector, even one as important as Western Europe."

As to the Germans, he stressed that all the talk and bickering about German rearmament had given the Germans the idea that "they can sit there and blackmail us." He explained that the Germans were saying that the price of their rearming and joining NATO was a restoration of their sovereignty, and that if they did not get it they just might have to turn to the Russians for help. To this threat, Eisenhower said, he had told the Germans, "I am not going to come down on my hands and knees for anything. If you people don't see your welfare lies with the free West, I am not going to beg you, a conquered nation." He added that "the Western European situation is really not going to be stable until that day arrives that we have Germany a decent respectable member, contributing its regular part."

It was a convincing performance. Two months later, Congress approved the dispatch of four divisions, plus supporting naval forces and air wings, to Europe. It voted increased appropriations for military aid.

With these American contributions, NATO by mid-1951 was beginning to create a genuine military force.

But it was only a start, as Eisenhower well knew, and in the months following his return to Europe he devoted most of his time to building more support for NATO both in Europe and back in the States. He called this goal his most important objective and carried out a brutal schedule to meet it—press conferences and numerous trips to the various capitals, where he was careful to talk not only to government figures but also to opposition party leaders, trade union officials, intellectuals, and molders of public opinion. "Our problem," he told Joe Collins, Army chief of staff, "is one of selling and inspiring."

In his extensive private correspondence with American leaders, Eisenhower concentrated on selling NATO. Most of the incoming letters were pleas that he run for the presidency; his standard reply was that he had no interest in politics, and that in any event the job he held was so important that he had to concentrate his full energy and time on it. Then he would launch into a sales pitch for NATO, usually ending by urging the recipient to spread the word.

The word was that "the future of civilization, as we know it, is at stake." The word was that the true defense of the United States was on the Elbe River. The word was that the American way of life was dependent upon raw materials that could come only from Europe and its colonies, and upon trade and scientific exchanges with Europe. The word was that by supporting European rearmament, the United States could buy as much security for itself by spending one dollar as it could by spending four dollars to build up American forces. The word was that only through collective security could the United States and Europe meet the Soviet threat.

He dealt head-on with the objection that the United States was committing itself to an indefinite defense of Europe, at a tremendous cost that would continually go higher. Eisenhower admitted that "we cannot be a modern Rome guarding the far frontiers with our legions." He recognized that the economic strength of the United States was the greatest asset the free world had, and he agreed that the expenditure of billions of dollars for defense would, in the long run, bankrupt the

United States, thus presenting the Soviets with "their greatest victory." But he insisted that support for NATO was a short-run proposition. He flatly declared, "If in ten years, all American troops stationed in Europe for national defense purposes have not been returned to the United States, then this whole project will have failed." He didn't really mean that, but it sounded good to the congressmen.

Within Europe, Eisenhower considered morale to be his biggest problem. NATO had only 12 divisions; the Red Army had 175. It seemed impossible to stop the Red Army without using atomic bombs, and if the Americans were going to use atomic bombs anyway, why bother to build European ground strength?

Eisenhower thought that sufficient conventional strength could be built and that it was both mad and immoral to rely upon the atomic bomb. Further, he felt that morale, which cost little or nothing to build, was with the West. "Civilian leaders talk about the state of morale in a given country as if it were a sort of uncontrollable event or phenomenon, like a thunderstorm or a cold winter," he complained in his diary, while "the soldier leader looks on morale as the greatest of all his problems, but also as one about which he can and must do something."

He told Averell Harriman, "The last thing that a leader may be is pessimistic if he is to achieve success." So he continued to urge, cajole, encourage. He asked the governments to remind each and every citizen daily "of his own conceptions of the dignity of man and of the value he places upon freedom; this must be accompanied by the reminder that freedom is something that must be earned every day that one lives!" On the seventh anniversary of D-Day, Eisenhower went to Normandy to deliver a Europe-wide radio broadcast that reminded the Europeans of what was at stake. "Never again," he said, "must there be a campaign of liberation fought on these shores."

On D-Day, British and American troops had fought side by side. The special relationship continued, but still the British, like the French, had to be wooed. The British were not so opposed to a German army as were the French, but a united Europe was "anathema to them." Eisenhower went after the Brits in his typical fashion—public speeches, private meetings with politicians, and an extensive correspondence with his many friends in the British government.

On July 4, he spoke in London. He issued a ringing call for a United States of Europe. He recognized the difficulties—"this project faces the deadly danger of procrastination, timid measures, slow steps and cautious stages"—then held out the vision of what could be gained: "With unity achieved, Europe could build adequate security and, at the same time, continue the march of human betterment that has characterized Western civilizations. Once united, the farms and factories of France and Belgium, the foundries of Germany, the rich farmlands of Holland and Denmark, the skilled labor of Italy, will produce miracles for the common good."

Throughout the year, Eisenhower pushed the United States of Europe project. To Harrison, he declared, "Every day brings new evidence that Western Europe must coalesce both politically and economically, or things will get worse instead of better. It seems remarkable that all European political leaders recognize the truth of this statement but just sit down and do absolutely nothing about it."

In April 1952, Eisenhower issued his NATO report. It was decidedly upbeat. "The tide has begun to flow our way and the situation of the free world is brighter than it was a year ago. Our active forces have increased to a point where they could give a vigorous account of themselves, should an attack be launched against us."

Then he resigned, to return to the States, to enter the Republican primaries, to keep Bob Taft from becoming president and ruining NATO.

He won, and for the next eight years he continued to make a strong, healthy NATO one of his top priorities. That meant bringing Germany into the organization as a full partner. It also meant working for German unity. The NATO ground commander, Field Marshal Montgomery, warned him to back off on German unity. Montgomery said that neither the French nor the Russians would ever allow it to happen. But Eisenhower had a different vision. He told Montgomery that "a steady social, political, military, and economic advance in West Germany would be like a magnet to the East Germans. It might even become impossible for the Communists to hold the place by force."

He wanted German unity even when Chancellor Adenauer did not. Adenauer gave public support to the idea, but privately he was opposed; as Secretary of State Christian Herter told Eisenhower, the Christian Democrats feared unity because they felt the Socialists in West Germany would team up with the East Germans to vote the Christian Democrats out of power. Eisenhower snorted, "If they get a true unification, they will have to take their chances with politics."

As president, his policy was to keep NATO strong in order to contain the Communists for so long as necessary, and wait for change. In 1959 he told congressional leaders, "Our most realistic policy is holding the line until the Soviets manage to educate their people. By doing so, they will sow the seeds of destruction of Communism." He warned that "this will take a long time," but he was sure that eventually what Thomas Jefferson called "the disease of liberty" would spread among an educated people, and when it did, Communism would join Nazism on the ash heap of history.

Not all of his hopes and dreams came true, but that one did. Others still could. He wanted an all-European army, in one uniform. He wanted a United States of Europe. He was the first commander of NATO forces; he was the first citizen of NATO; he was NATO's greatest friend and inspiration; we owe him a lot.

THE COLD WAR IN PERSPECTIVE

The Cold War is over. Communisim is dead. We won.

In 1991, as I write this piece, most Americans would agree whole-heartedly and enthusiastically with those simple declarative sentences. But I would quibble with the first, strongly object to the second, and wonder about the third. I will do so within the context of the central questions that need to be answered about every war. First, who won? Second, at what cost? Third, was it worth it? Fourth, was it inevitable? Fifth, could it have ended earlier?

My answers are based on my idea of victory, which was set in con-crete in 1945, when I was ten years old: victory means unconditional surrender. It means our troops occupy our enemies' country and that we teach them how to be good democrats.

If the Cold War is over and we won, why does the U.S. still maintain troops along the line of the Elbe River, naval bases in Greece, Italy and Scandinavia, missiles in Britain and other forces throughout the Mediterranean and Europe? They are not there as occupying troops. Why does the U.S. maintain combat-ready divisions along the 38th par-allel in Korea? They are not there as occupying troops. If the Cold War is over, why do the U.S. and the Soviet Union maintain thousands of nuclear-armed intercontinental missiles aimed at each other?

Communism is far from dead. More people in this world still live under Communist dictatorships than under any other system. This is obviously true in China, where one out of every four human beings live, in Cuba, through much of Southeast Asia, and still in parts of Eastern Europe. Even in the Soviet Union, where the Communist Party has ended up on the ash heap of history and where the one-party state has given way to a fledgling form of democracy, the economic system remains pretty much what it has been for the past seventy years.

If we won the Cold War, it has been a severely limited victory. We certainly did not win in China or Vietnam or Cambodia. In Europe the victory hardly compares to V-E Day and V-J Day. The Red Army is still the largest in the world, and has in addition one-half the world's nuclear weapons and missiles. There are still two hundred thousand Red Army troops in eastern Germany, no American or NATO troops in Moscow. We are not implementing a decommunization policy in the Soviet Union, teaching the Russians how to be good democrats.

Comparing the victory of 1945 with the victory of 1989–91 reveals many other striking contrasts. In 1945, our enemies' cities lay in ruins. The Japanese and German leaders were in prison, awaiting trial. Their armies were kaput, the pitiful survivors in POW cages. Our armed forces were more powerful than those of the remainder of the world combined. One-half of all the ships afloat in 1945, one-half of all the weapons made in that year, were built in the U.S. We had a monopoly on the atomic bomb. Our economy was poised to take off on the greatest boom in history.

In 1991, the cities of the former Soviet Union and Warsaw Pact nations are intact. So are their armies. Their leaders, most of them, freely walk the streets; some of them are still in power. Our military might, although far greater in its ability to destroy than in 1945, is relatively much weaker, certainly not superior to the rest of the world combined.

Obviously the Soviet Union faces terrible problems. Civil war threatens, there is massive unrest, possible famine coming this winter, the empire breaking up, the authority of the central government in question, desertion in the army and near-universal cynicism. Politics are volatile and extreme.

But this list of woes should not be carried too far. For all their problems, the Soviets in 1990 managed to build 140 new missiles, 2 new submarines, and 1,800 new tanks (while the U.S. built 12 missiles, 1 submarine, and 600 tanks). In 1991 the Soviets are still building at a frantic pace. And these are high-quality weapons; the Communists were abject failures in producing consumer goods ("they pretend to pay us, we pretend to work"), but they built good tanks, planes, and missiles.

Meanwhile, the U.S. in 1991 is considerably different from the U.S. in 1945. We have middle-class erosion, widespread discontent, homelessness, crime, drugs, race problems, scandals in our leading economic institutions and cynicism in government. Still, we are doing a lot better than our rival superpower, about which more later.

World War II pitted freedom and democracy—and Communism— against Nazism, fascism and Japanese militarism. When the latter surrendered unconditionally, the victorious allies went after each other: the Cold War pitted freedom and democracy against Communism. In many ways, that struggle continues; still, it is obvious that freedom and democracy have recently won some major battles. The real winners in those battles were the Poles, the East Germans, the Czechs, the Hungarians. These were stunning victories, comparable to the ones in 1945. Churchill said that the Nazi surrender was the signal for the greatest outburst of joy in the history of mankind, and he was right; but the tearing down of the Berlin Wall was not far behind. Can there be anyone among us who was not deeply moved when that hateful thing came down?

How does our contribution to the victories won in Central and Eastern Europe in 1989 compare to our contribution to the victories of 1945? In World War II, we sent planes, tanks, ships and fighting men to Europe, and aid to our allies. In the Cold War, we gave precious little support to the democratic forces in Poland, East Germany, Czechoslovakia, Yugoslavia and Hungary, and none at all to Bulgaria, Rumania, and Albania. We refused to recognize the Soviet annexation of the Baltic states but we also failed to give those countries any support whatsoever, other than rhetorical "captive nations" resolutions. The truth is, those nations in the region who are free liberated themselves. Neither

George Patton's Third Army nor its successors were anywhere to be seen.

The right wing in American politics is arguing today that we did make the essential contribution, by speeding up the arms race during the Reagan presidency. They claim that the Soviets were bankrupted by the attempt to keep up and thereby were forced to retreat from the advanced positions the Red Army had occupied in 1945. The Reagan build-up left us with a $3 trillion debt, but the right wing argues that that is a small price to pay for such a great victory.

That seems to me to be a strange argument for right-wingers to make. I would turn it around and say that Communism failed as a rotten system, and that it lasted as long as it did, in part, because the dictators could convince their people that they were under a threat from the West comparable to the threat of Hitler. (Parenthetically, the single redeeming feature of Communism is that it stopped Hitler; never forget that nine out of every ten Wehrmacht soldiers killed in World War II were killed by the men and women of the Red Army.)

In World War II we used every weapon in our arsenal, including atomic bombs, to force our enemies into unconditional surrender. In the Cold War, we used our weapons only in Korea and Vietnam, and even there we refused to make war as we had in World War II. One example will suffice: in World War II we bombed enemy cities without compunction, deliberately killing civilians by the hundreds of thousands. Very few voices were raised in objection. In the Vietnam War, when we bombed Hanoi in December 1972, the air force took care to avoid civilian targets, and civilian casualties were fewer than two thousand, which in 1945 would not even have rated a back-page one-paragraph story in the newspapers. But in 1972, there was a worldwide howl of protest, most of all from within the U.S.

Why the difference? The most basic cause for the moral revulsion over the Christmas bombing was the nature of the war itself. Between 1942 and 1945 the United States and her allies were fighting for their lives against foes who were not only pure evil but also powerful enough to threaten the entire world. In World War II there were no ongoing negotiations with the Germans and Japanese, only a demand for their unconditional surrender. In 1942–1945 the Allies were bombing in order to hasten that surrender.

But in 1972 no one believed that the United States was fighting for its life, or that the North Vietnamese could conquer the world, or that there could be no end to the war until Hanoi surrendered, or that more bombing would bring a quicker end to the war.

This brings up another contrast between World War II and the Cold War: until the fighting began in 1939, the Western democracies consistently, perversely underestimated the Japanese and German threats. In the Cold War, when the fighting between the main antagonists never did begin, the United States consistently, perversely overestimated the Communist threat. This is one of those cases in which one generation applied the wrong lesson from the preceding generation; in the same way, the American leaders in the pre–World War II period had applied the wrong lesson from their predecessors, thinking that the United States had made a mistake when it entered World War I, and that it had done so because American businessmen and bankers had sold so much and loaned so much to Britain and France that they had to protect their investment. Thus the pre–World War II leaders passed the various neutrality acts, forbidding trading with or loaning money to nations at war, which was a good way to avoid World War I but a terrible way to deal with the world crisis of 1938–1941. Let future leaders beware: whatever the lessons of the Cold War are, they will not apply to the crises of the future.

Another obvious major difference between World War II and the Cold War is that in the former we went on the offensive all around the world, contributing to the liberation of China and Southeast Asia, making possible the liberation of the Philippines, Korea, North Africa, and Western Europe. In the Cold War, we stayed on the defensive. Except for a brief foray into North Korea in 1950, we never attempted to liberate anyone. Containment, not liberation, was our policy. In the longest war in our history, we fought with self-imposed constraints. We never sent troops into North Vietnam, despite severe provocation; only once did we send troops into Cambodia, and then for less than two months;

we tried the impossible, fighting the tip of the spear without ever going after the spear itself, much less the spear-chucker or the spear-maker.

The reason for the restraint was the development of the atomic bomb and intercontinental missiles. That was also the reason for the remarkable fact that from 1945 to 1989, the U.S. and the Soviet Union spent enormous sums on military weapons without ever once firing even one of them against the enemy they were chiefly built to use against. The superpowers built tens of thousands of nuclear weapons, doing so with the hope that they would never be used. (It is my hunch that neither side ever gave serious consideration to a first strike.)

Four legacies from World War II dictated the manner in which the Cold War was waged. The first, actually dating to prewar years, had to do with the need to stand up against aggression. The second was fear of a surprise attack. The German invasion of the Soviet Union in June 1941 and the Japanese attack on Pearl Harbor in December of that year caught the U.S.S.R. and the U.S.A. completely by surprise. The leaders of the two countries throughout the Cold War were middle-aged or young men in 1945. Barbarossa and Pearl Harbor were burned into their souls. They vowed that never again would their countries be caught unprepared and by surprise.

The third legacy was technological: rockets and atomic weapons. Combined they made a potential World War III so obviously suicidal that it was unthinkable. But of course that was a judgement that was valid only so long as the other side had a rational leader, and the fourth legacy from World War II was Tojo's and Hitler's: the stark fact that great nations sometimes have insane murderers for leaders, men who are willing to destroy their own people rather than submit to superior force or logic. So the leaders of the superpowers built weapons they hoped/prayed/believed would never be used.

They have not been used. They have cost huge sums and made the world far more dangerous. But they have also prevented World War III, and acted as a constraint on the superpowers as they fought small wars against Third World countries, the U.S. in Korea and Vietnam, the Soviets in Afghanistan. (It is remarkable that nations powerful enough to destroy the world were defeated, or held in check, by the North Koreans, the North Vietnamese, and the Afghans.)

Thus a fifth legacy from World War II has been spurned throughout the Cold War, that of unconditional surrender. In 1941 the American people looked at Nazi Germany and militarist Japan and said, "These are evil nations imposing an unspeakably cruel, criminal dictatorship on their own people and those they have conquered. They must be crushed." In the Cold War, the American people looked at the Communists ruling the Soviet Union and said, "Theirs is an evil regime imposing an unspeakably cruel, criminal dictatorship on the territories of its own people and those they have conquered—and they must be contained."

The different reactions could not have been greater and they led to much frustration. The Republicans in the late forties and early fifties denounced containment as "cowardly." They wanted liberation—that is, total victory. But when Eisenhower became president in 1953, he ignored advice that he go over to the offensive, liberate North Korea, and then go to war against Communist China. Instead, he made peace, and then kept the peace. He explained to congressional leaders, "This Cold War is a continuous crisis that we will have to live with. Our most realistic policy is holding the line until the Soviets manage to educate their people. By doing so, they will sow the seeds of destruction of Communism. This will take a long time."

Eisenhower's counsel of patience, adopted by all his successors, has worked in Western Europe, South Korea, and Japan, but so far has been an utter failure in China and Vietnam, and it doomed two generations of Central and Eastern Europeans to slavery.

Because of the failures, the temptation to use the military option, up to and including nuclear weapons, was always there. But even our two most belligerent presidents resisted the temptation. John Kennedy came into office full of bellicose rhetoric. He wanted to go on the offensive worldwide and was ready to pay any price, bear any burden, to insure the triumph of freedom everywhere. He sponsored an invasion of Cuba—but then backed down at the critical moment. He took a strong stance on Berlin—and then backed down when Khrushchev built the wall. He faced down Khrushchev in the Cuban missile crisis—but only by paying a cost that has been a calamity for the Cuban people, his pledge that the U.S. would never invade, which has left them under Castro's control for thirty years. It is astonishing that the United States has spent trillions on her armed forces in those thirty years, and tolerated a sassy, provocative dictatorship that provides military bases to our enemy ninety miles off our coast.

Until he became president, Richard Nixon had been America's leading anti-Communist. In every crisis he raised his voice for more fire power, now. He wanted to liberate North Korea in 1953, to use atomic weapons against the Communists at Dien Bien Phu in 1954 and in China in 1955. He called for victory in Vietnam in 1964 and for the next four years was Johnson's leading critic—not for doing too much, but for doing too little.

But when he became president, he took the U.S. out of Vietnam, far short of victory. He decided the U.S. should aim for sufficiency, not superiority, in nuclear weapons and entered into the first arms control agreement of the Cold War, SALT I. He established detente with the Soviet Union. After twenty-two years of the most unrelenting hostility toward Communist China, he went to Peking to exchange toasts with Mao Tse-tung and Chou En-lai.

American presidents in the Cold War, including Kennedy and Nixon, have—in general and on the really big issues—followed a policy of realistic restraint. The one great exception was Vietnam. There we entered on a wave of hubris. We were completely unrealistic about the nature of the war and what we needed to do to win it. We exhibited a remarkable, and, since we had gone to war, foolish restraint—for example, by going along with the fiction that the war was limited to South Vietnam and that Laos and Cambodia were neutral. As noted, we fought with a restraint that stands in the sharpest possible contrast with how we fought World War II, but we fought in a way that exposed us to worldwide condemnation (the same can be said about the Red Army in Afghanistan).

During the Cold War, we built the most powerful armed forces we have ever had, but in forty-five years, while they won some battles, they never won a war. The first American victory since 1945 came in 1991, and then it was over Iraq in a war that had nothing to do with the Cold War for which the armed forces were built. But we can turn that around: we built armed forces that were so powerful in order to deter, to avoid war—and it worked.

This brings to the fore the second question about the Cold War: what was the cost? As compared to World War II, it was trivial. In World War II, nearly 50 million people died, among them more than a quarter-million American soldiers and sailors, but most of them Russians, Jews, Poles, Yugoslavs, Germans, Japanese, Chinese and Filipinos. In the Cold War, casualties were not nearly so high; only in Korea and Vietnam did the fighting even approach the intensity of World War II. In those two wars, about a hundred thousand U.S. soldiers and sailors were killed, a terrible price to pay to be sure, but not so high as World War II. To date, the Cold War has left the U.S. with a $3 trillion debt, a much greater sum than after World War II, when the national debt was $270 billion but, when adjusted for inflation, about the same.

A legacy from both wars has been the relative militarization of American society. Although the American defense establishment is much less pervasive than the Soviet Union's, or than Europe's had been in the late nineteenth and first four-and-a-half decades of the twentieth century, it is far more intrusive in the daily lives of Americans than had ever been the case before 1941. After World War II, while the Europeans were spending money on social welfare, the Americans were spending it on what has been called military welfare. This has led to a quip: after World War II the Americans were Prussianized while the Germans were Americanized.

Was the Cold War worth the cost? Unquestionably. No one can ever prove that the Truman doctrine of containment, and its chief implementing policies, NATO and the Marshall Plan, saved Western Europe from Communism—because we cannot know what would have happened had they not been implemented—but I believe it did. No one can ever prove that Communism would have collapsed in Central and Eastern Europe and the Soviet Union had there not been the Voice of America and Radio Free Europe and a consistent refusal by every Cold War president to accept as legitimate the Soviet domination of Central and

Eastern Europe—but I believe those were significant factors, and cite in evidence the polls that indicate that VOA and Radio Free Europe were the most popular radio programs in Eastern and Central Europe over the past four decades. No one can ever prove that American leadership was even helpful to, much less critical to, the triumphs of democracy that have taken place in many parts of the world in the past few years—but I believe it was.

Was the Cold War inevitable? Nothing in human affairs is inevitable; people must make choices. The West could have acquiesced in the Communist enslavement of the peoples of the Soviet Union and Eastern Europe; the policy is called appeasement. It is the policy we have followed with the Communist rulers who have enslaved China and Tibet. As the Chinese example shows, mortal combat between capitalism and freedom on the one hand and Communism and slavery on the other is not inevitable.

In the 1960s and 1970s Western scholars, including myself, tended to look at American policy when fixing the blame for the Cold War. Partly this was because we could study American documents but no Soviet documents; we knew what went on in the Truman and Eisenhower administrations, but not in Stalin's or Khrushchev's. Partly this revisionism was a response to the Vietnam War; young scholars extended their disapproval of that conflict backwards in time and successfully selected evidence from American archives that seemed to show American responsibility for the Cold War.

Today, things look different, at least to me. The easiest way to have avoided the Cold War would have been for Stalin to demobilize the Red Army in 1946 and live up to his pledge of free elections for Poland and Eastern Europe. But had he done that he would not have been Stalin. In that sense, and without pretending that this is in any way a conclusive answer, I'd say that the Cold War was inevitable so long as Stalin was in command and the Communist Party ruled the Soviet Union.

Could the Cold War have ended earlier? As my preceding remarks indicate, I don't see how. Communism had to collapse first. But, and this is a very big but, as I get older I discover that I have changed my mind on important questions so often that the only thing I know for certain is that I don't know anything for certain. As one example: for the first fifteen years of my scholarly career, I believed that Harry Truman made a terrible mistake when he used the atomic bomb in 1945 against Japan. For the second fifteen years of my career, I have believed that Truman had no choice and did exactly the right thing.

This is the glory of studying history in a free country. New documents are always coming to light, forcing new conclusions. For the historian, by the way, that is the difference between our system and the Communist system of studying the past. We change our minds when confronted with new evidence; they change their minds when confronted with a new dictator. Last November, I attended a conference in Moscow to discuss the Eisenhower administration. The sponsor was Georgi Arbatov of the Institute of the U.S. and Canada Studies. He opened the meeting by saying, "In my country the most unpredictable thing is the past." He was the editor of the official twelve-volume history of the Great Patriotic War. He said he had to change it every time the Soviet Union got a new leader, commenting, "It's value today is as toilet paper."

That is why in the next decade the most exciting place in the world to do research on the Cold War will be Moscow. As the archives there are opened to scholars, we will discover that we have an enormous amount to learn about the causes and conduct of the Cold War.

A little more than a decade ago, the president of the United States, Jimmy Carter, said we had a national malaise. Morale in the armed forces was disastrously low. Inflation was terribly high. America appeared to have abandoned her role of world leader. Vietnam hung heavy on our national outlook. We were deeply depressed by the discovery that the power to destroy is not the power to control, that to impose your will you must be able to put the man on the spot with the gun in his hand, and that the American people were not prepared to pay the cost to put him there when "there" was thousands of miles away and the evidence that "there" was important to or threatening us was inconclusive. These discoveries appeared to make Henry Luce's phrase "the American Century" a bitter joke.

Three years ago, our foreign policy was in disarray. The Iran-Contra scandal had almost made the president into an object of ridicule. The dynamic leaders of the world seemed to be Japanese, European, or Russian.

Today, President Bush is well on his way to reversing these trends. In his first major crisis he was able to mobilize public opinion within this country and around the world, thus demonstrating that the American president is still the most important person in the world. No other world leader could have put together the coalition that fought the Gulf War. In the process, Bush also demonstrated that no other nation could project so much power so far from home as the U.S. armed forces. In August of this year, Bush's condemnation of the coup in the Soviet Union as a criminal conspiracy, his support for Gorbachev and Boris Yeltsin, brought him praise and thanks from Soviet leaders, who said his policy was of fundamental importance to the democratic elements in Moscow.

As a result, the Cold War is entering its final stages, at least in Europe. Communism is dead in Europe and on the run elsewhere, even in China and Cuba. The forces of democracy have not won but are winning.

It is therefore time to look ahead to the postwar world. War always diverts attention from domestic problems, and for more than forty years the Cold War has done just that to America. So today we have problems of a crumbling infrastructure, banking, S&L and political scandals, a deteriorating environment, gross disparities in income between the rich and poor, widespread homelessness, awful race relations, crime, unemployment and much more. The question facing us now is, can we provide the kind of imagination and leadership in dealing with these problems that we did in fighting the Cold War? Should we adopt a policy of containing poverty at home, a Marshall Plan for America, liberation for our inner cities, detente in the manifold ethno-cultural-racial struggles within this country?

That is for the next generation to answer. My generation is leaving them with a huge debt and terrible problems—but also with an intact world in which Nazism, fascism, imperialism and colonialism are dead, and Communism is dying. These were our great victories and open the way for younger people to win theirs.

My favorite philosopher, James Thurber, advises us: "Don't look back in anger. Don't look forward with fear. Look around you with awareness." When you look around the U.S. today, for all its problems, you see the most diverse country in history, drawing its strength from peoples from around the world, not least the Cold War refugees from Eastern Europe, Russia, Vietnam, China and elsewhere. You see the finest system of higher education ever created—all the world wants to come to Berkeley or Harvard or Madison, Wisconsin, to study. You see a stable democracy. You see a nation that, for better or for worse, provides the cultural model for all the world.

A hundred and twenty-eight years ago Abraham Lincoln said that we were the last great hope of mankind. We still are.

WAR IN THE TWENTY-FIRST CENTURY

"The only thing I know about war are two things," President Dwight Eisenhower said in a 1955 news conference, in his typical jumbled syntax and with his usual wisdom. "The most changeable factor in war is human nature in its day-by-day manifestation; but the only unchanging factor in war is human nature. And the next thing is that every war is going to astonish you in the way it occurred, and in the way it is carried out." He added that anyone who thought differently was "merely exhibiting his ignorance of war." To display mine, I'm going to do some speculating about what war in the twenty-first century is likely to look like.

War is a political act, so the political situation will determine who fights whom, and how. Francis Fukuyama's provocative "The End of History" thesis dominates today's debate over the political/economic structure of the future. In brief, he argues that the collapse of imperialism, fascism, and Communism means an end to war, because there is no longer any serious challenge to liberal democracy and the marketplace economy. Not everyone has achieved such a system, but everyone is striving for it.

Leaving aside such obvious objections as "what about the Chinese?" and the current situation in the Persian Gulf, the end of the Cold War—

made official in Paris in November 1990, when the members of NATO and the Warsaw Pact signed a solemn pledge to act as friends and partners in the future—appears to prove the validity of Fukuyama's thesis.

Indeed, the Warsaw Pact dissolved in March 1991. Can NATO survive into the twenty-first century? Alliances, after all, have to have an enemy to exist. The argument that we need NATO in order to control the new Germany strikes me as unsupportable—what kind of an alliance is it that has as its main objective the restraint of the major European member of the alliance?

Fukuyama's argument is that liberal democracies do not fight each other. Perhaps, but nations certainly do, and the collapse of the world's last empire (the Soviet Union) and the probable breakup of NATO free the nations from Ireland across Europe and Asia all the way to Japan to pursue their own goals and aspirations. It is difficult to believe that they will not do so, that the end of history really means the return of history. The ideological wars of the twentieth century may well appear, one hundred years from now, to have been the aberration, while the nationalistic, ethnic, and religious wars of the past will appear the norm.

In short, what is already happening in the Persian Gulf will happen elsewhere; wars will be between Muslim and Christian, or Muslim and Jew, or Poles and Germans, or Russians and Ukrainians. What are these wars likely to be like, and what role will the United States play?

Some things seem obvious. They will be bloody beyond belief—the Iran-Iraq war of 1980–88 provides one example, the Gulf War another. This is because the world today is so fantastically armed. There are more rifles, rockets, planes, warships, ammunition, chemical and other weapons in the world today than there were in 1944 by a factor of ten or more.

This worldwide arms race is a consequence of the development of a military-industrial complex in the United States, the Soviet Union, the United Kingdom, France, Germany, Russia, Brazil, Italy, China, Eastern Europe, and elsewhere. These permanent arms industries need to sell their products in order to survive, meaning that the Third World is armed today in a way unimaginable only a few decades ago. The result is that Iraq, a nation of 17 million people, many illiterate, without any industrial base worth speaking of, can field the fourth largest army in the world, an army capable of inflicting heavy casualties, given good leadership.

Will the United States be willing to accept the human and money costs of fighting a war devoid of ideological content? Certainly we did in the Gulf, but there was minimal human loss, allies are paying the cost, it was quick. But in retrospect that looks like a unique war, because it is difficult to imagine any other nation being led by such a fool as Saddam.

The next war won't be bloodless, meaning that the pressure to end it will rise with every increase in the number of KIA. One obvious reason is television. The medium's impact on war has already been great, and, as worldwide instantaneous transmission continues to grow, will only increase. Had there been TV coverage of the Battle of Verdun (1916), it is possible to argue that the peoples of France and Germany would have created antiwar movements that would have led to a stalemated settlement in 1917. Had there been TV images of American boys stacked up in rows in the snow around Bastogne in December 1944, there might well have been an antiwar movement advocating a negotiated settlement with Hitler.

This is another way of saying that in the twenty-first century, there may be no wars fought to the finish, no unconditional surrenders, because neither side will run out of weapons and ammunition (which is essentially what happened to Germany in 1945), and because of antiwar movements on the home front. Korea provides an example, as does Afghanistan and Iran-Iraq, and even the Gulf War. Although there was no significant antiwar movement, surely President Bush was motivated in part to end the war so suddenly by the potential of such a movement. It seems possible to me that he did not order a march on Baghdad because once the Iraqi army was defending the city, it could not be outflanked. Street fighting is dangerous; one kid with a rifle shooting out a window can take a squad with him. We know now that Saddam saved enough firepower to possibly make that into the bloodbath he sought.

The civil war in Iraq is perhaps more indicative of the future of war than the preceding conflict in the Gulf. Around the world, nation states are beset by unhappy minorities. These minorities can usually get arms, most often from one of the superpowers or from European suppliers. Perhaps the worst scenario for the immediate future is a civil war within the former Soviet Union. In terms of quantity if not quality, it is the most heavily armed nation in the world, not even counting its atomic arsenal. The possibility of a "TIme of Troubles" is real; the dangers inherent in the situation are very great.

Civil war is also possible, even likely, in Yugoslavia, Czechoslovakia, the Philippines, throughout Central America and almost everywhere in Africa. But, as always in international affairs, there are contradictory trends. On the one hand, Europe is almost sure to create some form of a United States of Europe by the twenty-first century. The continent that had been the cockpit of war in the twentieth century (1914, 1939, the Cold War) is becoming the continent least likely to start a war in the twenty-first century.

The trend toward larger regional blocs is also evident in Asia and in North America. Japan, the great warmonger of Asia in the first half of the twentieth century, is busy creating a regional bloc dominated by the yen that poses no military threat to anyone (economics is another matter).

North America is not likely to form a single political entity, but the coming of free trade among the U.S., Mexico and Canada, the virtual disappearance of the borders to the north and south of the United States with regard to immigration as well as trade, means that the likelihood of war in North America is just about zero (unless Quebec starts a civil war in Canada). The U.S. has not fought its neighbor to the south since 1848 or its neighbor to the north since 1815. In Central America, however, as noted, civil war—which has been endemic since 1945—is almost certain to continue.

Whatever the politics, and no matter what nations are fighting, war in the twenty-first century will be a paradox—more impersonal, with greater personal impact. As in Iraq, it is the civilians who will be most affected by war. This is a consequence of modern weapons development, which has greatly extended the range, the accuracy, and the explosive power of the artillery shell, rocket, missile, intercontinental missile, submarine-launched missile, and more. This incredible, gigantic arsenal of weapons can carry an explosive force beyond imagination. A single B-52 today carries more explosive power than the sum total of all the explosions in all human history. The world today contains nuclear weapons that are equivalent to three tons of TNT for every man, woman and child on earth; this is 750 times all the high explosives used in all the wars in history. A single U.S. submarine carries about 200 warheads, enough to destroy every Soviet city with a population of more than 150,000 people.

These huge arsenals were built for the Cold War. Now that it is over—and many would say it ended without a real war precisely because of the threat of mutual suicide—what role do nuclear weapons have, especially in such numbers? It would seem to be common sense, and may well happen, that the two superpowers will actually reduce their stockpiles. But even an 80 percent reduction would leave them far ahead of all the rest.

It is with "all the rest" that the trouble lies. The problem is not so much with China, France, Britain, India, and other members of the nuclear club, but involves the relative ease with which *any* country, no matter how poor, can get a bomb. Such is the awesome efficiency of nuclear weapons that a grapefruit-sized chunk of plutonium can be made to detonate with a power equivalent to the amount of high explosive that would fill a train five miles long. And the plutonium is so plentiful that what to do with the waste from nuclear power plants is a major environmental worry. Given that this material is cheap and easy to get, it would seem inevitable that most countries will do so, always, of course, for "defensive" purposes; it seems likely that sometime over the next decades the weapons will be used, probably in the Middle East.

So war in the twenty-first century is likely to be even worse for civilians than war in the twentieth century has been.

A happier prediction is that bacteriologic warfare and chemical warfare are unlikely. This is because they do not make good military weapons. It takes time for bacteria to be effective; in war, time is everything. Also, bacteria don't know which side they are supposed to be on; typhus spread among your enemies has a way of coming back at you, as the Germans discovered in the Warsaw Ghetto. Chemicals drift in the wind, and countermeasures are, if cumbersome, possible; everybody has them and whoever uses them will be hit just as hard. Chemicals are a weapon to use against urban mobs, or villages in revolt, or other civilians; they are not a good weapon for armies.

This doesn't mean that research on them won't go forward, or stockpiles created and maintained. The U.S. has about thirty-eight thousand tons of chemical-warfare agents, one half mustard gas and the other half nerve gases. This is enough to kill everyone in the world—it takes only one drop of nerve gas to kill—four thousand times over. The West Germans have one thousand tons of nerve gas.

Research on all arms will go forward. Science researchers will be funded almost exclusively by the military; already about six hundred thousand scientists around the world work on military research and development. This is about 25 percent of all scientists employed on research. That percentage will grow. About 50 percent of the physicists and engineers, the men at the forefront of technological innovation, are working on military research and development. If one adds in all the technical people, the academics and bureaucrats hooked up with the weapons industry, and all the workers, it is possible to see what a huge lobby there is (not only here) for increasing military budgets and agitating for the development of every conceivable technological advance for military purposes.

Of course, as the machines take over, humans fade into the background. The next generation of military aircraft, for example, is likely to consist of planes without pilots. Already we are at the point where the pilot costs too much to train, takes up too much space in the cockpit, and has to be protected by armor, all at the expense of more electronic gadgets. Soon there will be tanks directed by radio from satellites.

The cost of staying competitive in automated warfare is horrendous. But the nations of the world will insist on staying competitive. Oil for weapons. Human bondage for weapons. Mass starvation for weapons. Anything for weapons, the latest and the best. An inevitable consequence is that most of the people of the world will remain very poor.

This is the new colonialism. The industrial countries provide the product, but instead of having to force it down poor people's throats, the poor people are clamoring for a chance to buy more. The arms trade is staggering in scope; it is the world's second biggest industry, after oil. The customers are the Middle East (45 percent), Africa (23 percent), the Far East (13 percent), Latin America (11 percent) and South Asia (9 percent). The profit goes to the arms makers.

But even the rich nations will suffer. Automated warfare will use munitions at an unprecedented rate. It will thus put a great premium on putting the economy on a permanent war footing. Can this be done without a total militarization of society? Possibly: we got through the effort of World War II with the democracy intact and secure. But there surely will be a political price.

Is there anything optimistic that can be said about the future of war? There is: the United Nations. In August 1990, the U.N. acted decisively in response to President Bush's leadership. This was not unique—the U.N. also acted decisively in 1950 in Korea, and in 1956 in forcing the British, French, and Israelis out of Egypt—but it was impressive. It is possible to believe that with the Cold War over, the United Nations will live up to the hopes of its founders, and the hopes of its real father, Woodrow Wilson, and be capable of acting as decisively as it did in the Gulf, thus ensuring collective security. Wilson and Franklin Roosevelt hoped that an international body that could isolate an aggressor and mobilize collective military action would guarantee peace. While the U.N. still finds it difficult, indeed impossible, to intervene in a civil war (as we saw in Iraq), it could fulfill Wilson's and Roosevelt's hopes, and abolish wars between nations. That would be a great leap forward for mankind. Strengthening the United Nations, as opposed to strengthening our own armed forces, would seem to be the best route to a secure, safe future for the United States—and the world.

War is terrible, a catastrophe, for the environment. Burning oil wells, oil spills, and nuclear winter threaten everyone, in somewhat the same way as bacteriological warfare does. Over the past hundred years, science fiction writers have played with the idea that the only way to abolish war is an outside threat—an invasion from Mars or from another galaxy. As usual, these writers have seized on a theme that works precisely because it speaks directly to the problem—we cannot do away with war unless we see an outside force that threatens us all. And by "us," the writers mean not "us Americans" or "us Russians" or "us Africans," but "us, the whole human race."

War itself is now that threat. We all breathe the same air, drink the same water, eat fish from the same sea. If the threat to that air, water, and sea come from war itself, can human beings long ignore this shared danger, and act to meet it, by abolishing war?